South-Western

DESKTOP PUBLISHING ACTIVITIES

Iris Blanc
Totenville High School
Staten Island, New York

Contributing Editor:

Elaine Langlois

JOIN US ON THE INTERNET
WWW: http://www.thomson.com
EMAIL: findit@kiosk.thomson.com A service of I(T)P®

South-Western Educational Publishing

an International Thomson Publishing company I(T)P®

Cincinnati • Albany, NY • Belmont, CA • Bonn • Boston • Detroit • Johannesburg • London • Madrid
Melbourne • Mexico City • New York • Paris • Singapore • Tokyo • Toronto • Washington

Managing Editor: Janie F. Schwark
Project Manager: Dave Lafferty
Editor: Becky E. Peveler
Marketing Manager: John Wills
Art and Design Coordinator: Mike Broussard
Cover Photo: Marjory Dressler

ISBN: 0-538-67790-2

I(T)P®
International Thomson Publishing

South-Western Educational Publishing is a division of International Thomson Publishing, Inc. The ITP logo is a registered trademark used herein under license by South-Western Educational Publishing.

1 2 3 4 5 6 7 8 H 04 03 02 01 00 99 98 97

Printed in the United States of America

CONTENTS

Part II CREATING PRESENTATION DOCUMENTS

PREFACE

With the proliferation of affordable and easy-to-use desktop publishing software, many businesses are producing a wide variety of printed materials within their own companies. The administrative support person responsible for producing business documents is being called upon to create attractive presentation documents using desktop publishing software. Personal computer users are finding that desktop publishing is a handy tool for creating a variety of professional-looking documents for personal and business use.

DESKTOP PUBLISHING ACTIVITIES introduces you to the newest and most commonly used desktop publishing features through skill-building exercises. You will use desktop publishing features to create and enhance letters, letterheads, logos, memos, reports, forms, resumes, invitations, announcements, flyers, news releases, advertisements, agendas, conference programs, brochures, menus, newsletters, presentation graphics, and documents formatted for Internet publication. Each hands-on, step-by-step exercise reviews previous concepts so that you can reinforce and build your desktop publishing skills as you work through the exercises.

Many of the exercises in DESKTOP PUBLISHING ACTIVITIES were designed by professional graphic design consultants on the desktop, expressly for this text.

Text Features

Part I of this text develops desktop publishing skills through 60 sequential applications and exercises. Each lesson in this section explains relevant desktop publishing concepts and vocabulary and provides numerous exercises in which you apply those concepts.

In 65 exercises in Part II, you will create 18 different types of business documents in attractive and sophisticated desktop-published formats. This part includes 15 "on-your-own" projects that will give you the opportunity to use the skills you have developed to design documents on your own. Part II concludes with a capstone simulation activity, in which you will take the part of a Publications Assistant to the busy Director of Communications of a city visitors bureau, designing and producing a variety of documents to promote tourism.

While creating your own desktop layouts does require some design skill, this book will give you, the non-designer, the information and background you need for document design. You will be surprised at how quickly you are producing professional-looking desktop-published documents on your own.

Before You Begin, Please Note the Following...

All the desktop publishing exercises in this text (and the text itself) were created using PageMaker 6.0 for Windows and an IBM-compatible PC. The exercises are generic in nature, however, and may be completed using most desktop publishing software packages and computers. Not all desktop publishing programs use all the features taught in this text. Your teacher will instruct you as to how to apply exercise concepts using the specific procedures for your software.

- The clip art used throughout this text is from the *Clip Art Folio* produced by South-Western Publishing Co. You may use any clip art to complete the exercises.
- Because desktop publishing programs differ, modifications may be necessary to complete an exercise. For example, if your software does not contain a directed type or line size, substitute the closest one available. Because printers and fonts vary, your line endings may not appear exactly as those in the exercises shown in this text.
- Most measurements used throughout this text are in inches. Fractions of an inch are usually expressed as decimals, except sometimes in reference to the rulers on the desktop publishing software screen.
- This text comes with a template disk containing 54 documents to be used in the exercises. The template disk files are provided in several popular word processing formats. For most exercises of any length, you will import the word processing files into your desktop publishing documents, as professional desktop publishers do. Using imported documents will also save you keying time.
- If you need practice using a mouse, working with menus and dialog boxes, or working with windows, turn to Appendix A of this text (page 239).
- After completing the 125 exercises and the capstone activity in this text, you will be able to desktop-publish with ease. Have fun and good luck!

ACKNOWLEDGMENTS

My heartfelt thanks go to those who have encouraged and assisted me with the production of this book:

- To my graphic design consultants, Cynthia Owczarek, New York City, and Jessica Murphy, New York City, thank you for your creative direction and your superb designs.
- To my editors, Kay Wagoner and Neil Wagoner, and to my reviewers, Elizabeth Ann Cobb and Wayne Skaret, thank you for your much-appreciated directions and suggestions.
- To my family, Alan, Pamela, Jaime, and Edith, and to my friends, Paul Bergman, Shirley Dembo, Cathy Vento, Ronnie Giordano, and Adrienne Frosch, thank you for your inspiration, support, and patience.

PART I INTRODUCTION TO DESKTOP PUBLISHING

In this part of the text, you will learn to use desktop publishing techniques to enhance business and personal documents.

Each new desktop concept is introduced with relevant vocabulary. A practice exercise will follow that will help you apply the concepts learned.

Carefully read and follow the step-by-step instructions to recreate the exercises to look as much like the illustrations as possible. Since printers and software vary, your final output may be different from the illustrations in the exercises. If a feature is unavailable on your software, substitute the closest one available.

As you work through the exercises, remember these two important points:

- Save often to avoid losing data.
- Do not become frustrated if you have difficulty completing an exercise. It takes a good deal of practice to feel comfortable manipulating the design elements found in desktop publishing.

After completing Part I, you will be ready to apply the concepts learned to create and enhance professional-looking desktop-published documents.

Learning Objectives

Load and exit from the software
Start a new publication
Learn publication window features
Move around in a publication
Change the screen view
Close a document without saving

Terms

- Rulers
- Toolbox
- Icons
- Scroll bars
- Grabber hand
- Default

Concepts

When you start a new publication, you will see a standard window. It will probably contain items like those in the illustration at the right. (If you need practice working with windows, turn to page 242.)

The page measures 8 1/2" x 11". Horizontal and vertical **rulers** on the top and left of the screen reflect this measurement. (On some software, rulers must be accessed.) As you move about the screen, the position of the pointer may be reflected in cross hairs on the rulers. These cross hairs help you see your position easily. (If you need practice working with a mouse, turn to page 239.)

A **toolbox** usually appears. The toolbox displays symbols or miniature pictures called **icons**, which represent selections for performing certain tasks.

You should first familiarize yourself with the document window and learn how to get around in a document. PageMaker documents have icons at the bottom representing document pages. Clicking on an icon moves you to that page. Most programs have a menu option for changing pages.

Clicking on a **scroll bar** arrow changes your view of the screen in small increments. Clicking on a larger rectangular part of a scroll bar moves you through a file in larger increments. You can drag the small square in a scroll bar (the scroll box) to move a precise distance.

Some software has a grabber hand, available when you press a certain key (Alt in PageMaker for Windows) and drag. The **grabber hand** is a very useful way of changing your view of the screen.

Most desktop programs allow you to magnify or reduce the screen view by various percentages. Some software has a zoom tool for this purpose (tools are usually selected by clicking on the tool). Often, by clicking the right mouse button, you can toggle between viewing the entire page and seeing a portion of the page at actual size. Placing your pointer where you want to work and clicking the right mouse button takes you to that area.

In this text, you will use the default selections for your software unless otherwise directed. A **default** is a preset condition that the software uses if no other option is selected. Each program has its own set of defaults for margins and other items.

INSTRUCTIONS

1. Load your desktop publishing program and start a new publication. Your instructor will help you if necessary.
2. If your software presents you with a document setup dialog box, accept the default options (for help in working with dialog boxes, see page 240). These options will be discussed on page 14.
3. Examine your document screen. Using your Help feature or manual, if necessary, identify each feature.
4. Open each menu and note the selections available (if you need practice working with menus, see page 240).
5. Using your Help feature or manual, if necessary, learn how to move from page to page, move around on the page, and change the screen view. Practice these skills.
6. Close your document without saving it. Your instructor will assist you, if necessary.
7. Exit from the program. Your instructor will assist you, if necessary.

EXERCISE

1

The PageMaker 6.0 (Windows) Document Window

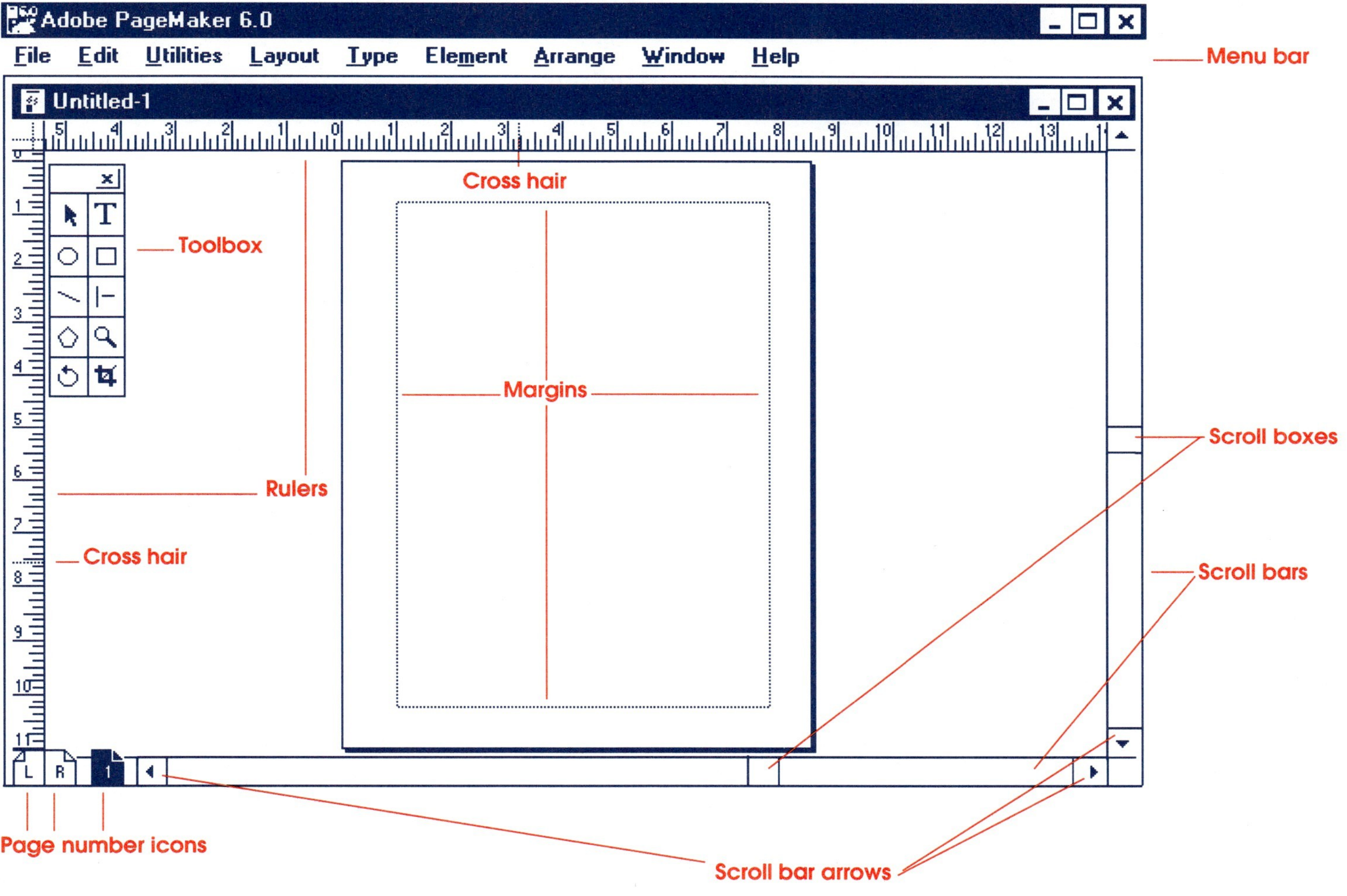

Learning Objectives

Enter text

Save a publication

Terms

- Text tool
- I-beam
- Clicking an insertion point
- Text cursor
- Flush left

Concepts

You can enter text into a desktop publishing document in two ways:

- Key the text directly on the page in the desktop software.
- Key the text in a word processing program and import it into the desktop software.

All except the shortest documents should be created in a word processing program. Word processors enable you to key and edit text much more quickly and efficiently than desktop software. For the first few exercises, however, you will key text in your desktop publishing program for practice. Importing text will be discussed in Lesson 4.

To key text on a page, you must select the **text tool** from the toolbox. In many programs, the pointer will change to a character that looks like the capital letter **I**, called an **I-beam.** Move the I-beam to the desired location and click. This action is called **clicking an insertion point.** A blinking vertical line or **text cursor** will appear at the insertion point location. You can then begin to key.

For most desktop software, text aligns by default **flush left** on the page (it will have an even left margin and a ragged right margin, like this text). As in a word processor, text will automatically wrap at the right margin to the next line.

To save your document, use the Save command in the File menu. The first time you save a document, you will be prompted to name it. Your software may have certain conventions you must follow for naming documents. After you have initially saved your document, you should save it again often to avoid losing work.

When you have finished work, save your file using the Save as command. Save as compresses the file, conserving disk space. Save as also enables you to save more than one version of a publication or to save a copy of a publication under another name.

INSTRUCTIONS

1. Load your desktop publishing program and start a new publication. Your instructor will help you, if necessary.
2. If your software presents you with a document setup dialog box, accept the default options. They will be discussed on page 14.
3. Select the text tool.
4. Click an insertion point at the left margin, 1" down from the top.
5. Magnify the page so text is visible.
6. Key the text on the right exactly as shown. Press Enter/Return twice at the end of each paragraph. Do not press Enter/Return within paragraphs; allow text to wrap automatically.
   - Do not worry about keying errors. Use the Backspace key to correct errors when you can. You will learn other correction methods later.
   - Press Enter/Return at the end of paragraphs.
   - Because fonts and default margins vary, your line endings may differ from those at the right.
7. Save the file; name it **RESUME.** Follow your software's filenaming conventions. Your instructor will help you, if necessary.
8. Close the file and exit from the program. Your instructor will help you, if necessary.

Exercise 2

James Constantino
43 Beacon Street
Amesbury, MA 01984-2234
(508) 555-8990

EDUCATION

Senior at Glover College
A.A., pending graduation
Major emphasis: Graphic design

Graduated Amesbury High School, 1995

SCHOOL ACTIVITIES

Sample Document (PageMaker 6.0 Windows)

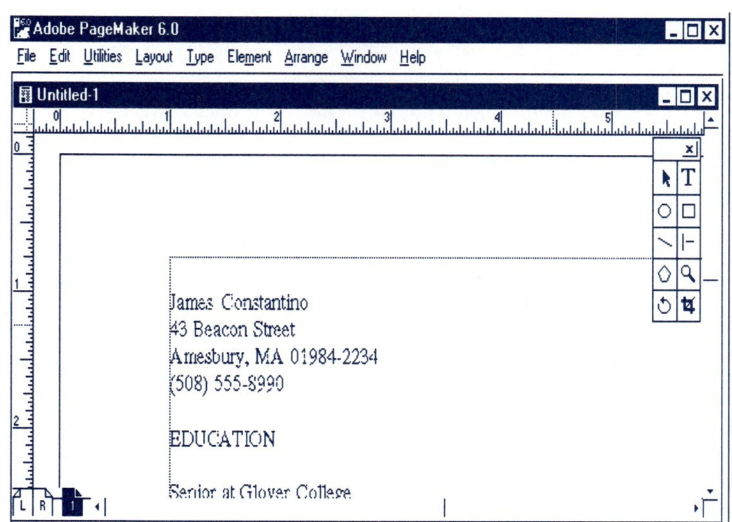

Production worker, Glover Weekly News, August 1996 to present. Work 15 hours a week designing pages and producing advertisements for college newspaper.

Dean's List, spring and fall 1996.

WORK EXPERIENCE

Publications intern, Stearns and Socol Advertising, Boston, MA, fall 1996. Produced flyers, newspaper advertisements, coupons, announcements, reports, and brochures.

EXERCISE 3

Learning Objectives

Enter text

Save a publication

INSTRUCTIONS

1. Load your desktop publishing program and start a new publication. Use the default page settings.
2. Select the text tool.
3. Click an insertion point at the left margin, 2" down from the top.
4. Magnify the page so text is visible.
5. Key the text on the right exactly as shown.
   - Do not worry about keying errors.
   - Remember to press Enter/Return only at the end of paragraphs.
   - Because fonts and default margins vary, your line endings may not match those in the exercise.
6. Save the file; name it **ECOLOG.**
7. Close the file. If you have finished working for the day, exit from the program.

For the remainder of the exercises, you will not be reminded to load or exit from your desktop publishing program.

Exercise 3

February 2, ----

Use four line returns between the date and the letter address and between the complimentary close ("Sincerely") and the name of the writer. Double-space between the rest of the letter parts.

Ms. Anne Sakamoto
Personnel Director
Ecological Solutions
897 Dane St.
Beverly, MA 01915-1259

Dear Ms. Sakamoto:

Thank you for meeting with me this morning concerning the Publications Assistant position. I greatly enjoyed learning more about Ecological Solutions and its innovative ideas for maintaining wetlands and restoring to ecological soundness some of our local harbors.

As we discussed, as a publications intern for Stearns and Socol Advertising and in desktop publishing classes at Glover College, I designed and produced many of the same types of publications Ecological Solutions requires. As you requested, I have enclosed a sample brochure.

I would welcome the opportunity to work for Ecological Solutions. If there is any additional information that would be helpful as you consider my application, please let me know.

Sincerely,

You will learn more about letter formatting in Exercise 13.

James Constantino

Enclosure

Learning Objectives

Enter text

Save two versions of a publication

INSTRUCTIONS

1. Start a new publication. Use the default page settings.
2. Select the text tool.
3. Click an insertion point at the left margin, 1" down from the top.
4. Magnify the page so text is visible.
5. Key half the exercise as noted and save it without closing the file; name it **ELEMENT.**
6. Key the remainder of the exercise.
7. Save the completed file as **ELEMENT1.** (Use the save as command.)
8. Close the file.

Exercise 4

DESIGN ELEMENTS

TYPEFACES
serif
sans serif

TYPE SIZES
6 point
12 point
24 point
36 point

TYPE STYLES
bold
italic
underline
strikethru

save the file

FONTS
Times 12-point bold
Helvetica 10-point italic

LEADING and ALIGNMENT (INCLUDING FORCE JUSTIFICATION)
This text is an example of 10-point type with 10-point leading (0 points between the lines), referred to as "10 on 10." This example is said to be "set solid." This left-aligned paragraph is even at the left edge.

This text is an example of 10-point type with 12-point leading (2 points between the lines), referred to as "10 on 12." A difference of two points between the type size and the leading is popular for body text. This centered paragraph is jagged on the left and right.

This is an example of 10-point type with 15-point leading (5 points between the lines), referred to as "10 on 15." This example is said to have "open leading." This right-aligned paragraph is even on the right and uneven on the left.

This last paragraph is set to 12-point type with "auto" leading. This setting is the default for some software. The paragraph will be aligned as justified text. Note all lines are even on both the left and the right, except the last.

save as

Learning Objectives

Enter text

Print a document

Terms

- Resolution
- Service bureau
- Portrait orientation
- Landscape orientation

Concepts

The objective of desktop publishing is to produce a high-quality printed document. Doing so requires a laser printer.

Laser printers suitable for desktop publishing must have a **resolution** (print quality) of 300 dots per inch or more. The more dots per inch a printer can produce, the better the quality of the printed document.

Most desktop documents will eventually be printed in large quantities. You can produce a master copy on your laser printer and give the copy to a print or photocopy shop for mass printing. If the final printed document must have a resolution comparable to that of books and magazines, you may want to take your publication on disk to a service bureau. **Service bureaus** provide a variety of services, including printing on high-resolution laser printers, converting graphics files to different formats, and making slides for presentations. If you decide to take your file to a service bureau, you should contact the service bureau beforehand (ideally, before you create the document) to ensure that your file copy will work with the service bureau's software and laser printer.

When you select the print option in your desktop publishing software, you will probably see a dialog box displaying additional options, such as the number of copies to be printed, the page range, and the destination printer. The software sets defaults for these options, but you can change them as desired. The default **orientation** is usually **portrait** (tall); the other option is **landscape** (wide). See the illustrations below.

Always do a final save of your file immediately before printing. Then, if anything should fail during the printing process, the file will remain intact.

Portrait

Landscape

INSTRUCTIONS

1. Start a new publication. Use the default page settings.
2. Click an insertion point at the left margin, 1" down from the top.
3. Key half the exercise as noted and save it without closing the file; name it **RULES.**
4. Key the remainder of the exercise.
5. Save the completed file as **RULES1.** (Use the save as command.)
6. Using all printer defaults, print one copy of **RULES1.**
7. Close the file.

EXERCISE
5

Exercise 5

COMPUTER ROOM RULES AND REGULATIONS

All software in the computer center is copyrighted and duplication of such material is strictly prohibited and illegal.

Do not bring outside software into the computer center.

Food and drinks are not allowed in the classrooms at any time.

Smoking is not permitted anywhere in the center.

Please clean up any scrap papers, printouts, etc., at your station before you leave for the day.

save

Do not rearrange any of the hardware in the center without checking with your teacher.

Do not connect or disconnect plugs without checking with your teacher.

Any changes made in the center's rules and procedures will be relayed to all users in written form or through their instructors.

save as

Learning Objectives

Understand stories
Understand text blocks
Enter text in separate stories
Print documents

Terms

- Story
- Text block
- Windowshades
- Windowshade handles

Concepts

In desktop publishing software, a single unit of text is called a **story.** A story may be as small as a single letter or as large as pages and pages of text. In each of the last four exercises, you have keyed a single story.

Documents may contain one story or many. This page, for example, contains four stories: the exercise number in the corner, the Learning Objectives, the Terms, and the Concepts. Having separate stories for these different elements is best. If text were inserted or deleted in one of the stories, the text in all the other stories would not be affected. The text in the other stories would not shift up or down, as it would if it were all in one story. Whether you key text in one story or several depends on what role the text will play in your document.

Stories are arranged in **text blocks.** A story can be contained in one text block or can be threaded through many text blocks. Text blocks can be moved from place to place, made wider or narrower to fit columns, and otherwise manipulated as you like.

To see a text block, click on some text with the pointer tool. Lines appear across the top and bottom of the block. They are called **windowshades.** The **handles** at either end of a windowshade are used to widen a text block or to make it narrower. For the top and bottom windowshade handles, an empty handle indicates the beginning (top) or end (bottom) of a story. If a handle contains a plus sign, there is more of the story in another text block. If a handle contains an arrow, you need to pull down that handle to reveal the rest of the story. To deselect a text block, move the pointer away from the text block and click.

In the next few exercises, you will create several separate stories in the same file. Starting a new story is easy. You simply click an insertion point outside the text block and start to key.

In Exercise 16, you will learn how to move text blocks and how to create separate text blocks from a single text block. In Exercise 17, you will learn how to widen and narrow text blocks.

Windowshades

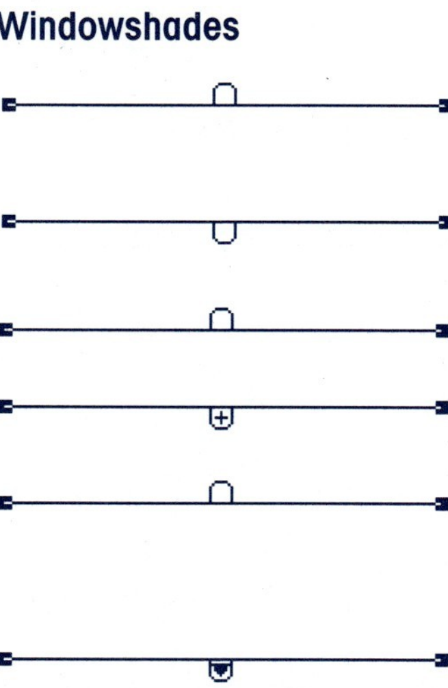

Stories and Text Blocks in a Newsletter

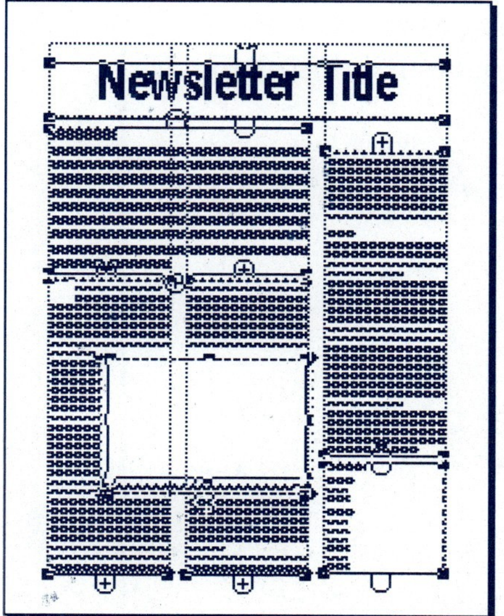

EXERCISE

6

INSTRUCTIONS

1. Start a new publication. Use the default page settings.
2. Key the first two lines on the right.
3. Key the rest of Exercise 6A as a separate story: Click an insertion point farther down the page and key. If you are not sure you are outside the text block of the first two lines, switch to the pointer tool, click on the first two lines, and note the bottom windowshade location. Then key the rest of the text below that location.
4. Save the file; name it **TEAM1**.
5. Using all printer defaults, print one copy.
6. Close the document.
7. Start a new publication. Use the default page settings.
8. Click an insertion point at the left margin, 1" down from the top.
9. Key the text in Exercise 6B as three separate stories. Begin each story at the vertical location indicated in the exercise. If you are not sure you are outside a text block, follow the procedures in Step 3.
10. Save the file; name it **YARDFILL**.
11. Using all printer defaults, print one copy.
12. Close the file.

Exercise 6A

West Pasadena High School
Athletics Department

1841 Shasta Highway Pasadena, CA 90246-8272 213-555-7474

In later exercises, you will format these two files into letterheads.

Exercise 6B

1" YARDFILL NURSERIES

1.5" 5 Magnolia Lane
Maplewood, NJ 09875-1813
Phone: 201-555-7676
Fax: 201-555-0816

2.5" Peter Moss, Proprietor

Learning Objectives

Enter text in separate stories
Print documents

INSTRUCTIONS

1. Start a new publication. Use the default page settings.
2. Key the three sections of text on the right as separate stories. If you are not sure you are outside a text block, follow the procedures in Step 3 on page 11.
3. Save the file; name it **DESSERT**.
4. Using all printer defaults, print one copy.
5. Close the file.

Exercise 7

COFFEE CUP
CAFE
Dessert
Menu

Coffee $1.00
Tea $1.00
Iced Tea $1.25
Iced Coffee $1.25
Espresso $1.25
Cappuccino $1.50
Iced Cappuccino $2.00
Cafe au Lait $1.10

$2.95
Blueberry Cheesecake
Chocolate Torte
Ice Cream Sundaes
Fudge Fantasy Cake
Coffee Toffee
Pumpkin Cheesecake
Great American Pie
Carrot Cake
Apple Pie
Lemon Squares
Brownies, Assorted Kinds
Fudge Fantasy
Chocolate Mousse Cake
Strawberries with Lemon Sorbet

Learning Objectives

Enter text in separate stories
Print documents

INSTRUCTIONS

1. Start a new publication. Use the default page settings.
2. Key the five sections of text on the right as separate stories.
3. Save the file; name it **PAUL**.
4. Using all printer defaults, print one copy.
5. Close the file.

Exercise 8

IT'S PAUL'S BIG DAY

He's going to be

5

Join us for a Party
at the Clown-Inn

Sunday, May 15, at 12:30 p.m. Come watch all the clowns make everybody smile as we wish Paul a Happy Birthday!

EXERCISE 9

Learning Objectives

Change default options
Learn about document setup
Change document setup options

Terms

- Page size
- Dimensions
- Target printer
- Double-sided
- Facing pages

Concepts

In the exercises so far, you have used the default document setup options for your software. In this exercise, you will learn about document setup options and how to change them.

You can change any of the default options for your software at any time. If you want the change to affect all future publications, you must make it with the program running but with no documents open. If you want the change to affect a single publication, you must open that publication and make the change. In this text, you will change defaults only for single publications.

When you start a new desktop publication, you must make some basic choices about format. These generally include the page size, page dimensions, orientation, number of pages, margins, and target printer.

Standard **page sizes** and **dimensions** include letter (8 1/2" x 11"), legal (8 1/2" x 14"), and tabloid (11" x 17"). When you select a page size, the dimensions are selected for you automatically. Desktop software often provides many page sizes and dimensions from which to choose. You can also key in figures for a custom size. You will use letter size for most of the activities in this text.

As you have learned, pages can have one of two orientations: portrait (tall) or landscape (wide). You will use both orientations in this text.

You set the **number of pages** and **margins** when you create the document. Pages can be added or deleted later as your needs dictate. Margins can easily be changed.

The **target printer** is the printer on which you will print the final version of your document. You may also be able to choose the resolution. This setting is standard for many printers.

Some programs have a **double-sided** option for documents that will be bound and printed on both sides of the page. With this option, you can set wider inside margins to accommodate binding. A **facing pages** option allows you to work with facing pages side by side. You will not use these two options in this text.

An option for **restarting page numbering** is used with multiple-publication documents. This option makes the software renumber pages in other documents automatically when the pagination in one publication changes.

INSTRUCTIONS

1. Start a new publication. Do not close the document setup dialog box.

2. Change some of the options in the dialog box and close it. Note the effect of your changes on the publication.

3. Continue to experiment with changing the different document setup options. If you want to learn more about an option, use the Help feature of your software or consult your software manual.

   You may need to go to other menus to change some of the document setup options that you chose initially. In PageMaker 6.0 for Windows, for example, if you want to add or delete pages after creating a document, you must go to the Layout menu.

4. Close the file without saving it.

Learning Objectives

Use typefaces

Terms

- Typeface
- Serif
- Sans serif
- Script
- Font

Concepts

In Lesson 2, you will learn about changing the appearance of text by altering such elements as the typeface, type style, and type size. In this exercise, you will learn about typefaces.

A **typeface** is a collection of all the characters of a single type design. Typefaces are often named after the designer, like Bodoni, or after the location where the design was created, like New York or Helvetica. The typefaces you choose for a publication can make a dramatic difference in communicating its message.

Most typefaces fall into three categories. **Serif typefaces** have lines or curves extending from the ends of the letters. **Sans serif typefaces** are straight-edged. **Script typefaces** resemble handwriting or hand-printing. There are also decorative or display typefaces consisting of symbols or designs.

The terms **typeface** and **font** are often used interchangeably, but in strict publishing terminology, they are different. A **font** is one style and size of a particular typeface. Palatino is a typeface. Ten-point Palatino bold is a font. You will learn about type sizes and type styles in the next two exercises.

Although more than 5,000 typefaces are available, desktop publishers usually use only two or three in a document, changing the type size and type style when variety is needed. Using just a few typefaces gives a publication an appearance of unity, consistency, and clarity.

Some Examples of Typefaces

Times	Helvetica	Nuptial
Palatino	Avant Garde	BrushScript
Bookman	Bauhaus	Tekton
Garamond	Kabel	❄✱▼❏✍ Zapf Dingbats

INSTRUCTIONS

1. Start a new publication. Use the default page settings.
2. Access the type or font option.
3. Key the name of each typeface available in your software in that typeface. For a symbol typeface, key some symbols; then key the name of the typeface in a different typeface.
4. Using all printer defaults, print one copy.
5. On the printout, write next to each typeface whether it is a serif, sans serif, script, or decorative typeface.
6. Close the file without saving.
7. In groups, if possible, pick six different types of publications, such as magazines, books, newsletters, and advertisements. Choose from your list of typefaces two or three that could be used to produce those publications. Consider the appearance, message, and needs of readers in making your decisions.
8. Make a list of the six publications and chosen typefaces, along with a brief explanation of each of your choices.

Learning Objectives

Use type styles
Open/recall a publication
Select text with the text tool

Terms

- Type style
- Roman (normal, medium)
- Retrieve (open, get, recall)
- Select (block)

Concepts

Type style refers to modification of typefaces to add emphasis or contrast. Most desktop publishing programs permit you to apply at least four styles to type: **Roman** (also called *normal* or *medium*), italic, bold, and bold/italic. Other type styles available in some desktop publishing software are outline, underline, double underline, strikethru, all caps, small caps, reverse, and shadow.

These attributes should be used sparingly and consistently for good effect. Use bold type for text that should stand out: heads and subheads, for example. Use italics for emphasis; foreign expressions; definitions; words used as words (the word *type*); names of ships, trains, aircraft, and spacecraft; and major titles (for example, books, newspapers, magazines, journals, long poems, plays, operas, long musical compositions, artwork, movies, and radio and television programs).

In this exercise, you will retrieve a file you keyed previously. In different software, retrieving a file may be referred to as *opening*, *getting*, or *recalling* it.

You will change typefaces and type styles for some of the text in the document. To make such modifications to previously keyed text, you must **block** or **select** it. To select text, use the text tool to drag over the text so that it is highlighted. Desktop publishing programs have different selection shortcuts, such as double-clicking to select a word or triple-clicking to select a paragraph. Often, the Edit menu has a select all command.

Some Type Styles

bold	~~strikethru~~
italic	reverse
bold/italic	underline

When text is set to reverse, it disappears from view. Actually it becomes white and will appear only when it is placed on a non-white background.

INSTRUCTIONS

1. Open **RESUME.**
2. Using the text tool, select the indicated text and change the typeface and type styles as shown in the exercise. Use the same sans serif typeface for all sans serif elements.
3. Using all printer defaults, print one copy.
4. Save and close the file.

Exercise 11

James Constantino
43 Beacon Street
Amesbury, MA 01984-2234
(508) 555-8990

Make the first four lines sans serif bold.

EDUCATION

Make the headings "EDUCATION," "SCHOOL ACTIVITIES," and "WORK EXPERIENCE" sans serif bold.

Senior at Glover College
A.A., pending graduation
Major emphasis: Graphic design

Graduated Amesbury High School, 1995

SCHOOL ACTIVITIES

Italicize the name of the student newspaper.

Production worker, *Glover Weekly News*, August 1996 to present. Work 15 hours a week designing pages and producing advertisements for college newspaper.

Dean's List, spring and fall 1996.

Make "Production worker," "Dean's List," and "Publications intern" bold.

WORK EXPERIENCE

Publications intern, Stearns and Socol Advertising, Boston, MA, fall 1996. Produced flyers, newspaper advertisements, coupons, announcements, reports, and brochures.

EXERCISE 12

Learning Objectives

Use different type sizes
Understand measurement options
Understand and change leading
Align text

Terms

- Points
- Picas
- Leading

Concepts

Type is measured in **points,** from the highest part of the tallest letter to the lowest descending part of a letter. There are 72 points to an inch. Although desktop publishing programs allow you to work with inches and other units of measurement, printers and desktop publishers generally work with **picas.** There are 12 points to a pica and 6 picas to an inch.

Leading (pronounced *ledding*) is the vertical distance between lines of type. Desktop publishing programs compute the leading for you automatically. The default automatic leading is usually 120 percent of the point size (10-point type would have 12-point leading). Desktop publishers often set the leading manually; for example, tightening the leading for headlines and opening it to make body text more readable.

Type size and leading play an important role in readability. Body text should be from 9 to 12 points in size. Headlines should be at least 1 or 2 points larger than the body text. A good rule of thumb for body text is to use at least 1 point more of leading than the type size; 2 or 3 points makes text even more readable.

You have already learned about flush left alignment, the default in many desktop publishing programs. Other alignment options include right, centered, justified, and force-justified.

Text Alignment

Flush left text has a friendly, informal look. It is good for narrow columns, body text, heads, captions, short lines, and large type. Contemporary style accepts flush left alignment in all areas of a publication.

Justified text has even left and right margins. It conveys formality and orderliness. Justified text can be read more rapidly because of its consistent column width. Justification accommodates more type and is a good choice for long works requiring unbroken reading and concentration.

Right alignment should be used sparingly for special effects such as headings or captions.

Centered alignment is usually reserved for headlines or other display text, announcements and invitations, pull quotes (short quotations set in large type sizes and used to draw attention to an article), and captions.

FORCE-JUSTIFIED ALIGNMENT IS USED FOR HEADINGS AND SPECIAL EFFECTS. THIS OPTION IS NOT USED FOR BODY TEXT.

INSTRUCTIONS

1. Open **ELEMENT1.**
2. Change the typefaces, type styles, type sizes, leading, and alignment as shown in the exercise.
   - Set all text to Courier, except where indicated.
   - If your software does not contain an element indicated, substitute another.
3. Access the measurement option for your software.
4. Change the measurement option to different units of measurement. Note the effects on the rulers in your document.
5. Return the measurement system option to inches.
6. Using all printer defaults, print one copy.
7. Save and close the file.

EXERCISE
12

Exercise 12

DESIGN ELEMENTS — 14-point sans serif bold, center-aligned

TYPEFACES — 14-point bold
serif — 12-point serif (other than Courier)
sans serif — 12-point sans serif

Set all text to Courier except where noted.

TYPE SIZES — 14-point bold
6 point
12 point
24 point
36 point

Set these four lines to the sizes noted.

TYPE STYLES — 14-point bold
bold
italic
underline
~~strikethru~~

Set these four lines to the styles noted.

FONTS — 14-point bold
Times 12-point bold
Helvetica 10-point italic

Set these two lines to the font noted.

Set this paragraph 10/10, left-aligned.

Set this heading 14-point bold, force-justified.

LEADING and ALIGNMENT (INCLUDING FORCE JUSTIFICATION)

This text is an example of 10-point type with 10-point leading (0 points between the lines), referred to as "10 on 10." This example is said to be "set solid." This left-aligned paragraph is even at the left edge.

Set the next paragraph 10/12, center-aligned.

This text is an example of 10-point type with 12-point leading (2 points between the lines), referred to as "10 on 12." A difference of two points between the type size and the leading is popular for body text. This centered paragraph is jagged on the left and right.

Set the next paragraph 10/15, right-aligned.

This is an example of 10-point type with 15-point leading (5 points between the lines), referred to as "10 on 15." This example is said to have "open leading." This right-aligned paragraph is even on the right and uneven on the left.

Set this last paragraph 12/auto, justified.

This last paragraph is set to 12-point type with "auto" leading. This setting is the default for some software. The paragraph will be aligned as justified text. Note all lines are even on both the left and the right, except the last.

EXERCISE 13

Learning Objectives

Change type size, type style, leading, and alignment

Create a letterhead

Learn personal-business letter format

Terms

- Letterhead
- Personal-business letter
- Block format
- Open punctuation
- Mixed punctuation
- Enclosure/attachment notation

Concepts

In this exercise, you will create and format a letterhead. **Letterhead** is stationery used by an individual or company that contains name and address information. Letterheads are designed at the top, sides, or bottom of a page, giving maximum space for writing the communication. You will use the type features you have learned in the last three lessons to format your letterhead. Other special features that can be used to enhance letterheads will be covered later in this text.

You will add this letterhead to the letter you keyed in Exercise 3 and format the letter as a personal-business letter. As the name implies, a **personal-business letter** is used for correspondence between an individual and a business.

In a personal-business letter (see the model at the right), the return address and date, if the letter does not have a letterhead, or just the date, if the letter does have a letterhead, is keyed 2 inches from the top. The side margins may be at the software default settings or at 1 inch. A double space (DS) separates all letter parts except the date and letter address and the complimentary close and name of the writer; for those two exceptions, a quadruple space (QS) separates letter parts.

The letter at the right is in **block** format, a popular format format for both personal and business correspondence. In block format, all letter parts begin at the left margin.

Letters may be formatted with **open** or **mixed punctuation.** The letter at the right uses mixed punctuation: a colon following the salutation and a comma following the complimentary close. A letter formatted with open punctuation has no punctuation following the salutation or the complimentary close.

When a separate item is included with a letter, an **enclosure** or **attachment notation** is keyed a double space below the the author's name. If the item is attached to the letter, the word *Attachment* is used; if the item is not attached to the letter, the word *Enclosure* is used.

INSTRUCTIONS

1. Open **ECOLOG.**
2. Create the letterhead shown at the top of the page (just inside the top margin) in 10-point sans serif bold, center-aligned. Use five spaces between the street and the city, and between the ZIP Code and the telephone number.
3. Make the body text of the letter 10/12 in a serif typeface.
4. Add bold to the body text as indicated in the model.
5. Using all printer defaults, print one copy.
6. Save and close the file.

EXERCISE
13

Exercise 13

Letterhead

James Constantino
43 Beacon Street Amesbury, MA 01984-2234 (508) 555-8990

Date February 2, ---- Begin text at 2" (or center the letter vertically).

QS

Letter address
Ms. Anne Sakamoto
Personnel Director
Ecological Solutions
897 Dane St.
Beverly, MA 01915-1259

DS

Salutation Dear Ms. Sakamoto:

DS

Body Thank you for meeting with me this morning concerning the **Publications Assistant** position. I greatly enjoyed learning more about **Ecological Solutions** and its innovative ideas for maintaining wetlands and restoring to ecological soundness some of our local harbors.

DS

1" or software default As we discussed, as a publications intern for Stearns and Socol Advertising and in desktop publishing classes at Glover College, I designed and produced many of the same types of publications **Ecological Solutions** requires. As you requested, I have enclosed a sample brochure. 1" or software default

DS

I would welcome the opportunity to work for **Ecological Solutions.** If there is any additional information that would be helpful as you consider my application, please let me know.

DS

Complimentary close Sincerely,

QS

Writer James Constantino

Personal-Business Letter

DS

Enclosure notation Enclosure

At least 1"

Learning Objectives

Insert, delete, and replace text

Proofread work

Concepts

Editing text in a desktop publishing program is quite similar to editing text in a word processor.

To insert new text into existing text, simply click an insertion point where you want the new text, and key. Text that is inserted into existing text will pick up the same formatting as the character to its left. When the insertion point is flashing, changes to the formatting may be made through the menus. The new formatting will then affect the text to be inserted.

To delete text, select the text to be deleted and press the Backspace or Delete key. To replace text (insert new text over old text), select the text to be replaced and key the new text over the old.

Since you have now learned to make corrections to text, you will be expected from this point on to proofread and correct all exercise copy before handing it in to your instructor. The key to effective proofreading is working systematically. Many professional proofreaders check printed matter twice, first by reading it against the original copy and then by reading it alone. To read a proof (the printed text) against copy (the original), place the two documents side by side. Use two envelopes to match the proof line by line with the copy. Covering up text you haven't yet reached helps you focus your attention on each line of text individually. Do not read for content. As if you were trying to detect differences between two nearly identical pictures, carefully compare the two lines of text.

After checking the proof against the copy, read the proof again (without referring to the copy) for coherence and completeness. Does it make sense? Is anything missing?

For large or complex proofreading tasks, consider working with another person: one reads from the copy while the other checks the proof for correctness. This method is especially useful for checking lists of numbers and other statistical material.

Some proofreader's marks used in this exercise appear on the right.

INSTRUCTIONS

1. Open **RULES1.**
2. Edit the text as shown at the right. If you do not understand a proofreader's mark, refer to the key below.
3. Using all printer defaults, print a draft copy.
4. Proofread the draft copy, using the methods described at the left. If further corrections are needed, make them, and print another copy.
5. Save and close the file.
6. Turn in the final copy to your instructor.

Proofreader's Marks

^ = insert

≡ = capitalize

EXERCISE 14

Exercise 14

COMPUTER ROOM RULES AND REGULATIONS

All software in the computer center is copyrighted ~~and~~ duplication of such material is strictly prohibited and illegal.

Insert two line returns here.

Do not bring outside software into the computer center.

Bring Food and drinks ~~are not allowed~~ in to the classrooms at any time.

e

Smok~~ing is not permitted~~ anywhere in the center.

Leave

~~Please clean up~~ any scrap papers, printouts, etc., at your station ~~before you leave for the day~~.

~~Do not~~ rearrange ~~any of~~ the hardware in the center without checking with your teacher.

's permission

~~Do not~~ connect or disconnect plugs without ~~checking with~~ your teacher.

~~Any changes made in the center's rules and procedures will be relayed to all users in written form or through their instructors.~~

EXERCISE 15

Learning Objectives

Insert, delete, replace, and format text

Proofread work

INSTRUCTIONS

1. Open **RESUME.**
2. Edit the text as shown at the right.
   - In the first four lines, the brackets] [mean that the text between the brackets should be centered.
   - Under "Publications Intern," "Designed and" goes before "produced."
3. Using all printer defaults, print a draft copy.
4. Proofread the draft copy, using the methods described on page 22. If further corrections are needed, make them, and print another copy.
5. Save and close the file.
6. Turn in the final copy to your instructor.

For the remainder of the exercises, you will not be reminded to proofread your work.

Proofreader's Marks

]\[= center

Exercise 15

]**James Constantino**[
]**43 Beacon Street**[
]**Amesbury, MA 01984-2234**[
]**(508) 555-8990**[

EDUCATION

~~Senior at~~ Glover College, 1997
A.A., ~~pending graduation~~
~~Major emphasis:~~ Graphic design,

Senior Designer, Glover College Yearbook, spring 1997. Worked with student committee to re-design the college yearbook on desktop publishing software.

High School Diploma,
~~Graduated~~ Amesbury High School, 1995

SCHOOL ACTIVITIES

Production worker, *Glover Weekly News*, August 1996 to May 1997 ~~present~~. Worked 15 hours a week designing pages and producing advertisements for college newspaper.

Dean's List, spring and fall 1996, spring 1997

WORK EXPERIENCE

Publications intern, Stearns and Socol Advertising, Boston, MA, fall 1996. Produced flyers, newspaper advertisements, coupons, Designed and announcements, reports, and brochures.

Intern, Olivera Publishing, Salem, MA, spring 1997. Designed and produced technical manuals and sales catalog.

Volunteer, Glover Outreach Project, spring 1997. Worked Saturday afternoons doing repairs and light carpentry for low-income citizens.

REFERENCES

References available upon request.

Learning Objectives

Cut, copy, and paste text

Terms

- Cut
- Copy
- Paste
- Clipboard

EXERCISE

16

Concepts

In a desktop publishing program, the method you use for moving and copying text depends on where and how you want the text to appear.

In most instances, you will use the text tool to select text for moving and copying. (Two exceptions will be discussed below.) After selecting the text, you will choose the **cut** or **copy** command from the Edit menu.

For most programs, cut or copied material resides in the **clipboard,** a temporary storage area in memory, from which it can be pasted repeatedly until something else is cut or copied to the clipboard.

To paste text into existing text, click an insertion point where you want the cut or copied text and choose the **paste** command from the Edit menu. To paste text as a separate text block, choose the pointer tool before executing the paste command, or click an insertion point outside the existing text blocks.

Text in the clipboard can be pasted into different documents in your desktop publishing program and generally into different applications as well. Keyboard shortcuts for cutting, copying, and pasting usually work across programs in the same operating system or environment.

Here are the two instances in which you would use the pointer tool rather than the text tool to select text to be moved or copied:

- To move a text block from one story into a different story, select the text block with the pointer tool, choose the cut command, click an insertion point where you want to insert the text, and choose the paste command.
- To move a text block, select it with the pointer tool, place the pointer anywhere on the text block except on a handle, and drag the text block to the new location. With this method, of course, the text block is not copied to the clipboard. For many programs, you can move a text block straight horizontally or straight vertically if you press a designated key (the Shift key, for example) while dragging.

INSTRUCTIONS

1. Open **ELEMENT.**
2. Select some text with the text tool and cut it.
3. If possible, open the clipboard to see the cut text. Then close the clipboard.
4. Paste the cut text into existing text in the document.
5. Change to the pointer tool, and paste the cut text again. Note how the cut text is now a separate text block.
6. Practice moving the text block by dragging it with the pointer tool.
7. Practice cutting, copying, and pasting text, both within existing text and as a separate text block. Select text blocks and insert them into other stories. Move text blocks, including straight vertically and straight horizontally.
8. If your instructor asks you to, print one copy of the document, using all printer defaults.
9. Close the file without saving.

EXERCISE 17

Learning Objectives

Move the zero marker
Create a layout grid
Adjust the size of text blocks
Drag-place text
Turn off hyphenation

Terms

- Grid
- Ruler guides
- Zero marker
- Drag-place

Concepts

In this exercise, you will create a layout grid to help you arrange text. A **grid** is a setup of nonprinting lines that can include the margin guides, column guides, and ruler guides. In this exercise, you will add ruler guides. **Ruler guides** can be added, moved, or deleted at any time. In some programs, the screen will show a grid of non-printing lines, like graph paper, that fulfills the same function.

Desktop publishing software often has a snap-to option that causes text and graphics to "snap" to the nearest guide. This snap-to function makes placement much easier.

In placing ruler guides, you will often find it helpful to reposition the zero marker. Desktop publishing programs with rulers often have a zero marker in the upper left corner where the rulers intersect. The **zero marker** resets where zero appears on a ruler. The marker can be dragged horizontally and/or vertically to any position. For example, to set a ruler guide 4 inches in from the right margin, you can drag the zero marker to the right margin. The horizontal ruler setting at the right margin will then be zero, and you can set your ruler guide at the 4-inch mark to the left of zero.

In this exercise, you will adjust the size of text blocks to fit the grid. Widening and narrowing text blocks is easy. Simply drag a right or left handle in the direction you want to go. Remember that when you narrow a text block, you may need to pull down the bottom windowshade handle or the bottom of the text block to re-display all the text.

You will cut some text and then **drag-place** it. Drag-placing is used when you want to create a text block at a precise size, particularly in an area where you do not have margin or column guides (margin and column guides, unlike ruler guides, restrict the flow of text). To drag-place, position the text cursor at the desired left boundary of the text block. Drag to outline the right and bottom boundaries. Then execute the paste command. Drag-placing is more efficient than pasting the text, moving the text block, and adjusting its size, but the effect is the same.

Finally, you will turn off the hyphenation feature for this document so that text will not be divided inappropriately. You will learn more about hyphenation in a future exercise.

INSTRUCTIONS

1. Open **RULES1.**
2. If your software has a snap to guides option, select it.
3. If possible on your software, reposition the zero marker to the right margin.
4. If your software uses ruler guides, place a vertical guide 4" in from the right margin and a horizontal ruler guide 2.5" down from the top of the page.
5. Drag the top left handle of the text block to the 4" vertical ruler guide. The text block is now 4" wide and at the right side of the page.
6. Drag down the bottom windowshade handle (or the bottom of the text box) so all text is visible.
7. Set all text to a sans serif typeface. Turn off hyphenation.
8. Move the text block below the horizontal ruler guide while keeping it to the right of the vertical ruler guide. ***(HINT:*** If your software has a function for dragging straight vertically, use it.)
9. Cut the heading. Drag-place it, beginning just below the top margin and to the right of the vertical ruler guide. Use the right margin as the right boundary of the dragged text.
10. Change the type styles, type sizes, and leading as shown in the exercise.
11. Using all printer defaults, print one copy.
12. Save and close the file.

EXERCISE
17

Exercise 17

Make the title 30-point bold with auto leading.

COMPUTER ROOM RULES AND REGULATIONS

ruler guide at 4"

ruler guide at 2.5"

Make this paragraph 14/16. →

All software in the computer center is copyrighted. Duplication of such material is strictly prohibited and **illegal.**

↖Bold

18-point bold italic →

DO NOT

Set the rest of the text at 18/20. ↓

Bring outside software into the computer center.

Bring food and drinks into the classrooms at any time.

Smoke anywhere in the center.

Leave any scrap papers, printouts, etc., at your station.

Rearrange the hardware in the center without checking with your teacher.

Connect or disconnect plugs without your teacher's permission.

The text and spacing in this exercise have been reduced to make the exercise fit on the page.

EXERCISE 18

Learning Objectives

Learn resume format
Create a layout grid
Cut, paste, and adjust text blocks
Drag-place text
Format text

Terms

- Resume

Concepts

A **resume** lists your experience, skills and abilities. It provides an overview of what you have to offer an employer for a particular job and provides a picture of who you are.

A resume is often sent to an employer and forms the basis for getting the interview. At the interview, the resume serves as discussion material. Since a resume leaves an employer with an impression of you, it should highlight your most positive qualities.

A resume should include identifying information (name, address, and so forth), a section on education, and a section on work experience. Recent graduates often include a section on school activities. You may list references (with their permission) or use the statement "References available upon request." Other optional materials may include special skills, course work, hobbies, or interests pertinent to the position being applied for; special honors or awards; and community activities.

While resumes may vary in format, the information should be easy to read. Unless work history is extensive, resumes should not exceed one page.

INSTRUCTIONS

1. Open **RESUME.**
2. Change the top margin to 1.5" and all other margins to 1".
3. Set a horizontal ruler guide at 1 3/8" *from the top margin.* Set two vertical ruler guides at 1.5" and 2" *from the left margin.*
4. Adjust the text block to fit the side margins. Drag the text down to just below the horizontal ruler guide. ***(HINT:*** If your software has a function for dragging straight vertically, use it.)
5. Change the leading for all the text to 14-point. Turn off hyphenation.
6. Cut the first four lines and paste them just inside the top margin. "EDUCATION" should be just below the horizontal ruler guide (you may have to delete a line return).
7. Change "James Constantino" to all capital letters, 14-point type.
8. Justify the body text.
9. Add "HONORS" as a heading before "Dean's List."
10. Under "WORK EXPERIENCE," switch the order of the first two entries.
11. For the body text of the resume, shorten the text block so its left boundary is the vertical ruler guide at 2". You may need to pull down the bottom windowshade handle (or the bottom of the text box) so all text is visible.
12. Cut each of the headings and drag-place them at the left margin, with their right boundary being the vertical ruler guide at 1.5". Do not worry about horizontal placement; you will adjust them in Step 15.
13. Right-align each of the headings.
14. Go through the body text of the resume and insert line spaces so that each major section is separated by four line returns.
15. Place horizontal ruler guides underlining the first line of each section of body text.
16. Drag each section heading to the appropriate ruler guide. Make sure the headings do not move horizontally as you drag them. Their right boundary should still be the 1.5" vertical ruler guide.
17. Using all printer defaults, print one copy.
18. Save and close the file.

EXERCISE
18

Exercise 18

ruler guide at 1.5"

ruler guide at 2"

ruler guide at 1 3/8"

Use ruler guides to align headings with body text.

JAMES CONSTANTINO
43 Beacon Street
Amesbury, MA 01984-2234
(508) 555-8990

Resume

EDUCATION

A.A., Graphic Design, Glover College, 1997

High School Diploma, Amesbury High School, 1995

SCHOOL ACTIVITIES

Senior Designer, *Glover College Yearbook*, spring 1997. Worked with student committee to re-design the college yearbook on desktop publishing software.

Production Worker, *Glover Weekly News*, August 1996 to May 1997. Worked 15 hours a week designing pages and producing advertisements for college newspaper.

The text and spacing in this exercise have been reduced because of space constraints.

HONORS

Dean's List, spring and fall 1996, spring 1997.

WORK EXPERIENCE

Intern, Olivera Publishing, Salem, MA, spring 1997. Designed and produced technical manuals and sales catalog.

Publications Intern, Stearns and Socol Advertising, Boston, MA, fall 1996. Designed and produced flyers, newspaper advertisements, coupons, announcements, reports, and brochures.

Volunteer, Glover Outreach Project, spring 1997. Worked Saturday afternoons doing repairs and light carpentry for low-income citizens.

REFERENCES

References available upon request.

EXERCISE 19

Learning Objectives

Edit text with story editor
Copy a publication

Terms

- Story editor

Concepts

As you have learned, text should be keyed and edited in a word processing program rather than in desktop publishing software. Word processors not only enable users to key text more quickly than desktop publishing software, but also provide a wealth of features for editing text. For those occasions when you do need to edit text in a desktop publishing program, however, you can avail yourself of the story editor feature available in many programs.

The **story editor** is a mini-word processor. As the name implies, in story editor, you work with stories (remember, a *story* is a single unit of text). Only the text of a story is displayed, not the layout, so the screen redraws itself rapidly. Copy appears as straight text in a standard font, so you can move through it quickly and easily. You can apply formatting to text in story editor, but generally you will not see the formatting until you return to layout view. The story editor usually contains a simple spelling checker and a find/replace feature.

Spelling checkers do not detect words that have been spelled correctly but used incorrectly; for example, "to" instead of "too." It is generally best to run a spell-check after finishing a document and then proofread your work.

In this exercise, you will work with a copy of a data file. One way to copy a file is to open it and to save it immediately under a different filename using the save as command. If your software has an option for opening a copy of a publication instead of the original, use that option instead, since it opens an untitled copy of the document, leaving no chance that you might accidentally modify the original. You then save and name the document as usual.

INSTRUCTIONS

1. Open **DESSERT** (or open a copy of **DESSERT** if your software has that option).
2. Save the document as **DESSERT1.**
3. Spell-check the first story.
4. In the second story, replace all instances of "$1.00" with "$1.25." Then spell-check the story.
5. In the third story, replace each instance of "Cheesecake" with "Pie." Then spell-check the story.
6. Using all printer defaults, print one copy.
7. Save and close the file.
8. Open **ECOLOG** and **ELEMENT1.** Spell-check each document. If a spell-check results in corrections, print a corrected copy of the document. Then save and close it.

Learning Objectives

Format text with the control palette

Terms

- Control palette
- Character view
- Paragraph view
- Paragraph

Concepts

A disadvantage to formatting text in desktop publishing software is that you often have to access several different commands to apply all the formatting you want to selected text. Some desktop publishing programs offer a **control palette** that eliminates this inconvenience. When you are working in story editor or working with the text tool in layout view, you can use the control palette to assign several different types of formatting to text simultaneously. The control palette can be used to change the typeface, type style, type size, leading, alignment, and other attributes of selected text.

The control palette can be displayed on the screen like the toolbox. When text is selected or an insertion point is clicked in the text, the control palette displays the attributes of that text.

In PageMaker, the control palette has two displays for changing text. In **character view,** you can change attributes such as the typeface, type style, type size, and leading for selected text. In **paragraph view,** you can change formatting features such as alignment and indents for one or more paragraphs. (In desktop publishing software, a **paragraph** is any unit in text that ends in a hard return, even if it consists of one sentence, a few words, or even just a hard return itself.)

To change text formatting with the control palette, display the palette, select the text, and click on the appropriate control palette buttons. If no text is selected when changes are made in the Control palette, the publication defaults will be changed. To change paragraph attributes for just one paragraph, you need only click an insertion point in the paragraph and then make the change.

An even more efficient method of applying several different types of formatting to text is to use **styles.** You will learn about styles, and other text and graphics attributes that can be changed through the control palette, in later exercises.

The PageMaker 6.0 (Windows) Control Palette—Character View

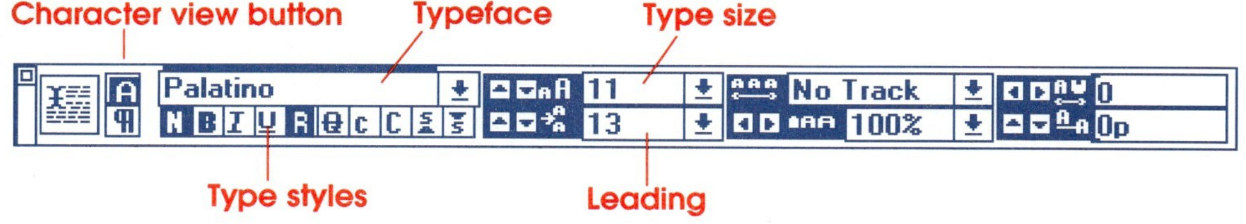

INSTRUCTIONS

1. Open **RULES**.
2. Display the control palette.
3. Practice using the control palette to change the typeface, type style, type size, leading, and alignment of selected text.
4. Using all printer defaults, print one copy.
5. Close the file without saving.

EXERCISE 21

Learning Objectives

Create squares, rectangles, circles, ovals, and polygons

Use fills (shades)

Select, resize, move, and delete objects

Change the stacking order

Terms

- Drawing tools
- Crossbar
- Layering shapes

Concepts

Most desktop publishing programs contain **drawing tools** that enable you to create simple objects or designs for your publication.

A **rectangle tool** enables you to draw squares and rectangles. To draw squares or rectangles with rounded corners, you may have a **rounded-corner tool** or a menu option. An **ellipse tool** permits you to draw circles or ovals. With a **polygon tool,** you can create basic polygons. **Line tools** will be discussed in Exercise 22.

When you select a drawing tool from the toolbox, the mouse pointer changes to a **crossbar** (+). To draw a circle, oval, square, rectangle, or polygon, select the appropriate tool, place the crossbar where you want the object to begin, and drag diagonally down. To make a circle, square, or polygon with equilateral sides, you must usually hold down a key while you drag (the Shift key, for example). Release the mouse button before releasing the key.

To resize, delete, or move an object, you must first select it by clicking on it with the pointer tool. (For "empty" objects like the circle at the upper left of the next page, you must click on the edge of the object to select it.) Handles will appear around the object, as in the illustration below. To resize the object, drag the appropriate handle. To delete it, press the Delete or Backspace key. To move it, place the pointer anywhere on the object except on a handle, and drag. (For "empty" objects like the circle at the upper left of the next page, you must drag by the edge, but not by a handle.)

A shape may be filled with tints, colors, and patterns, which are selected using appropriate menu commands. The fill patterns are opaque and will hide anything behind them. A "paper" fill is white.

When shapes are **layered** or stacked on top of each other, shadowing and other effects can be created. To rearrange the order of stacked objects, you can often use "send to back" and "bring to front" commands. Many programs have a special keyboard command (Control-click, for example) to select an object in the next layer.

To cut or copy an object, select it with the pointer tool and execute the appropriate command, just as you would for text. The object will appear in the Clipboard, from which you can paste it again and again until another object is cut or copied to the clipboard. Copying and pasting would be the best method for creating the shadow box at the bottom left of Exercise 21, because you would then be sure that both boxes were the same size.

INSTRUCTIONS

1. Start a new publication. Set the left margin at .75".
2. Position vertical ruler guides at 2" and 3" and horizontal ruler guides at 2", 3", 5", and 7".
3. Using the appropriate drawing tools, create the shapes and fills within the ruler guides (and margins) as shown in the exercise.
4. Save the file; name it **SHAPES.**
5. Using all printer defaults, print one copy.
6. Close the file.

A Selected Object

EXERCISE
21

Exercise 21

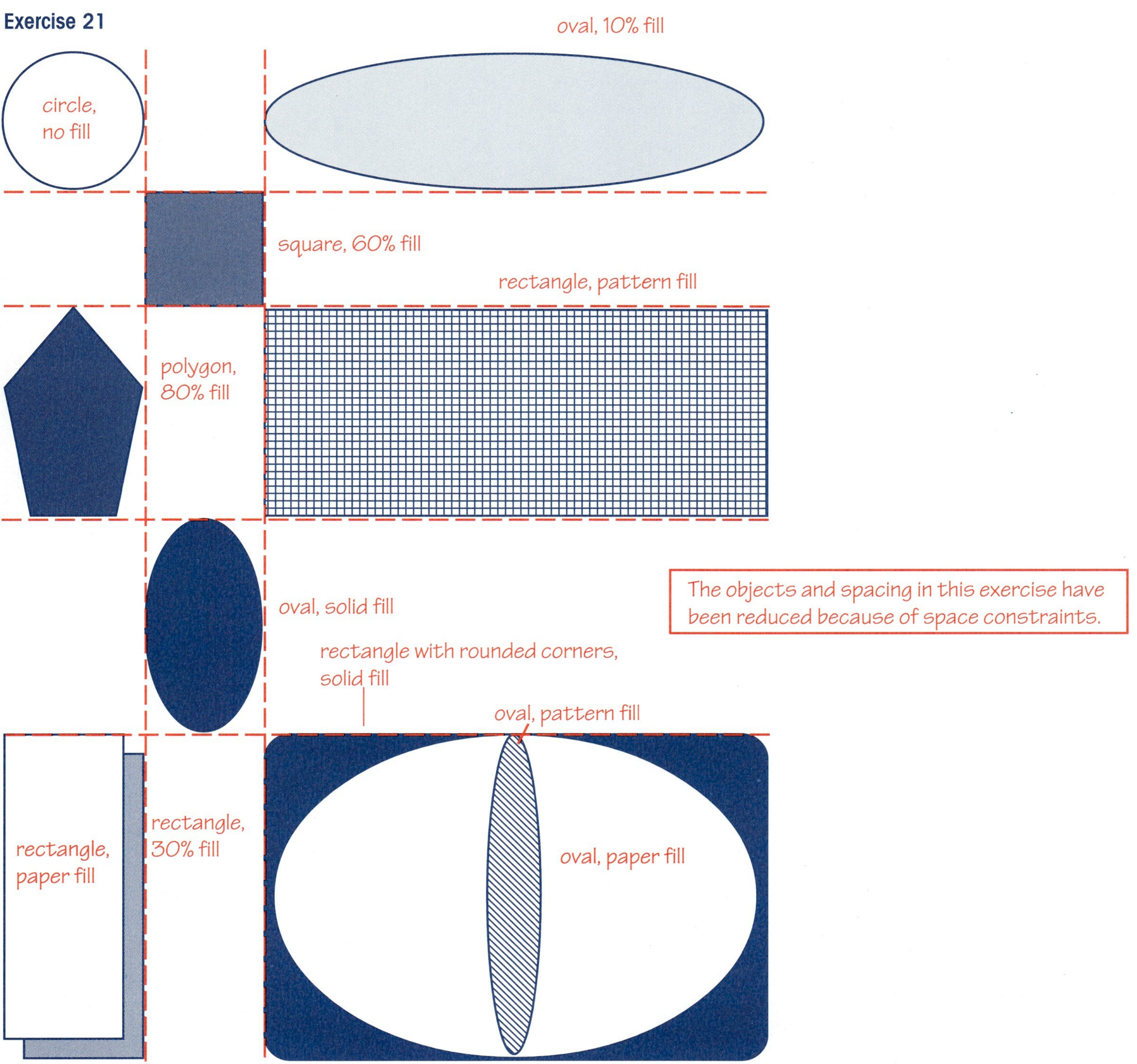
oval, 10% fill
circle, no fill
square, 60% fill
rectangle, pattern fill
polygon, 80% fill
oval, solid fill
The objects and spacing in this exercise have been reduced because of space constraints.
rectangle with rounded corners, solid fill
oval, pattern fill
rectangle, 30% fill
rectangle, paper fill
oval, paper fill

Learning Objectives

Draw lines (rules)
Choose line sizes and patterns
Edit drawn shapes
Change a polygon to a star
Use the power paste feature

Terms

- Lines/rules
- Line tool
- Constrained-line tool
- Power paste
- Offset

Concepts

Most desktop publishing programs contain two line tools: a **line tool,** which draws lines at any angle, and a **constrained-line tool,** which draws lines at any 45-degree angle. Lines are referred to as **rules** in some software.

Desktop publishing software offers a variety of line widths and designs from which to choose. Often, you can set your own custom sizes as well. The line widths and designs may be used not only for drawn lines, but also for the border of any rectangle, square, oval, polygon, or circle. You may select "none" from the line options if you do not want a border to appear around a shape. Line options also include reverse (the line turns white and can only be seen against a shaded background), as well as transparent (for dashed and similarly patterned lines, the spaces between the lines will show the color of the background rather than white).

Lines, like other drawn objects, may be selected with the pointer tool and deleted, moved, resized, or copied. You must usually press a key (the Shift key, for example) to avoid distorting a line drawn with the constrained-line tool while resizing it. Pressing this key while drawing or resizing a line drawn with the line tool results in a line at a 45-degree angle.

Software with a polygon option may offer a feature for changing the polygon to a star.

Many desktop publishing programs have a **power paste** option for pasting multiple copies of an object. You may be able to set the horizontal and vertical **offset,** or distance, between the objects. This option prevents your having to measure, place ruler guides, and drag when you want objects at a set distance from one another.

PageMaker Line Options

INSTRUCTIONS

1. Open **SHAPES** (or open a copy of **SHAPES** if your software has that option).
2. Save the document as **SHAPES1.**
3. Delete the top right oval and the square.
4. Resize shapes and change borders as noted. If a border is unavailable, substitute the closest one available. For the rectangle in the lower left corner, remember to copy and paste to create the shadow box effect.
5. Change the polygon into a star, if your software has that option.
6. Create the new objects: three rings, musical note, toothbrush, and eyeglasses. Use copy and paste where duplication of shapes is necessary. If a power paste feature is available, use it.

   HINT: To create the "bridge" of the eyeglasses: draw a white oval without a border between the two "lenses." Then layer a black oval over the white oval.
7. Using all printer defaults, print one copy.
8. Save and close the file.

EXERCISE
22

Exercise 22

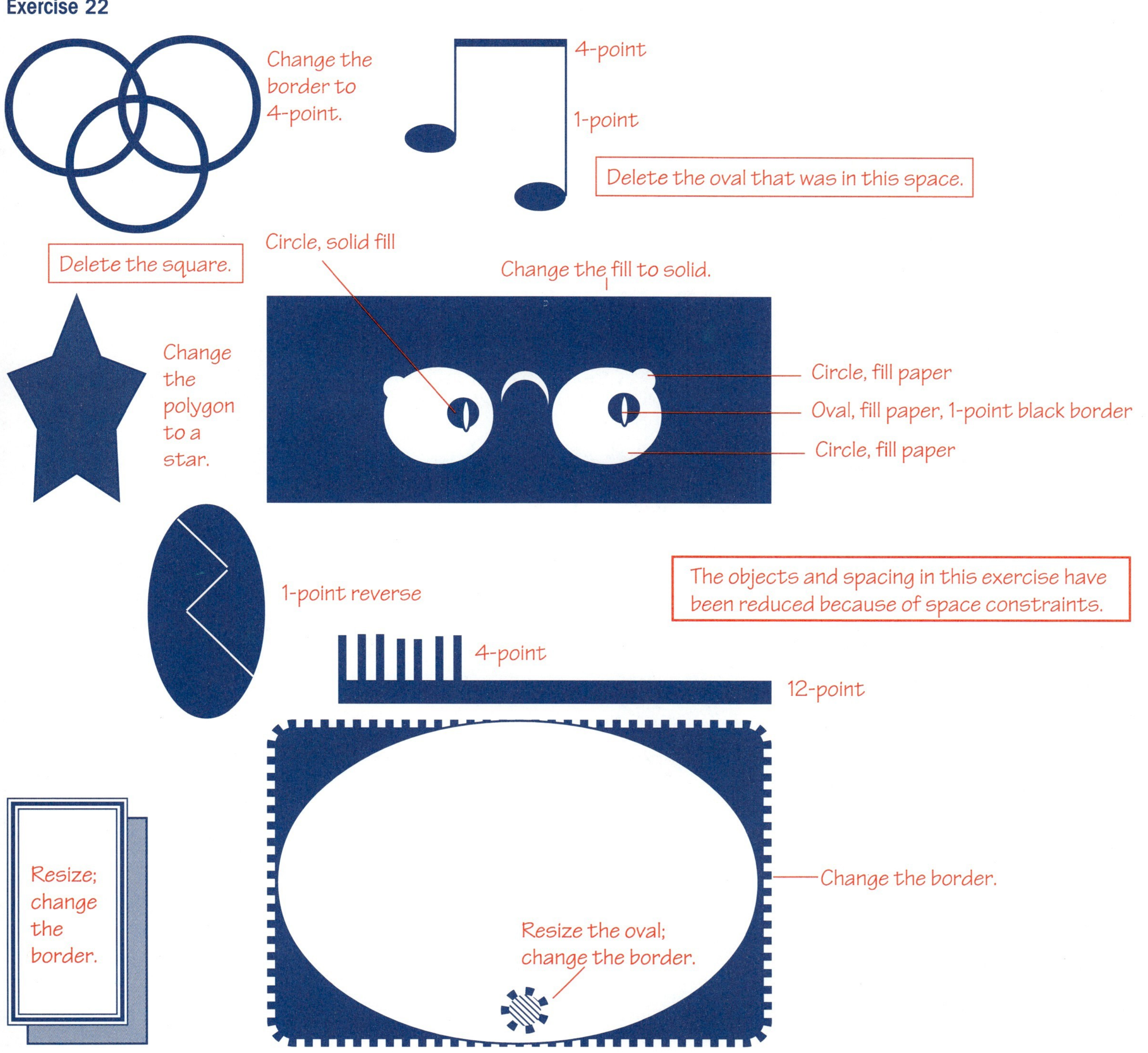
Change the border to 4-point.
4-point
1-point
Delete the oval that was in this space.
Delete the square.
Circle, solid fill
Change the fill to solid.
Change the polygon to a star.
Circle, fill paper
Oval, fill paper, 1-point black border
Circle, fill paper
1-point reverse
The objects and spacing in this exercise have been reduced because of space constraints.
4-point
12-point
Resize; change the border.
Change the border.
Resize the oval; change the border.

Learning Objectives

Create objects with drawing tools
Select multiple objects
Work with grouped objects
Align and distribute objects

Terms

- Marquee
- Grouping objects
- Aligning objects
- Distributing objects

Concepts

Every desktop publishing program offers a way of selecting and copying or moving several objects at the same time. The method can be as simple as pressing a key (the Shift key, for example) as each object is selected. You may also be able to drag with the pointer tool to draw a **marquee**, or box, around objects to select them all.

The methods described above group objects only until you deselect them. Some programs offer a **grouping** option through a menu command that enables you to group selected objects permanently (or at least until you decide to split them up using another menu command). Grouped objects can be moved and resized together as a unit, as well as individually. You can see how a grouping option might be useful for the objects on page 37.

In Exercise 22, you learned that you may be able to use a power paste option to paste objects with a specific horizontal or vertical distance between them. Some programs offer a related option for objects already on the page. An **align** option lines objects up; a **distribute** option puts an even amount of space between objects. Objects can be aligned or distributed based on a common edge or on their centers.

INSTRUCTIONS

1. Start a new publication. Use the default page settings.
2. Using the appropriate drawing tools, create the seven objects shown in the exercise. Place and size them as desired.
   - Use the copy and paste procedure where duplication of shapes is necessary.
   - Use the power paste or align and distribute feature (if available) to create Object 6.

   HINT: *To create the coffee cup and plate:*

   - Draw an oval to create the plate; use a 1-point line for the border.
   - Copy the oval, size it smaller than the plate, use a 10% fill with no border, and place it inside the larger oval to create the shadow.
   - Draw a large oval and use a paper fill to create the cup.
   - Draw an oval on top of the cup and use a paper fill to create the rim.
   - Draw an oval inside the rim of the cup and use a solid fill to create the coffee.
   - Draw a circle handle; use a paper fill.
   - Draw a smaller circle and place it inside the larger circle to complete the handle.

   To create the steam:

   - Draw small circles; use a 10% fill for some and a paper fill for others. Place the paper-filled circles in the coffee; place the others outside the coffee as shown.
3. If your software has a grouping option, group the objects of which the cup (Object 3) is composed. Copy the group and resize the copy as shown. *If your software does not have an option that enables you to resize grouped objects as a unit, do not complete this part of the exercise.*
4. Save the file; name it **OBJECTS.**
5. Using all printer defaults, print one copy.
6. Close the file.

EXERCISE

23

Exercise 23

1

3

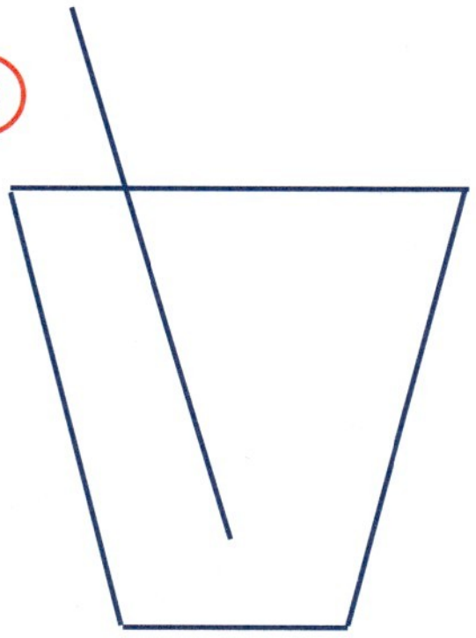

Create the smaller cup only if you have a grouping option that allows you to resize grouped objects as a unit.

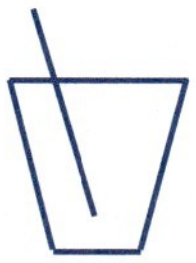

2

4

5

7

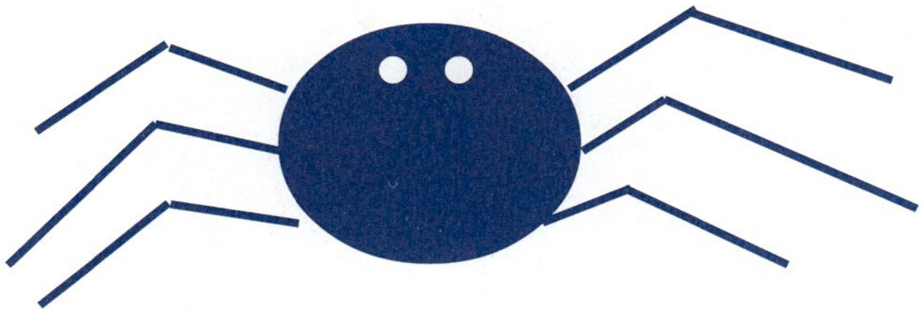

6

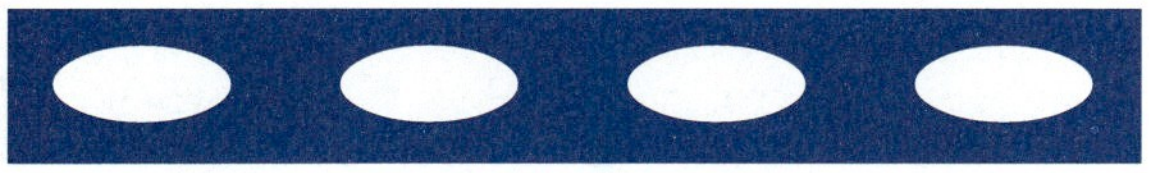

The objects and spacing in this exercise have been reduced because of space constraints.

EXERCISE 24

Learning Objectives

Create objects with drawing tools

INSTRUCTIONS

1. Open **YARDFILL**. Set all margins at .75".
2. Right-align the address text block; set the type to sans serif 14-point.
3. Drag the "Peter Moss, Proprietor" text block temporarily to a blank area on the page (not at the bottom).
4. Delete the "Y" in "yardfill." Move the "ardfill Nurseries" text block so it is just inside the top margin and begins at 2" on the horizontal ruler. Set the type to sans serif 24-point bold.
5. To create the tree:
   - Draw two 8-point lines (approximately 1 1/8" long) to create the V-shaped branches.
   - Draw a 12-point line to create the tree trunk.
   - Create a circle approximately .25" in diameter using a 20% fill and no border. Copy the circle to create the foliage. Use the power paste feature, if available. You may also wish to use the align and distribute options. Note that your foliage will extend above the top margin. Your foliage does not have to match the foliage in the exercise.
6. To create the grass:
   - Draw a solid-fill rectangle .5" tall and extending from the left margin to the right. The bottom of the rectangle should be at the bottom margin.
   - Draw 2-point lines to create grass blades of varying heights. The tallest blade should not be more than 1" high. Your grass does not have to match the grass in the exercise.
7. Set the "Peter Moss, Proprietor" text block to sans serif 14-point reverse. Center-align it and drag it onto the rectangle. Drag the side handles to extend to the left and right edges of the rectangle (this forces the text to center-align across the rectangle automatically).
8. Using all printer defaults, print one copy. If some of the foliage is cut off, select everything at the top of the page including the address information, move it down (if you have a grouping option, use it), and adjust the size of the tree trunk. Then print another copy.
9. Save and close the file.

EXERCISE 24

Exercise 24

20% fill, no border

ARDFILL NURSERIES —24-point bold

5 Magnolia Lane
Maplewood, NJ 09875-1813
Phone: 201-555-7676
Fax: 201-555-0816

14-point

8-point

12-point

Set all text to sans serif.

The text, objects, and spacing in this exercise have been reduced because of space constraints.

Set "Peter Moss, Proprietor" in 14-point reverse.

2-point

Peter Moss, Proprietor

rectangle, solid fill

Learning Objectives

Create objects with drawing tools

Concepts

An **invitation** is a request for someone to be present at a special event or to celebrate an occasion. Invitations may be formal (such as a request to be present at a company dinner) or informal (such as a request to attend a friend's party).

Invitations are sometimes printed on paper or card sizes other than the standard 8 1/2" x 11" paper. Changing paper size for invitations will be covered in a future exercise.

Invitation text is usually centered horizontally and vertically on the page. Other formats may be used, however. Bold and italics may be used to emphasize text. In later exercises, you will see how desktop publishing can further enhance an invitation to help convey a sense of the formality and tone of the occasion.

INSTRUCTIONS

1. Open **PAUL.** Set the left margin at 1" and all other margins at .75".
2. Create a dashed-line border to frame the margins.
3. Position horizontal ruler guides at 1.75", 2.5", 6.25", 7.25", and 8.5".
4. For all the type blocks except "5," choose a sans serif typeface, set the type size as shown in the exercise, and center-align the text.
5. Select each text block and check that the handles extend to both margins so text will center-align correctly. For the last text block, drag the side handles in 1" from the margin on each side. Drag each text block except "5" so that the first line of the text block rests on the appropriate ruler guide, as shown on page 41.
6. To create the plate, draw an oval approximately 5.25" wide by 1" tall. Use a 2-point line for the border. Place the oval so that it is centered between the side margins and sitting on the 6.25" horizontal ruler guide. For the inner ring, copy the oval and size it smaller than the plate. Use a 1-point line for the border and place it inside the larger oval.
7. To create the cake, draw the bottom of the cake to fit on top of the smaller oval plate; use a 40% fill and no border. Note the rounded corners. Draw an oval to fit on top of the cake; use a 20% fill and no border.
8. To create the candles:
   - Create a rectangle .75" tall by 1/8" wide; use a paper fill and a 1-point border.
   - Use a 4-point line to create the wick.
   - Create a star or an oval using a hairline border to represent the flame. The example uses a polygon with edited settings.
   - Select the completed candle; group it using the grouping option, if available; copy it; and drag it onto the cake.
   - Paste four copies of the candle, using the power paste option and horizontal and vertical offset, if available. Alternatively, you can use the align and distribute options, if available, to create an attractive candle arrangement. You can also simply drag the candles. Your arrangement does not have to match that in the exercise.
9. Set the "5" to a sans serif typeface, 24-point reverse, center-aligned. Drag it to the middle of the cake (adjust the side handles to the sides of the cake so the text will align properly).
10. Using all printer defaults, print one copy.
11. Save and close the file.

EXERCISE 25

Exercise 25

1.75"
IT'S PAUL'S BIG DAY—24-point bold
2.5"
He's going to be—18-point
Invitation
5
6.25"
Make this text block 24-point.
7.25"
Join us for a Party
at the Clown-Inn
Make this text block 24-point.
8.5"
Sunday, May 15, at 12:30 p.m.
Come watch all the clowns
make everybody smile as we
wish Paul a Happy Birthday!

The text, objects, and spacing in this exercise have been reduced because of space constraints.

Learning Objectives

Create objects with drawing tools

Concepts

A **flyer** is a communication that is meant to be posted in public or distributed. Its purpose is to attract immediate attention to inform the reader of a special event, service, or product. A flyer is sometimes thought of as an informal advertisement.

The text of a flyer, like the text of an invitation or an announcement, is usually centered horizontally and vertically on the page. Other formats may be used, however. Bold, italics, and spacing techniques may be used to emphasize text. In upcoming exercises, you will apply other desktop publishing techniques to enhance flyers.

INSTRUCTIONS

1. Open **RULES1.** Set the bottom margin at .5".
2. You should already have a horizontal ruler guide at 2.5" and a vertical ruler guide at 4" (if you do not, place them). Add horizontal ruler guides at 2.25" and 4.5" and a vertical ruler guide at 5". If you have a power paste option with control of horizontal and vertical offset, or an align option, you do not need to add any more ruler guides. If you do not have either of these options, set additional horizontal ruler guides at 4.75", 6.5", 6.75", 8.5", and 8.75".
3. Create a circle 1.75" in diameter; use an 8-point line for the border. As shown in the exercise, set the circle in the 2.5" and 4.5" horizontal ruler guides, centered horizontally between the left margin and the vertical ruler guide at 5".
4. *If you have a power paste option with control of horizontal and vertical offset,* copy the circle and set your power paste feature to paste it three times with a horizontal offset of 0" and a vertical offset of 2".

   Alternatively, if you have an align option, copy the circle and paste three copies of it aligned roughly vertically underneath. Then align the circles on their center axes with a vertical distribution of 2".

   If you have neither of these options, copy the circle and place each copy, using the ruler guides as shown on the right.
5. Draw each object inside each circle as shown; center each object within the circle. *If you have a grouping option that allows you to resize grouped objects as a unit, instead of recreating the cup and cigarette,* open **OBJECTS,** copy the cup group, and resize the copy. Group the cigarette objects, copy the group, and resize the copy.
6. Draw a diagonal line through each circle as shown, using an 8-point line.
7. Using a 12-point line, draw three horizontal lines as follows *(lines can extend outside the top and bottom margins)*: (1) above the heading, from the left margin to the right margin; (2) below the heading, along the 2.25" horizontal ruler guide, from the 4" vertical ruler guide to the right margin; (3) at the bottom margin, extending from the 4" vertical ruler guide to the right margin.
8. Draw a dashed border around the borders of the document as shown. The border will probably fall outside at least some margins.
9. Using all printer defaults, print one copy.
10. Save and close the file.

EXERCISE 26

Exercise 26

Flyer

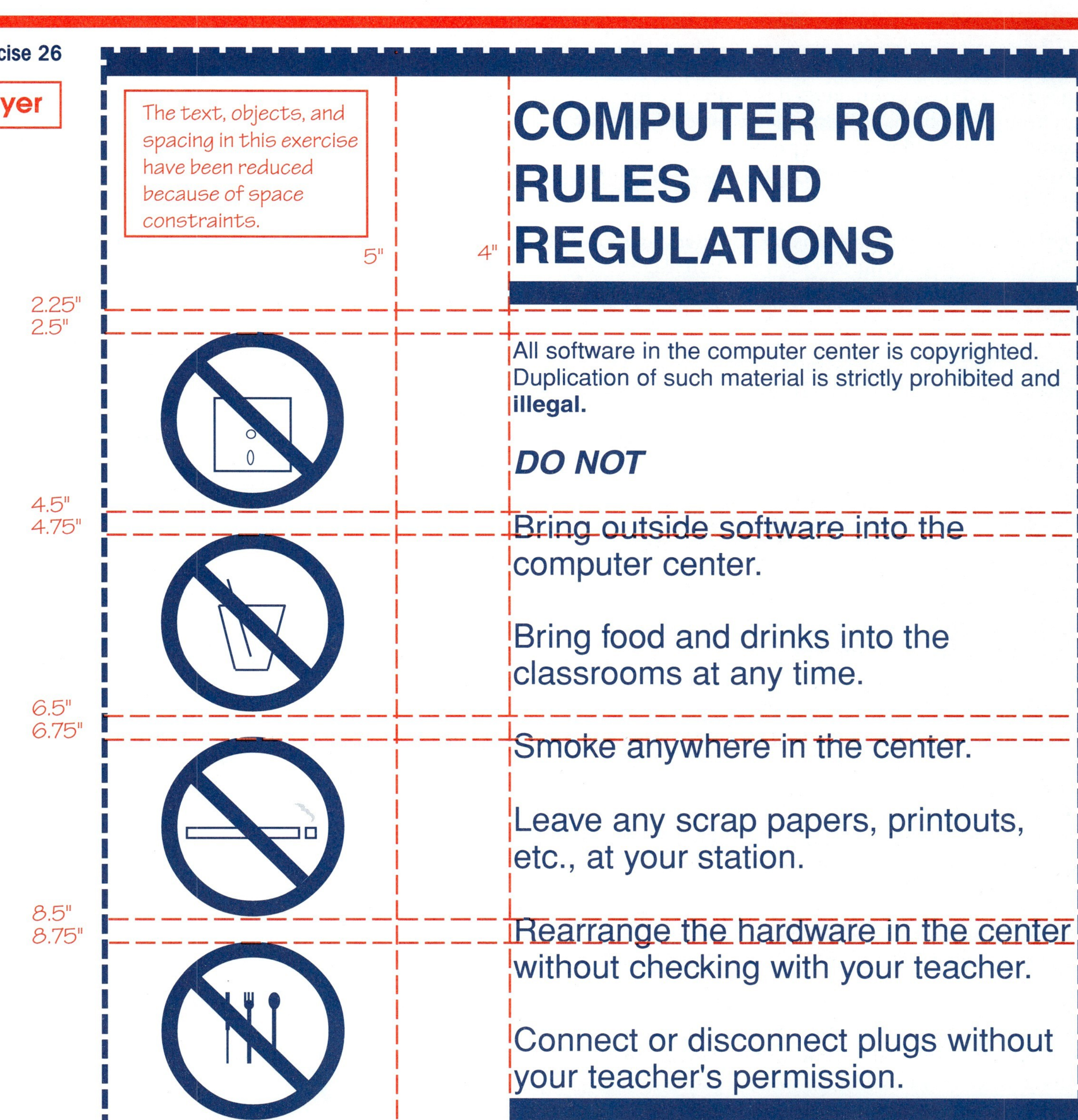
The text, objects, and spacing in this exercise have been reduced because of space constraints.
5"
4"
2.25"
2.5"
4.5"
4.75"
6.5"
6.75"
8.5"
8.75"
COMPUTER ROOM RULES AND REGULATIONS
All software in the computer center is copyrighted. Duplication of such material is strictly prohibited and **illegal.**
DO NOT
Bring outside software into the computer center.
Bring food and drinks into the classrooms at any time.
Smoke anywhere in the center.
Leave any scrap papers, printouts, etc., at your station.
Rearrange the hardware in the center without checking with your teacher.
Connect or disconnect plugs without your teacher's permission.

EXERCISE 27

Learning Objectives

Import word-processed text

Concepts

In earlier exercises, you entered text directly into your page layout program. As you have learned, however, text is usually more easily created and edited in a word processing program. Thus, text should be created in a word processing program and then imported into desktop publishing software.

Desktop publishing programs do not always support all the formatting that can be done in a word processor. As you might expect, more recent versions of desktop publishing software retain more imported formatting than older versions. When you are preparing a file in your word processor that you plan to import into a desktop publishing program, check your software manuals to determine what formatting will import. Since you can generally format more quickly and easily in a word processor than in desktop publishing software, format the document to the extent your desktop publishing software will accept. Do the rest of the formatting in your desktop publishing program. Here are some general guidelines:

- If you do not know what formatting will import, use only the simplest formatting in your word processor: bold and italics, for example.
- Single-space text.
- Use word wrap (press Enter/Return only at the end of a paragraph).
- Delete special formatting and codes; for example, footnotes, headers, footers, and page numbers.
- Delete returns at the top of document (the document should begin at the top of the screen) and at the bottom.
- Do a final spelling check and proofread the file before importing.

You may need to follow special filenaming procedures for word-processed files to be recognized by your desktop publishing program. Consult your software manual. You will need to navigate to the drive and directory or folder where the word-processed file resides.

In this exercise, you will import a prepared file from your template disk. The file is provided in several popular word processor formats. Your instructor will assist you in choosing a format and placing the file.

Text is imported as one text block. When text is imported, it will flow to fit within margin and column guides. In some software, you must specify how you wish the text to flow and where on the page you wish the text flow to begin. You will learn more about text flow options in Exercise 28.

INSTRUCTIONS

1. Start a new publication. Set 2" left and right margins and .5" top and bottom margins.
2. Place **FUN** at the top margin.
3. Select all the text and change it to a serif typeface, 12/18. Turn off hyphenation.
4. Set the title text to sans serif 18-point bold and center-align it.
5. Draw 8-point lines across the top and bottom margins, extending from the left to the right margin.
6. Select the text block and center it vertically between the two 8-point lines.
7. Save the file as **FUN1.**
8. Using all printer defaults, print one copy.
9. Close the file.

EXERCISE
27

Exercise 27

VACATION MEANS DIFFERENT THINGS TO DIFFERENT PEOPLE

To some, the roar of the ocean waves crashing on the sandy shore means relaxation and enjoyment. To others, a place with grassy, rolling hills enveloping a duck-filled lake in the country is the perfect getaway. There are many different ideas of the ideal vacation.

Those accustomed to a frenetic daily pace may seek a time just to sit back and unwind, rest at home, rent movies, and eat at local restaurants. Others may choose from many different vacation options depending on individual tastes. A getaway to the tropics provides for tanning, resting on the beach, sailing, or snorkeling by day and dancing and dining by night. There is seldom much sight-seeing to do—the purpose of these vacations is to escape to glorious weather and spend a lot of time at the beach. A trip to the country allows one to horseback-ride; golf; drive through fields of multicolored foliage; and take in the pure, clean air. Evenings may be spent sitting around a fireplace or campfire sipping hot cocoa or going to country fairs.

Vacations to big cities usually involve seeing major landmarks and points of interest. Most of the day may be spent touring the metropolis and shopping for souvenirs. Nights may be spent sampling the native cuisine and seeing local night spots.

How people choose to spend their vacation depends on what they find enjoyable. The main goal is always the same: HAVE FUN!

left margin 2"

right margin 2"

The text, objects, and spacing in this exercise have been reduced because of space constraints.

EXERCISE
28

Learning Objectives

Import word-processed text
Create multiple columns
Use text flow options
Align text across columns

Terms

- Gutter
- Automatic text flow
- Semiautomatic text flow
- Manual text flow
- Dummy text/*lorem ipsum*/ copyfit file

Concepts

Columns should always be set in the desktop publishing software rather than in the word processor. When you select the number of columns for your publication, your software will generally determine for you the column width and the **gutter** (the space between columns). On some software, you can create custom columns by manually dragging a column guide to the desired location or by keying the width of each column and/or the gutter in the column setup dialog box.

Desktop publishing programs may offer different options for flowing text into your document. With **automatic text flow,** you click the icon where you want the text to begin, and text placement proceeds automatically until all text has been placed. When you click a text flow icon using **manual text flow,** text flows to the bottom of the column or page and stops. If there is more text to be placed, a plus sign appears in the bottom windowshade handle. You must click on the plus sign and then click the resulting text flow icon where you want text to continue. When you click a text flow icon using **semiautomatic text flow,** text flows to the bottom of the column or page, and the text flow icon appears, ready for you to click where you want text to continue (the step of clicking on the plus sign is eliminated). The different text flow options may have distinct icons.

In this exercise and in some future exercises, you will use a **"dummy"** text file from the template disk to practice setting text in columns and other desktop publishing options. Desktop publishers often flow dummy text into a publication when they are designing it and want an idea of how the finished design will look with text. Some software provides a dummy text file for this purpose; it may be called a ***lorem ipsum*** or ***copyfit*** file. Really, any file can serve as practice text.

To make your multi-column publication look professional, try to align the text in the columns across the page. If your software supports ruler guides, the best way to align text is to place a ruler guide so that a line of text sits on it and then shift the other column(s) up or down slightly so that one line of all the text, reading across, sits on that same ruler guide. Aligning text in this way cannot always be accomplished, particularly when your story contains headings and other elements with different type sizes and spacing, but when you can align text across columns fairly easily, you should do so. You will learn other methods in later exercises.

INSTRUCTIONS

1. Start a new publication. Use the default settings.
2. Create 3 columns; use the default gutter size.
3. Use automatic text flow, if available, to import the template disk file **PF**. If the text does not extend to 3 columns, select it and increase the size until it does.
4. Select the story and delete it from your document.
5. Import the template disk file again. Use semiautomatic text flow, if available. Then delete the story again.
6. Continue to place and delete the file until you are comfortable with all text flow options. When finished, delete the story as usual.
7. Change the column settings to 2 columns with the default space between columns. Set horizontal ruler guides at 1.5" and 3".
8. Place **PF** again. Use the text flow option of your choice.
9. Format the text as shown.
10. Drag the text in the second column below the 3" horizontal ruler guide. Align the text across the page.
11. Draw a 6-point line on the 3" horizontal ruler guide across the second column.
12. Draw a .5-point vertical line in the gutter from the top to the bottom margin.
13. Key the heading as shown.
14. Save the file; name it **PF1.**
15. Using all printer defaults, print one copy.
16. Close the file.

EXERCISE 28

Exercise 28

USING PRACTICE TEXT

This is practice or "dummy" text that you can use for importing, placing, and playing purposes. Desktop publishers often use dummy text. When you are first designing a publication, you can flow a dummy text file in to see how your design will look with type. Desktop publishers also use dummy text for publications that will be produced periodically, such as a monthly newsletter. The dummy text serves as a placeholder for the different articles that will appear in each issue. You will learn more about using dummy text in this way in later exercises.

Some desktop publishing programs give you practice or "dummy" text that looks like Latin (but it's not). It is called a *lorem ipsum* file. Really, any file can serve as dummy text. The more it looks like the kind of text you will be using in your final publication, the better. You can manipulate and move sections of practice text as you desire. You can experiment with different elements such as typefaces, type styles, type sizes, and leading.

Later in this book, you will be given the opportunity to create your own projects. Before you tackle them, you will learn to plan your publication ahead by drawing a "thumbnail" sketch on a piece of blank paper. Drawing a thumbnail will give you direction in creating your page layout on the computer. The sketch should define the approximate positions of all the text and graphic elements that will appear on each page. Of course, the design may be changed as you are working on your project in the desktop publishing program.

There are countless ways to design a document. Professional designing requires education and skill, but you do not have to be a professional designer to create simple, attractive publications in your desktop publishing software. The exercises in this book will give you the general guidelines you need for document design, as well as ideas to consider and examples to follow. Looking at different publications will give you other ideas to try.

Desktop publishing software often comes with sample documents, or *templates*, already designed and formatted for you. Your software may provide templates for letters, memos, newsletters, reports, and other common documents. Templates can be used as is or modified as needed. You will learn more about templates later in this text.

When you begin to design a publication, try different typefaces, type styles, type sizes, and leading options. Change the margins, and vary the space between columns. Stretch your text boxes to varying lengths. Don't be afraid to experiment! If you are not happy with your work, delete the story, or close your desktop publishing file without saving it and place the file again. You can place files as many times as you like without altering them.

Remember, this is practice text. You can read the copy if you like, but all the information contained here will be given to you formally in later exercises.

Ruler guide at 1.5"

Make the heading 30-point sans serif bold, right-aligned, hyphenation off, each word on a separate line. Place it so the word "USING" rests on the 1.5" horizontal ruler guide.

Ruler guide at 3"

To align text across columns, draw a ruler guide so that a line of the text in the first column sits on the guide. Adjust the second column so the adjacent line of text in that column sits on the ruler guide, too.

Set the body text in a serif typeface, 12/18, fully justified. Turn off hyphenation.

The text, objects, and spacing in this exercise have been reduced because of space constraints.

EXERCISE 29

Learning Objectives

Use different column layouts

Terms

- White space

Concepts

Columns make a page easier to read and add interest to it. Your software probably allows you to create a large number of columns in any document, but publications generally use from one to six.

A document with a single text column per page is the simplest pattern. This format is often used for business and educational reports, proposals, and other simple internal documents. Single-column layouts generally call for easily readable typefaces with generous leading.

A two-column format, like you used in Exercise 28, has a more designed and polished look. It is used in many brochures, reports, and catalogs.

The three-column format is the most commonly used in desktop publishing. Three-column documents are usually the most readable, because narrow columns are easier for the eye to scan. Since the columns are narrower, you may need to choose a smaller type size and left alignment for better readability.

Four columns is a good number to use in a magazine. This format results in short lines of text, and space can be used economically. Four columns lends itself well to a document with several short articles.

As in Exercise 28, rules are sometimes used to separate columns and make text more readable. **White space**—the nonprinted space of margins and gutters—is an important factor in readability.

INSTRUCTIONS

1. Start a new publication. Use the default settings.
2. As you did in Steps 2-5 of Exercise 28, experiment with importing the template disk file **PF.** Try changing the number of columns, the typeface, the type size, the leading, the justification, the margins, and the gutter. Try adding rules between the columns. Using all printer defaults, print your better efforts.
3. Submit up to three of your best documents to your instructor.
4. Close the file without saving.

One-column layout

COUNTY FAIR

ROSS COUNTY FAIR

This is practice or "dummy" text that you can use for importing, placing, and playing purposes. Desktop publishers often use dummy text.

- When you are first designing a publication, you can flow a dummy text file in to see how your design will look with type.
- Desktop publishers also use dummy text for publications that will be produced periodically, such as a monthly newsletter. The dummy text serves as a placeholder for the different articles that will appear in each issue.

Some desktop publishing programs give you practice or "dummy" text that looks like Latin (but it's not). It is called a *lorem ipsum* file. Really, any file can serve as dummy text.

Three-column layout

POLITICS

WEIGHING THE COST OF ENVIRONMENTAL POLICY

by Russell Rossmeyer
Congress faces some tough decisions.

This is practice or "dummy" text that you can use for importing, placing, and also for playing purposes. Desktop publishers often use dummy text. When you are first designing a publication, you can flow a dummy text file in to see how your design will look with type. Desktop publishers also use dummy text for publications that will be produced periodi-

This is practice or "dummy" text that you can use for importing, placing, and playing purposes. Desktop publishers often use dummy text. When you are first designing a publication, you can flow a dummy text file in to see how

This is practice or "dummy" text that you can use for importing, placing, and playing purposes. Desktop publishers often use dummy text. When you are first designing a publication, you can flow a dummy text file in to see how your design will look with type. Desktop publishers also use dummy text for publications that will be produced

Four-column layout

FOOD FOR THOUGHT

LIGHT ITALIAN

Desktop publishers often use dummy text. When you are first designing a publication, you can flow a way in later exercises.

Some desktop publishing programs give you practice or "dummy" text that looks like Latin (but

This is the practice or "dummy" text that you can use when you are working with your design.

HEALTHY HERBS

Desktop publishers often use dummy text. When you are first designing a Desktop publishers often lishers often

This dummy text can be used when you are testing a design.

SUMMER SALADS

Desktop publishers often use dummy text. When you are first designing a Desktop publishers often use dummy text. Desktop publishers. publishers

ORGANIC FRUITS

This is practice or "dummy" text that you can use for importing, placing, and playing purposes. Desktop publishers often use dummy

EXERCISE 30

Learning Objectives

Divide words, lines, and paragraphs appropriately

Use the hyphenation feature

Use the widow/orphan feature

Terms

- Hyphenation zone
- Widow
- Orphan

Concepts

Word division should be avoided when possible. Divided words can be confusing and can hinder comprehension. You must balance the visual appearance of the text and the demands of the layout against the rules of hyphenation.

In general, you can hyphenate:

- At a natural syllable break.
- Between the elements of a compound word.
- At the syllable break closest to the middle of the word.
- After a prefix or before a suffix.
- Using existing hyphens (*mother-in-law*).

In general, do not hyphenate:

- So as to leave a syllable of only one or two letters.
- At the end of the last full line of a paragraph.
- At the end of the first full line of a paragraph.
- At the end of consecutive lines.
- At the end of a page or column.

Most desktop publishing programs have a word division feature. Typically, the user can choose automatic or manual word division. The user can set the **hyphenation zone**—the area at the end of the line in which words will be divided. A narrower hyphenation zone means a flush left margin will be less ragged; a wider zone means fewer hyphens. The user can also set the number of consecutive lines that can end with a hyphen.

Another rule for desktop publishers is not to divide paragraphs between pages unless at least two lines remain on the first page and at least two lines are carried to the second page. Most desktop publishing programs have a **widow/orphan** feature that can automatically correct such violations. (The first line of a paragraph appearing by itself at the bottom of a column or page is called a **widow.** The last line of a paragraph appearing by itself at the top of a column or page is called an **orphan.**)

INSTRUCTIONS

1. Open **PF1** (or open a copy of **PF1** if your software has that option).
2. Save the document as **PF2.**
3. Select all the text, left-justify it, turn on hyphenation (set the number of consecutive lines that can be divided as 1), and turn on widow/orphan protect (set the number of lines at 1).
4. Go through the text and correct violations of the rules for hyphenation where you consider appropriate. In each case, balance the rules against the visual appearance of the text. If the last paragraph extends below the document and you cannot correct this problem by hyphenation, delete the paragraph.
5. Using all printer defaults, print one copy.
6. Save and close the file.

Learning Objectives

Work with multi-page documents
Reset tabs
Use the paragraph feature to adjust spacing

Concepts

Tabs set in a word processor usually import into a desktop publishing program without difficulty (check your software manuals). Even tabs that import correctly, however, may seem too large or too small when you are working with different typefaces and type sizes. Therefore, you may sometimes want to set or adjust tabs in your desktop publishing program. Setting tabs in desktop publishing software is similar to setting tabs in a word processor, with left, right, center, and decimal-aligned tabs and dot leaders.

Desktop publishing programs usually have a feature for identing paragraphs on the left and right and for adding space before and after paragraphs. Desktop publishers often use this feature rather than an extra line return to "double-space" between paragraphs, adding slightly less space than a double space would take. Headings usually have more space above than below.

In this exercise, you will work for the first time with a multiple-page document. As you may remember, you can set the number of pages when you create a document.

continued on page 52

INSTRUCTIONS

1. Create a new two-page publication. Set page options for a single-sided page. Set .75" margins.
2. On page 1, set three columns using a .25" gutter. Position horizontal ruler guides at 2.5" and 3". Draw a 1-point rectangle around the page, slightly outside the margins, as shown. Draw an 8-point line just above the 2.5" ruler guide extending from one side of the rectangle to the other. Draw hairline rules down the middle of each column from the 8-point line to the bottom of the rectangle.
3. On page 2, create two columns using a .25" gutter, the second a custom column that begins 2.75" from the left edge of the page. Position horizontal ruler guides at 2" and at 2.5". Draw an 8-point line just above the guide extending across the second column.
4. Create the address information at the bottom of the left column. Set it in a serif typeface, 9/13, center-aligned, with .01" left indent and .008" right indent. Draw a box around the text extending the width of the column with a 2-point line and a 10% fill.
5. Turn on widow/orphan protect (set the number of lines at 1). Turn on hyphenation.
6. Return to page 1 and import the template file **SEATRIP** using manual or semiautomatic text flow as shown in the exercise.
7. Save the file; name it **SEATRIP1.**
8. Cut the heading to the clipboard.
9. On page 1, drag-place the heading in the rectangle created by the top, left, and right margins and the 8-point line. Right-align the heading, turn off hyphenation, and set the text in a sans serif font with auto leading. Make the first two lines 12-point and the last two 30-point. Add .2" of space after "presents."
10. Select all the text and make the following changes: choose a serif typeface, 12/18; and add a tab at .25".

continued on page 52

EXERCISE **31**

Exercise 31 continued on page 53

Voyages Travel Consultants, Inc.
presents...

Cruising to the Islands of the Caribbean

Ruler guide at 2.5"

Ruler guide at 3"

The vast Caribbean Sea is home to thousands of islands—large and tiny, breathtakingly beautiful, newly developed and ancient, peopled and uninhabited. They represent diverse and blended cultures, with an infinite variety of foods, crafts, music, and art. The Caribbean offers the most rich and rewarding vacation experience you can imagine.

The islands have a natural splendor. The fine beaches, beautiful waters, lush vegetation, and breathtaking coral reefs will satisfy any lover of natural beauty. With their tropical rain forests, magnificent caverns, sulfur springs and volcanic rock, and protected habitats and reserves for many rare and endangered species, the islands offer you an unforgettable experience of the wonders of the natural world.

The islands also have a rich history. There are serene, quaint Dutch villages on islands like Aruba, Curacao, and Bonaire, off the northern coast of South America. The great houses of Barbados, the 1500s Spanish architecture of Old San Juan, and the ruins of St.-Pierre on Martinique, destroyed by a volcano, are some of the stops on our tour for history buffs.

If swimming, sunning, boating, fishing, or any water sport is your desire, the Caribbean is your ideal destination. You can lounge on pristine, white beaches. You can cruise, in glass-bottomed boats, aqua, blue, and emerald crystal-clear waters, with visibility from 200 to 300 feet. The exquisite coral reefs and sunken ships, teeming with exotic marine life, offer incomparable conditions for scuba diving and snorkeling.

Those who enjoy hiking, biking, or horseback riding will find scenic jaunts through towns and along nature trails. Cricket, soccer, and polo matches will entice lovers of fast-paced sports. Golfers will find well-designed courses amid breathtaking scenery. Tennis buffs will enjoy well-kept courts and matchless views.

For those who enjoy fine dining and an exciting night life, we offer city tours with shopping in duty-free boutiques and leisurely dinners in world-class restaurants. You can end your evening in a nightclub or dance hall with reggae, jazz, calypso, or steel-band music.

Every Voyages cruise offers luxurious accommodations, a panoply of recreational activities from swimming to shuffleboard, big-band dancing, our own Voyages dance and musical show, and sumptuous meals prepared by premier chefs. Our seasoned crews will devote every effort to making sure your cruise is a memorable one.

Travelers with special needs receive special treatment with Voyages. Older travelers, families with young children,

The text, objects, and spacing in this exercise have been reduced because of space constraints.

Align the text across the bottom.

EXERCISE 31

Concepts continued from page 50

When working with text in multiple columns, desktop publishers try to adjust the windowshades in each column so that the columns end on the same line. See, for example, the exercise on page 51.

INSTRUCTIONS continued from page 50

11. On page 2, in the left column, adjust the bottom windowshade handle so the box you created in Step 4 is revealed.
12. Adjust the text on page 2 so that the tour information appears in the large right column as shown in the exercise. Depending on the serif typeface you use, you may need to reduce the leading of the article (not the tour information, the rest of the article) so that it ends before the boxed information as shown.
13. Set each heading in a 14/18 sans serif typeface with .29" space above and .08" space below. You may need to adjust the leading of the tour information to fit it all as shown.
14. Go through the article and check for violations of the rules for hyphenation. On page 1, adjust the columns so that they are even across the bottom.
15. Re-save the file.
16. Using all printer defaults, print one copy.
17. Close the file.

EXERCISE

31

Exercise 31 continued from page 51

and disabled individuals will find that our tours can be specially designed to accommodate their needs.

Voyages has created six fabulous tours to the most exciting ports in the Caribbean. Every package includes airfare, accommodations, and entertainment and meals on the cruise ship. It might be difficult to pick just one of the tour packages in this brochure. Plan your vacation now, for the fine spring weather, or take advantage of our off-season rates. Contact any of our representatives at Voyages Travel Consultants, Incorporated, at the numbers below to get details and to make your reservation. And visit our Web site to check out the latest destinations and prices!

VOYAGES TRAVEL CONSULTANTS, INC.
46 South Street
Columbus, Ohio 43215-3406
Phone: 614-555-9544
Or 1-800-555-9995
Fax: 614-555-4321
Visit our Web site at
wxx.vyg.com.

Ruler guide at 2"

Ruler guide at 2.5"

CARNIVAL AT SEA

A twelve-day major island tour of Puerto Rico, the Dominican Republic, Trinidad, and Jamaica. Enjoy the spectacular sights of the Trinidad Carnival during your stay.

DIVER'S DELIGHT

A ten-day expedition to the splendid coral reefs of Cozumel, Aruba, St. Bonaire, and Curacao. Scuba and snorkel through mosaics coral teeming with marine life. Diving gear and expert instruction included.

CUISINE ADVENTURE

A one-week jaunt to Martinique, St. Martin, Guadeloupe, and Montserrat. Partake of the finest cuisine in world-class restaurants.

The text, objects, and spacing in this exercise have been reduced because of space constraints.

HISTORY AND MYSTERY

Six days of exploring the historic sites of Puerto Rico, Antigua, Martinique, and Barbados. From French and Spanish colonial mansions to a city devastated by a volcanic eruption, you will immerse yourself in the stories of these islands in times past.

SHOPPER'S PARADISE

Spend eight days sightseeing and shopping on the duty-free islands of St. Thomas, St. Croix, St. Martin, and St. John. Save your money for the bargains you will get!

ECO-TOUR

Seven days of stepping lightly through some of the most beautiful land in the world. Tropical rain forests, volcanic islands, coral reefs, and rare wildlife are some of the natural wonders you will experience.

EXERCISE 32

Learning Objectives

Work with multi-page documents
Work with a master page

Terms

- Master pages
- Feathering

Concepts

Master pages are a feature of most desktop publishing software. Guides, text, and graphics set on the master page(s) will appear automatically on every page in the publication.

Setting repeating elements on a master page saves time and effort and reduces the change of making errors. Suppose, for example, that you were working on a long report and you wanted a border around every page. If you set the border on the master page, it would appear automatically on all pages of the publication. If you later decided to change the border to a double rule, you would need to make the change only once, on the master page. The change would be made automatically on all pages of the publication.

You can suppress master elements on any one publication page by deselecting a menu option. If you want one master page item to be suppressed, but others to appear (for example, reports and other documents usually do not have a page number on the first page), you could "hide" the page number by covering it with a paper-filled box with no border. Some programs allow you to display printing and nonprinting master page items separately on individual pages.

continued on page 56

INSTRUCTIONS

1. Start a new three-page publication. Set page options for a single-sided page. Set 1.5" left and right margins and 1" top and bottom margins.

COMPLETE STEPS 2–7 ON THE MASTER PAGE:

2. Create 2 columns with 0.3" gutter space.
3. Position horizontal ruler guides at 3", 3 3/8", 81/8", and 9 7/8" and vertical ruler guides at 1/4" *outside* the left and right margins.
4. Draw a hairline box to frame the margins. The box should extend vertically from the top to the bottom margin and horizontally from one ruler guide to the other (the sides of the box will fall outside the side margins).
5. Draw an 8-point horizontal line just above the 3" ruler guide, extending from one side of the rectangle you just drew to the other.
6. On the ruler guide at 9 7/8", key the following address information in sans serif 8-point, centered, and with five spaces between parts as shown in the exercise: "Voyages Travel Consultants, Inc.   46 South Street   Columbus, Ohio 43215-3406   614-555-9544."
7. Key "Page" plus an automatic page numbering code in a serif typeface, 10-point, in the upper right corner (below the top margin).
8. On page 3, set a custom column that begins 3" from the left edge of the page.
9. On page 1, create a box with no border and a paper fill over "Page 1" to hide the page number.
10. Turn on widow/orphan protect (set the number of lines at 1). Turn on hyphenation.
11. Import the template file **SEATRIP** as shown using manual or semiautomatic text flow.
12. Save the file; name it **SEATRIP2.**

continued on page 56

EXERCISE

32

Exercise 32 continued on page 57

Voyages Travel Consultants, Inc.,
presents...

Cruising to the Islands of the Caribbean

3"

3 3/8"

The vast Caribbean Sea is home to thousands of islands—large and tiny, breathtakingly beautiful, newly developed and ancient, peopled and uninhabited. They represent diverse and blended cultures, with an infinite variety of foods, crafts, music, and art. The Caribbean offers the most rich and rewarding vacation experience you can imagine.

The islands have a natural splendor. The fine beaches, beautiful waters, lush vegetation, and breath-taking coral reefs will satisfy any lover of natural beauty. With their tropical rain forests, magnificent caverns, sulfur springs and volcanic rock, and protected habitats and reserves for many rare and endangered species, the islands offer you an unforgettable experience of the wonders of the natural world.

The islands also have a rich history. There are serene, quaint Dutch villages on islands like Aruba, Curacao, and Bonaire, off the northern coast of South America. The great houses of Barbados, the 1500s Spanish architecture of Old San Juan, and the ruins of St.-Pierre on Martinique, destroyed by a volcano, are some of the stops on our tour for history buffs.

If swimming, sunning, boating, fishing, or any water sport is your desire, the Caribbean is your ideal destination. You can lounge on pris-tine, white beaches. You can cruise, in glass-bottomed boats, aqua, blue, and emerald crystal-clear waters, with visibility from 200 to 300 feet. The exquisite coral reefs and sunken ships, teeming with exotic marine life, offer incomparable conditions for scuba diving and snorkeling.

8 1/8". Align text across the bottom.

Voyages Travel Consultants, Inc. 46 South Street Columbus, Ohio 43215-3406 614-555-9544

9 7/8"

The text, objects, and spacing in this exercise have been reduced because of space constraints.

EXERCISE 32

Concepts continued from page 54

Text or graphics placed on a master page cannot be edited or moved on a publication page. You must return to the master page to edit or move the material. Master page guides can be customized on publication pages, however.

In this exercise, you will set up automatic page numbering on the master page. Desktop publishing software generally has a code that you key to set up page numbering. You will also set a running foot on the master page that contains company name and address information.

You will need to make the bottoms of columns of text line up in this exercise as you did in Exercise 31. To align the text, you may need to use feathering. **Feathering** means adding small amounts of space after individual paragraphs or increasing the leading slightly.

INSTRUCTIONS continued from page 54

13. Cut the heading to the clipboard.
14. On page 1, drag-place the heading in the rectangle created by the top, left, and right margins and the 8-point line. Center the heading, turn off hyphenation, and set the text in a sans serif typeface. Set the first two lines to 12/12 and the last two to 30/30. Add .2" of space after "presents." Center the heading vertically in the rectangle created by the top, left, and right margins and the 8-point line.
15. Select all the body text and set it to a serif typeface, 12/16, with .097" of space after.
16. On pages 1 and 2, align the text across the bottom. You may need to feather one or more paragraphs to get the last lines of the column even.
17. On page 3, adjust the text so the cruise package descriptions begin in the second column. Set the cruise description text to sans serif italic, 11/13, with no space after paragraphs and justify it. Set the headings to sans serif 12/12, no italic, with .1" of space before and .06" of space after.
18. Go through the article and check for violations of the rules for hyphenation.
19. Re-save the file.
20. Using all printer defaults, print one copy.
21. Close the file.

For the remainder of the exercises, you will be expected, without being told, to turn off the double-sided option, to turn on hyphenation (unless otherwise directed), to turn on widow/orphan protect, and to check your work for violations of the rules for hyphenation.

EXERCISE 32

Exercise 32 continued from page 55

Page 2

Those who enjoy hiking, biking, or horseback riding will find scenic jaunts through towns and along nature trails. Cricket, soccer, and polo matches entice lovers of fast-paced sports. Golfers will find well-designed courses amid breathtaking scenery. Tennis buffs will enjoy well-kept courts and matchless views.

For those who enjoy fine dining and an exciting night life, we offer city tours with shopping in duty-free boutiques and leisurely dinners in world-class restaurants. You can end your evening in a nightclub or dance hall with reggae, jazz, calypso, or steel-band music.

Every Voyages cruise offers luxurious accommodations, a panoply of recreational activities from swimming to shuffleboard, big-band dancing, our own Voyages dance and musical show, and sumptuous meals prepared by premier chefs. Our seasoned crews will devote every effort to making sure your cruise is a memorable one.

Travelers with special needs receive special treatment with Voyages. Older travelers, families with young children, and disabled individuals will find that our tours can be specially designed to accommodate their needs.

Voyages has created six fabulous tours to the most exciting ports in the Caribbean. Every package includes airfare, accommodations, and entertainment and meals on the cruise ship. It might be difficult to pick just one of the tour packages in this brochure.

3 3/8"

8 1/8"

Voyages Travel Consultants, Inc. 46 South Street Columbus, Ohio 43215-3406 614-555-9544

Page 3

Plan your vacation now, for the fine spring weather, or take advantage of our off-season rates. Contact any of our representatives at Voyages Travel Consultants, Inc., at the numbers below to get details and to make your reservation. And visit our Web site to check out the latest destinations and prices!

Insert "at wxx.vyg.com."

CARNIVAL AT SEA

A twelve-day major island tour of Puerto Rico, the Dominican Republic, Trinidad, and Jamaica. Enjoy the spectacular sights of the Trinidad Carnival during your stay.

DIVER'S DELIGHT

A ten-day expedition to the splendid coral reefs of Cozumel, Aruba, St. Bonaire, and Curacao. Scuba and snorkel through mosaics coral teeming with marine life. Diving gear and expert instruction included.

CUISINE ADVENTURE

A one-week jaunt to Martinique, St. Martin, Guadeloupe, and Montserrat. Partake of the finest cuisine in world-class restaurants.

HISTORY AND MYSTERY

Six days of exploring the historic sites of Puerto Rico, Antigua, Martinique, and Barbados. From French and Spanish colonial mansions to a city devastated by a volcanic eruption, you will immerse yourself in the stories of these islands in times past.

SHOPPER'S PARADISE

Spend eight days sightseeing and shopping on the duty-free islands of St. Thomas, St. Croix, St. Martin, and St. John. Save your money for the bargains you will get!

ECO-TOUR

Seven days of stepping lightly through some of the most beautiful land in the world. Tropical rain forests, volcanic islands, coral reefs, and rare wildlife are some of the natural wonders you will experience.

Voyages Travel Consultants, Inc. 46 South Street Columbus, Ohio 43215-3406 614-555-9544

The text, objects, and spacing in this exercise have been reduced because of space constraints.

Learning Objectives

Learn block business letter format
Use reference initials
Convert quotes and apostrophes
Key em and en spaces
Use paragraph rules

Terms

- Reference initials
- Em space
- En space
- Paragraph rule
- Footer

Concepts

In this exercise, you will prepare a business letter in block format. As you have learned, in block format, all letter parts begin at the left margin. The top margin may be 2 inches, or the letter may be centered vertically. The side margins may be at the software default settings or at 1 inch. A double space (DS) separates all letter parts except the date and letter address and the complimentary close and name of the writer; for those two exceptions, a quadruple space (QS) separates letter parts.

Like personal-business letters, business letters may be formatted with open or mixed punctuation. To review open and mixed punctuation, see page 20.

If someone other than the author of the letter keys the letter, that person's initials, which are called the **reference initials,** appear in lowercase letters at the left margin, a double space below the writer's name, title, or department, whichever comes last.

Beginning in this exercise, you will make sure that your work uses true typeset apostrophes and quotation marks, like that of professional desktop publishers. Most desktop publishing programs have a special keyboard combination that you can key to convert quotation marks and apostrophes that look like this ' " " to true typeset apostrophes and quotation marks that look like this ’ “ ”. Quotation marks and apostrophes keyed in word processing software usually, but not always, import as true typeset marks in desktop publishing software. Whether they import depends on the software used. An option to convert quotation marks and apostrophes may appear in the dialog box for placing files.

In this exercise, you will also use em spaces and en spaces, units of measure used by professional typesetters. An **em space** equals the point size of your type. An **en space** equals half an em space. Em and en spaces are produced with special keyboard combinations.

Finally, you will use a **paragraph rule** to format text, if your software has that feature. Some desktop publishing software allows you to set rules above and below a paragraph automatically, without having to draw them. Being able to set a rule as part of a paragraph saves time and effort. The software draws the rule for you; and if the paragraph moves, the rule moves automatically with it. The paragraph rule will be used to format a footer that is part of the letterhead. A **footer** is text that appears at the bottom of a page.

INSTRUCTIONS

1. Open the data file **TEAM1.**
2. Place and format the "West Pasadena High School" text block as shown.
3. Format the address text block as a footer as shown. If your software does not have a paragraph rule feature, draw the rule instead.
4. Import the template file **TEAM** 2" from the top of the page.
5. Save the file; name it **TEAM2.**
6. Set the body text to serif 11/13.
7. Insert text as shown, using true typeset quotation marks and apostrophes.
8. Check the rest of the letter to ensure that apostrophes are true typeset apostrophes.
9. Re-save the file.
10. Using all printer defaults, print one copy.
11. Close the file.

EXERCISE 33

Exercise 33

Business Letter in Block Format

Letterhead

West Pasadena High School
Athletics Department

Place the text block at 1". Set it in sans serif 12/auto bold, center-aligned.

Date

October 19, ——

Begin text at 2" (or center the letter vertically).

QS

Letter address

Mr. Bill Javenski
Head Coach
Western University
234 Belleflower Boulevard
Pasadena, CA 90246-8272

Clara Martinez of the *Pasadena Herald* recently said, "Pete Johnson's ability to lead the fast break and hit the open man makes him invaluable to the team's success."

DS

Salutation

Dear Mr. Javenski

DS

Body

Attached to this letter is West Pasadena High School's home basketball schedule for this season. I sincerely hope that you will have an opportunity to come to West Pasadena High to observe some of our team members' playing ability.

DS

Two seniors on our team merit particular attention. I have detailed the attributes of two of our most valuable senior players: **Pete Johnson** and **Brian Wilcox.** Knowing the type of team you have, I feel that Pete and Brian will adapt well to your team's style of play.

DS

1" or software default

Pete Johnson has averaged 23 points per game, with 10 rebounds and 6 assists.

1" or software default

DS

Brian Wilcox has averaged 18 points per game and is our best defensive player, blocking 6 shots a game and keeping the opponent's offensive threat down to scoring well below his per-game average.

DS

I look forward to having you or your scouts attend one or more of our games. I know you will not be disappointed with our team members' playing ability. You will be impressed with what you will see. If you have any questions, please phone me at **213-555-7474.**

DS

Complimentary close

Sincerely

QS

The text, objects, and spacing in this exercise have been reduced because of space constraints.

Writer

Alan H. Savoy
Athletic Director

DS

Reference initials

bcd

DS

Attachment notation

Attachment

Set the address text in a sans serif typeface, 10/auto, bold, center-aligned, with a 1-point paragraph rule .167" above the paragraph.

em space + en space

1841 Shasta Highway Pasadena, CA 90246-8272 213-555-7474

em space + en space

At least 1" (but footer may appear below 1" margin)

EXERCISE 34

Learning Objectives

Format text with bullets
Use hanging indents

Terms

- Bullets
- Hanging indent

Concepts

In this exercise, you will create a bulleted list. **Bullets** are special characters used (1) for emphasis (to call attention to important points), (2) in lists instead of numbers when the order of the items does not matter, and (3) to add graphic interest. Most desktop publishing programs have a feature for inserting bullets manually or automatically. You can also use special characters from symbol typefaces or graphic elements as bullets.

To insert bulleted items, you may need to format paragraphs to create a hanging indent. In a **hanging indent,** the first line of the paragraph begins farther to the left than the remaining lines in that paragraph. Desktop publishing programs have different methods for creating hanging indents.

INSTRUCTIONS

1. Start a new publication. Set 1" margins.
2. Create the letterhead as shown.
3. Import the template disk file **HEARINGS.**
4. Save the file; name it **HEARING1.**
5. Set all body text to serif 11/12.
6. Format text with bullets as shown. Bullets should appear .5" from the left margin of the letter. The text following the bullets should appear .75" from the left margin of the letter. Use the symbol of your choice for the bullets.
7. Center the letter vertically on the page.
8. Re-save the file.
9. Using all printer defaults, print one copy.
10. Close the file.

EXERCISE

34

Exercise 34

Saybrook Planning Board 16/auto sans serif bold

632 Magnolia Street • Westbrook, CT 25876-0312 • 203-555-1215

9/auto sans serif bold, bullets preceded and followed by an em space, 1-point paragraph rule below with auto space before the baseline

November 5, ——

Ms. Sarabeth Mosler
876 Harbor Way
Westbrook, CT 25876-1105

Dear Ms. Mosler:

The Saybrook Planning Board will hold a series of public hearings on zoning and land uses throughout our county. Saybrook County is the first northeast county to address important issues that will affect homeowners. The program will include:

- **Commercial vs. residential zoning changes.** This hearing will redefine areas in which new housing may be built. Some of the previous commercial zoning will now become residential.
- **Use of natural resources.** Many new energy sources will be defined that will lead to cleaner air and less water pollution.
- **Maintenance of parks and recreational areas.** Three new parks are planned. Discussion will include the priority building order and the taxes necessary to support the recreational improvement.
- **Proposed building of the seaport in the downtown area.** The seaport will have a major impact on the local economy. We would like to hear comments on this proposal.

The locations and dates of the hearings appear on the enclosed table. We urge you to attend. While we feel that the proposals will have a major positive effect on homeowners, it is the homeowners themselves who must decide. Some have already raised preliminary concerns on the cost of these endeavors. Please make your voice heard. Serve your community by attending.

Cordially,

Victor Zolo, President
Saybrook Planning Board

js

Enclosure

The text, objects, and spacing in this exercise have been reduced because of space constraints.

Learning Objectives

Import, resize, and move graphics

Terms

- Clip art

Concepts

You have already learned how to create simple graphics using the drawing tools in your desktop publishing program. In this lesson, you will begin to work with imported graphics. In addition to drawings, imported graphics can include photographs, charts, and graphs.

In the next few exercises, you will work with clip art. **Clip art** is a collection of ready-made illustrations available in different topics and themes, which may be purchased on disk, installed on your computer, and imported into publications. Some software comes with clip art. You will learn about other sources of illustrations for desktop publishing in Exercise 36.

When you purchase a clip art package, examine the legal restrictions on use carefully. Generally, clip art can be used in a publication if the clip art publisher has been credited and is the copyright owner of the images. You cannot make copies of clip art to distribute to others. With some clip art services, you pay for the right to use images or modify them.

Imported graphics are placed as text is. They are moved, copied, resized, deleted, grouped, aligned, and distributed as drawn objects are.

- To move a graphic, select it with the pointer tool. With the mouse pointer inside the graphic (not on a handle), drag the graphic to its new location.
- To delete a graphic, select it and press the Delete or Backspace key. Alternatively, you can use the Clear option (if available) on one of the menus.
- To resize a graphic, use the pointer tool to select the graphic and drag a handle. On some software, you can resize a graphic proportionally by holding down a key (the Shift key, for example) while dragging a handle. Resizing graphics disproportionately can often make them look awkward. In this exercise, for example, stretching the car graphic horizontally makes it look like a limousine; shrinking it makes it look like a compact car.

INSTRUCTIONS

1. Start a new one-page publication. Set 1" margins.
2. Position horizontal ruler guides at 2", 4.5", and 8" and vertical ruler guides at 2" and 4.5", dividing the page into 12 areas of various sizes as shown. ***NOTE:*** *The page division will make resizing each graphic easier.*
3. Import four different graphics. Place and size each within the "box" shown in Part 1.
4. Save the file; name it **GRAPHIC.**
5. Using all printer defaults, print one copy.
6. Move and size each graphic as shown in Part 2.
7. Re-save the file.
8. Using all printer defaults, print one copy.
9. Close the file.

EXERCISE 35

Exercise 35-Part 1

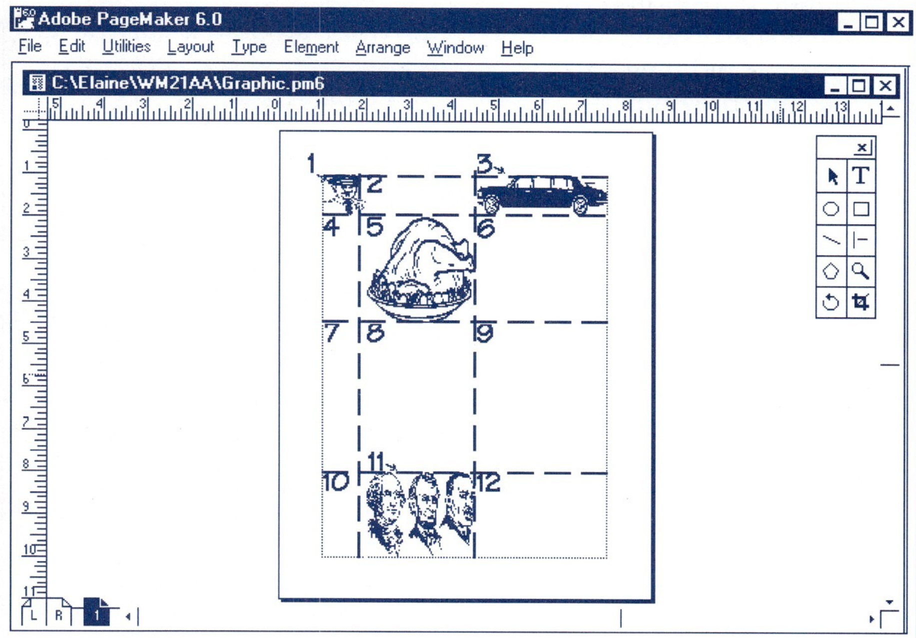

Exercise 35-Part 2

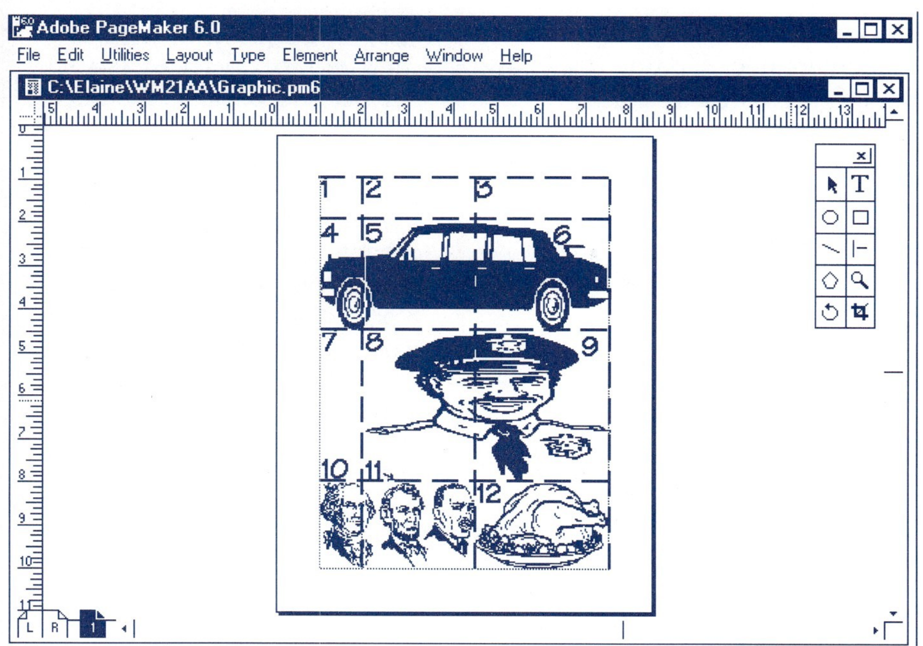

EXERCISE 36

Learning Objectives

Know sources of artwork for desktop publishing

Understand graphics formats

Import, resize, and move graphics

Terms

- Text art
- Screen captures
- Scanning
- Resolution

Concepts

The desktop publisher has many resources for illustrations. In addition to drawing objects and importing clip art, you can create **text art:** raised or dropped capital letters, text boxes using different typefaces and type sizes, shadow boxes, rotated text, and so on. Desktop publishing programs also allow you to do some modification of imported graphics, like cropping (trimming) them and adjusting the lightness, darkness, and contrast. You will create text art and modify imported graphics in upcoming exercises.

You can create more sophisticated graphics using a paint, draw, or PostScript-based illustration program. These programs can also be used to modify artwork. Many computers come with simple paint and draw programs. Charts and graphs created in a spreadsheet or presentation program can often be imported directly into a desktop publishing document. **Screen captures**—shots of the computer screen made with standard or separately purchased software—can be converted to a compatible file format and imported.

If you have a piece of hard-copy art that you would like to use on the computer, you can have it scanned. **Scanning** makes a digitized copy of the image, which you can place in a desktop publishing document like any other graphic. Alternatively, you can ask a commercial printer to photograph it, reduce it if necessary, and place it for you.

Many of the graphics you will import will have been created in paint, draw, or PostScript-based illustration programs. Illustrations created in draw or PostScript-based programs resize better and require less storage space than those created in paint programs. These illustrations also represent curved shapes more faithfully. The **resolution,** or sharpness, of images created in paint programs is limited by the resolution of the monitor, printer, or scanner used.

Graphics created in different types of programs have different formats. Paint graphics created on the Macintosh (Mac) are often saved in the PNTG or TIFF file format. For personal computers (PCs), popular bit-mapped file formats are PCX, TIF, and BMP. Some widely used formats for draw images are EPS (PC and Mac), PICT2 (Mac), and WMF (PC). Files created in PostScript-based illustration programs are usually in the Encapsulated PostScript (EPS) format. Encapsulated PostScript files can only be printed on PostScript printers. Some paint, draw, and illustration programs have their own proprietary formats.

INSTRUCTIONS

1. Open the data file **SEATRIP2**.
2. On the master page, position a horizontal ruler guide at 9 5/8". You should already have a horizontal ruler guide at 8 1/8". If you do not, add one.
3. Save the file; name it **SEATRIP3.**
4. On pages 1 and 2, import several graphics (at least two per page) that relate to the topic of the article. Place and size them to fall between the ruler guides at 8 1/8" and 9 5/8". The exercise at the right should serve as an example, but use your own judgment in deciding how many graphics to place, what size they should be, and how they should be arranged. Keep them between the ruler guides, though.
5. Re-save the file.
6. Using all printer defaults, print one copy each of pages 1 and 2.
7. Close the file.

EXERCISE

36

Exercise 36

Voyages Travel Consultants, Inc.,

presents...

Cruising to the Islands of the Caribbean

The vast Caribbean Sea is home to thousands of islands—large and tiny, breathtakingly beautiful, newly developed and ancient, peopled and uninhabited. They represent diverse and blended cultures, with an infinite variety of foods, crafts, music, and art. The Caribbean offers the most rich and rewarding vacation experience you can imagine.

The islands have a natural splendor. The fine beaches, beautiful waters, lush vegetation, and breath-taking coral reefs will satisfy any lover of natural beauty. With their tropical rain forests, magnificent caverns, sulfur springs and volcanic rock, and protected habitats and reserves for many rare and endangered species, the islands offer you an unforgettable experience of the wonders of the natural world.

The islands also have a rich history. There are serene, quaint Dutch villages on islands like Aruba, Curacao, and Bonaire, off the northern coast of South America. The great houses of Barbados, the 1500s Spanish architecture of Old San Juan, and the ruins of St.-Pierre on Martinique, destroyed by a volcano, are some of the stops on our tour for history buffs.

If swimming, sunning, boating, fishing, or any water sport is your desire, the Caribbean is your ideal destination. You can lounge on pristine, white beaches. You can cruise, in glass-bottomed boats, aqua, blue, and emerald crystal-clear waters, with visibility from 200 to 300 feet. The exquisite coral reefs and sunken ships, teeming with exotic marine life, offer incomparable conditions for scuba diving and snorkeling.

8 1/8"

9 5/8"

Voyages Travel Consultants, Inc. 46 South Street Columbus, Ohio 43215-3406 614-555-9544

Page 2

Those who enjoy hiking, biking, or horseback riding will find scenic jaunts through towns and along nature trails. Cricket, soccer, and polo matches entice lovers of fast-paced sports. Golfers will find well-designed courses amid breathtaking scenery. Tennis buffs will enjoy well-kept courts and matchless views.

For those who enjoy fine dining and an exciting night life, we offer city tours with shopping in duty-free boutiques and leisurely dinners in world-class restaurants. You can end your evening in a nightclub or dance hall with reggae, jazz, calypso, or steel-band music.

Every Voyages cruise offers luxurious accommodations, a panoply of recreational activities from swimming to shuffleboard, big-band dancing, our own Voyages dance and musical show, and sumptuous meals prepared by premier chefs. Our seasoned crews will devote every effort to making sure your cruise is a memorable one.

Travelers with special needs receive special treatment with Voyages. Older travelers, families with young children, and disabled individuals will find that our tours can be specially designed to accommodate their needs.

Voyages has created six fabulous tours to the most exciting ports in the Caribbean. Every package includes airfare, accommodations, and entertainment and meals on the cruise ship. It might be difficult to pick just one of the tour packages in this brochure.

Voyages Travel Consultants, Inc. 46 South Street Columbus, Ohio 43215-3406 614-555-9544

The text, objects, and spacing in this exercise have been reduced because of space constraints.

EXERCISE 37

Learning Objectives

Use text flow and text wrap options

Terms

- Text wrap
- Text flow
- No wrap
- Column break
- Jump over
- Wrap all sides
- Offset/boundary/standoff

Concepts

On some software, you can control the way text flows around a graphic by selecting the graphic and then selecting a **text wrap** and **text flow** option. Being able to program a graphic so that text flows around it automatically prevents you from having to adjust windowshades. It is particularly useful in long documents and in documents such as newsletters that may have a graphic in the same place from issue to issue.

The default text wrap option is generally **no wrap** (text flows through the graphic). If you choose to have text wrap around a graphic, you can choose a **column break** option, in which text flows above a graphic and then jumps to the next column; a **jump over** option, in which text flows above the graphic, jumps over it, and continues flowing beneath it; or a **wrap all sides** option, in which text flows around all sides of the graphic. When you choose the last option, you can customize the wrap to come in close around the graphic. You will use custom wrap in the next exercise.

When text is wrapped around a graphic, the software establishes how much space will appear between the edge of the graphic and the beginning of the text. This space is called the **offset,** the **boundary,** or the **standoff**. Most software uses a default offset measurement; however, on some software, you may change this measurement.

When text wrap is used, it is often necessary to adjust the placement of the graphic so that the text does not break in an awkward place. This is particularly true when using a custom wrap.

INSTRUCTIONS

1. Open the data file **PF1** (or open a copy of **PF1** if your software has that option).
2. Save the document as **PF3.**
3. Import a graphic. Note that text flows through the graphic (the default text wrap option).
4. Re-size the graphic so it fits in the left column as shown.
5. Select the graphic and choose the column break option.
6. Import a second graphic, and re-size it so it fits in the right column as shown.
7. Select the graphic and choose the jump over option.
8. If necessary, adjust the placement of the two graphics so text does not break awkwardly (does not leave a widow or orphan, for example).
9. Delete text at the end of the story so it does not extend below the bottom margin, as shown.
10. Re-save the file.
11. Using all printer defaults, print one copy.
12. Close the file.

EXERCISE 37

USING PRACTICE TEXT

Exercise 37

This is practice or "dummy" text that you can use for importing, placing, and playing purposes. Desktop publishers often use dummy text. When you are first designing a publication, you can flow a dummy text file in to see how your design will look with type. Desktop publishers also use dummy text for publications that will be produced periodically, such as a monthly newsletter. The dummy text serves as a placeholder for the different articles that will appear in each issue. You will learn more about using dummy text in this way in later exercises.

Some desktop publishing programs give you practice or "dummy" text that looks like Latin (but it's not). It is called a *lorem ipsum* file. Really, any file can serve as dummy text. The more it looks like the kind of text you will be using in your final publication, the better. You can manipulate and move sections of practice text as you desire. You can experiment with different elements such as typefaces, type styles, type sizes, and leading.

Later in this book, you will be given the opportunity to create your own projects. Before you tackle them, you will learn to plan your publication ahead by drawing a "thumbnail" sketch on a piece of blank paper. Drawing a thumbnail will give you direction in creating your page layout on the computer. The sketch should define the approximate positions of all the text and graphic elements that will appear on each page. Of course, the design may be changed as you are working on your project in the desktop publishing program.

There are countless ways to design a document. Professional designing requires education and skill, but you do not have to be a professional designer to create simple, attractive publications in your desktop publishing software. The exercises in this book will give you the general guidelines you need for document design, as well as ideas to consider and examples to follow.

The text, objects, and spacing in this exercise have been reduced because of space constraints.

Learning Objectives

Use text flow and text wrap options
Perform a custom wrap

INSTRUCTIONS

1. Open the data file **PF1** (or open a copy of **PF1** if your software has that option).
2. Save the document as **PF4.**
3. Delete the rule between the columns.
4. Import a graphic. Re-size it, if necessary, and place it in the middle of the page as shown.
5. Select the graphic, and select the wrap all sides option.
6. Try to ensure text does not break inappropriately. You may need to hyphenate manually or automatically or to move or fine-tune the size of the graphic.
7. Pull up the bottom windowshade in the right column to make sure text does not extend below the bottom margin.
8. Re-save the file.
9. Using all printer defaults, print one copy.
10. Save the file as **PF5.**
11. Customize the text wrap, as shown in the exercise on the right.
12. Try to ensure text does not break inappropriately. Delete text at the end of the story so it does not extend below the bottom margin, as shown.
13. Re-save the file.
14. Using all printer defaults, print one copy.
15. Close the file.

EXERCISE

38

Exercise 38

USING PRACTICE TEXT

This is practice or "dummy" text that you can use for importing, placing, and playing purposes. Desktop publishers often use dummy text. When you are first designing a publication, you can flow a dummy text file in to see how your design will look with type. Desktop publishers also use dummy text for publications that will be produced periodically, such as a monthly newsletter. The dummy text serves as a placeholder for the different articles that will appear in each issue. You will learn more about using dummy text in this way in later exercises.

Some desktop publishing programs give you practice or "dummy" text that looks like Latin (but it's not). It is called a *lorem ipsum* file. Really, any file can serve as dummy text. The more it looks like the kind of text you will be using in your final publication, the better. You can manipulate and move sections of practice text as you desire. You can experiment with different elements such as typefaces, type styles, type sizes, and leading.

Later in this book, you will be given the opportunity to create your own projects. Before you tackle them, you will learn to plan your publication ahead by drawing a "thumbnail" sketch on a piece of blank paper. Drawing a thumbnail will give you direction in creating your page layout on the computer. The sketch should define the approximate positions of all the text and graphic elements that will appear on each page. Of course, the design may be changed as you are working on your project in the desktop publishing program.

There are countless ways to design a document. Professional designing requires education and skill, but you do not have to be a professional designer to create simple, attractive publications in your desktop publishing software. The exercises in this book will give you the general guidelines you need for document design, as well as ideas to consider and examples to follow. Looking at different publications will give you other ideas to try.

Desktop publishing software often comes with sample documents, or *templates*, already designed and formatted for you. Your software may provide templates for letters, memos, newsletters, reports, and other common documents. Templates can be used as is or modified as needed. You will learn more about templates later in this text.

When you begin to design a publication, try different typefaces, type styles, type sizes, and leading options. Change the margins, and vary the space between columns. Stretch your text boxes to varying lengths. Don't be afraid to experiment! If you are not

USING PRACTICE TEXT

This is practice or "dummy" text that you can use for importing, placing, and playing purposes. Desktop publishers often use dummy text. When you are first designing a publication, you can flow a dummy text file in to see how your design will look with type. Desktop publishers also use dummy text for publications that will be produced periodically, such as a monthly newsletter. The dummy text serves as a placeholder for the different articles that will appear in each issue. You will learn more about using dummy text in this way in later exercises.

Some desktop publishing programs give you practice or "dummy" text that looks like Latin (but it's not). It is called a *lorem ipsum* file. Really, any file can serve as dummy text. The more it looks like the kind of text you will be using in your final publication, the better. You can manipulate and move sections of practice text as you desire. You can experiment with different elements such as typefaces, type styles, type sizes, and leading.

Later in this book, you will be given the opportunity to create your own projects. Before you tackle them, you will learn to plan your publication ahead by drawing a "thumbnail" sketch on a piece of blank paper. Drawing a thumbnail will give you direction in creating your page layout on the computer. The sketch should define the approximate positions of all the text and graphic elements that will appear on each page. Of course, the design may be changed as you are working on your project in the desktop publishing program.

There are countless ways to design a document. Professional designing requires education and skill, but you do not have to be a professional designer to create simple, attractive publications in your desktop publishing software. The exercises in this book will give you the general guidelines you need for document design, as well as ideas to consider and examples to follow. Looking at different publications will give you other ideas to try.

Desktop publishing software often comes with sample documents, or *templates*, already designed and formatted for you. Your software may provide templates for letters, memos, newsletters, reports, and other common documents. Templates can be used as is or modified as needed. You will learn more about templates later in this text.

When you begin to design a publication, try different typefaces, type styles, type sizes, and leading options. Change the margins, and vary the space between columns. Stretch your text boxes to varying lengths. Don't be afraid to experiment! If you are not happy with your work, delete the story, or close your desktop publishing file without saving it and place the file again. You can place files as many times as you like without altering them.

The text, objects, and spacing in this exercise have been reduced because of space constraints.

Learning Objectives

Create a pull quote
Perform custom wraps

Terms

- Placeholder
- Pull quote

Concepts

You can wrap text around other objects besides imported graphics. On some software, you can wrap text around drawn graphics and around any group, even one including text.

Desktop publishers sometimes draw an empty shape such as a box and set up text flow around it; the shape serves as a **placeholder** for a graphic that will come later. Placeholders are used when you are planning a document. They are also often used for documents that will be produced more than once, such as newsletters. Customizing the wrap allows you to create odd shapes out of the placeholder.

In this exercise, you will create a piece of text art called a **pull quote.** Pull quotes consist of important, interesting, or provocative text from the body copy. Like other graphic elements, a pull quote is intended to attract the reader to the story.

INSTRUCTIONS

1. Open the data file **PF1** (or open a copy of **PF1** if your software has that option).
2. Save the document as **PF6.**
3. Delete the rule between the columns.
4. Create a pull quote like that shown on the right. Choose your own quote from the practice text file. Set the quote in a sans serif typeface, bold/italic, with generous leading.
5. *If your software allows you to group objects and wrap text around the group,* create a shadow box like that shown (use the power paste or align and distribute feature, if available), group the finished pull quote, and wrap text around the group.

   If your software does not have a group option, omit the "shadow," create the pull quote with just one box, and wrap text around it. You may need to adjust the pull quote text block (handles, type size, and/or leading) to fit inside the drawn box, so the text is not bumped outside by the standoff.
6. If necessary, adjust the placement of the pull quote so text does not break awkwardly.
7. Delete text at the end of the story so it does not extend below the bottom margin, as shown.
8. Re-save the file.
9. Using all printer defaults, print one copy.
10. Close the file.
11. Open the data file **PF1** (or open a copy of **PF1** if your software has that option).
12. Save the document as **PF7.**
13. Delete the rule between the columns.
14. Draw a small square with no border in the center of the document, and choose the wrap all sides option.
15. To customize the wrap into the shape of a diamond as shown, add handles on the boundary opposite the *middle* handles on each side (add four handles in all). Drag each of the four handles outward, away from the graphic.
16. If necessary, move the diamond so text does not break awkwardly.
17. Delete text at the end of the story so it does not extend below the bottom margin, as shown.
18. Re-save the file.
19. Using all printer defaults, print one copy.
20. Close the file.

EXERCISE 39

Exercise 39

USING PRACTICE TEXT

This is practice or "dummy" text that you can use for importing, placing, and playing purposes. Desktop publishers often use dummy text. When you are first designing a publication, you can flow a dummy text file in to see how your design will look with type. Desktop publishers also use dummy text for publications that will be produced periodically, such as a monthly newsletter. The dummy text serves as a placeholder for the different articles that will appear in each issue. You will learn more about using dummy text in this way in later exercises.

Some desktop publishing programs give you practice or "dummy" text that looks like Latin (but it's not). It is called a *lorem ipsum* file. Really, any file can serve as dummy text. The more it looks like the kind of text you will be using in your final publication, the better. You can manipulate and move sections of practice text as you desire. You can experiment with different elements such as typefaces, type styles, type sizes, and leading.

There are countless ways to design a document.

Later in this book, you will be given the opportunity to create your own projects. Before you tackle them, you will learn to plan your publication ahead by drawing a "thumbnail" sketch on a piece of blank paper. Drawing a thumbnail will give you direction in creating your page layout on the computer. The sketch should define the approximate positions of all the text and graphic elements that will appear on each page. Of course, the design may be changed as you are working on your project in the desktop publishing program.

There are countless ways to design a document. Professional designing requires education and skill, but you do not have to be a professional designer to create simple, attractive publications in your desktop publishing software. The exercises in this book will give you the general guidelines you need for document design, as well as ideas to consider and examples to follow. Looking at different publications will give you other ideas to try.

Desktop publishing software often comes with sample documents, or *templates*, already designed and formatted for you. Your software may provide templates for letters, memos, newsletters, reports, and other common documents. Templates can be used as is or modified as needed. You will learn more about templates later in this text.

When you begin to design a publication, try different typefaces, type styles, type sizes, and leading options. Change the margins, and vary the space between columns. Stretch your text boxes to varying lengths. Don't be afraid to experiment! If you are not happy with your work, delete the story, or close your desktop publishing file without saving it and place the file again. You can place files as many times as you like

USING PRACTICE TEXT

This is practice or "dummy" text that you can use for importing, placing, and playing purposes. Desktop publishers often use dummy text. When you are first designing a publication, you can flow a dummy text file in to see how your design will look with type. Desktop publishers also use dummy text for publications that will be produced periodically, such as a monthly newsletter. The dummy text serves as a placeholder for the different articles that will appear in each issue. You will learn more about using dummy text in this way in later exercises.

Some desktop publishing programs give you practice or "dummy" text that looks like Latin (but it's not). It is called a *lorem ipsum* file. Really, any file can serve as dummy text. The more it looks like the kind of text you will be using in your final publication, the better. You can manipulate and move sections of practice text as you desire. You can experiment with different elements such as typefaces, type styles, type sizes, and leading.

Later in this book, you will be given the opportunity to create your own projects. Before you tackle them, you will learn to plan your publication ahead by drawing a "thumbnail" sketch on a piece of blank paper. Drawing a thumbnail will give you direction in creating your page layout on the computer. The sketch should define the approximate positions of all the text and graphic elements that will appear on each page. Of course, the design may be changed as you are working on your project in the desktop publishing program.

There are countless ways to design a document. Professional designing requires education and skill, but you do not have to be a professional designer to create simple, attractive publications in your desktop publishing software. The exercises in this book will give you the general guidelines you need for document design, as well as ideas to consider and examples to follow. Looking at different publications will give you other ideas to try.

Desktop publishing software often comes with sample documents, or *templates*, already designed and formatted for you. Your software may provide templates for letters, memos, newsletters, reports, and other common documents. Templates can be used as is or modified as needed. You will learn more about templates later in this text.

When you begin to design a publication, try different typefaces, type styles, type sizes, and leading options. Change the margins, and vary the space between columns. Stretch your text boxes to varying lengths. Don't be afraid to experiment! If you are not happy with your work, delete the story, or close your desktop publishing file without saving it and place the file again. You can place files as many times as you like

Use a 10% fill and a 1-point rule for the first pull quote box. For the second, use a solid fill with no rule.

The text, objects, and spacing in this exercise have been reduced because of space constraints.

Learning Objectives

Crop and pan graphics
Follow guidelines for cropping

Terms

- Cropping
- Panning

Concepts

Cropping is the ability to cut out part of a graphic image. On most software, cropping is accomplished by choosing the cropping tool from the toolbox, selecting the graphic, and dragging handles to cut away part of the image. Some programs also allow you to crop using the control palette.

Although cropping makes an image look like it has been trimmed, the rest of the image is still there, but hidden. If you wish to "uncrop" the image, reverse the cropping procedure.

After you have cropped an image, you can move it around within its frame, if you wish, to display exactly the part of the image you want. Moving a cropped image around in its frame is referred to as **panning** the image and is usually accomplished with a key/mouse combination, such as **Alt + drag.**

These guidelines should help you when cropping an image:

- Crop out the parts of the image that have little meaning, are extraneous, or are distracting.
- Focus on the area of the image that gives it meaning.
- With people, parts of the body can be cropped.
- Crop for compatibility with the page layout.

INSTRUCTIONS

1. Open the data file **PF1** (or open a copy of **PF1** if your software has that option).
2. Save the document as **PF8.**
3. Delete the rule between the columns.
4. Import a graphic that has elements that you can crop away.
5. Crop the graphic so it is displayed attractively. Pan it, if necessary.

   NOTE: *In this exercise, two of the faces were cut out of the original graphic.*
6. Place the graphic in the center of the page, and choose the wrap all sides option as shown.
7. If necessary, adjust the graphic so text does not break awkwardly. You may need to change the stand-off on one or more sides.
8. Delete text at the end of the story so it does not extend below the bottom margin, as shown.
9. Re-save the file.
10. Using all printer defaults, print one copy.
11. Close the file.

EXERCISE **40**

Exercise 40

USING PRACTICE TEXT

The text, objects, and spacing in this exercise have been reduced because of space constraints.

This is practice or "dummy" text that you can use for importing, placing, and playing purposes. Desktop publishers often use dummy text. When you are first designing a publication, you can flow a dummy text file in to see how your design will look with type. Desktop publishers also use dummy text for publications that will be produced periodically, such as a monthly newsletter. The dummy text serves as a placeholder for the different articles that will appear in each issue. You will learn more about using dummy text in this way in later exercises.

Some desktop publishing programs give you practice or "dummy" text that looks like Latin (but it's not). It is called a *lorem ipsum* file. Really, any file can serve as dummy text. The more it looks like the kind of text you will be using in your final publication, the better. You can manipulate and move sections of practice text as you desire. You can experiment with different elements such as typefaces, type styles, type sizes, and leading.

Later in this book, you will be given the opportunity to create your own projects. Before you tackle them, you will learn to plan your publication ahead by drawing a "thumbnail" sketch on a piece of blank paper. Drawing a thumbnail will give you direction in creating your page layout on the computer. The sketch should define the approximate positions of all the text and graphic elements that will appear on each page. Of course, the design may be changed as you are working on your project in the desktop publishing program.

There are countless ways to design a document. Professional designing requires education and skill, but you do not have to be a professional designer to create simple, attractive publications in your desktop publishing software. The exercises in this book will give you the general guidelines you need for document design, as well as ideas to consider and examples to follow. Looking at different publications will give you other ideas to try.

Desktop publishing software often comes with sample documents, or *templates*, already designed and formatted for you. Your software may provide templates for letters, memos, newsletters, reports, and other common documents. Templates can be used as is or modified as needed. You will learn more about templates later in this text.

When you begin to design a publication, try different typefaces, type styles, type sizes, and leading options. Change the margins, and vary

Original Graphic

EXERCISE 41

Learning Objectives

Mask graphics

Terms

- Mask

Concepts

On some desktop publishing software, it is possible to **mask** out part of an object so that only a portion of it appears. The mask itself is created with the software drawing tools. The mask is placed over the graphic to be masked, both items are selected, and the masking command is chosen. The software groups the items and masks the graphic beneath the drawn object.

INSTRUCTIONS

1. Start a new document. Use the default page settings.
2. Set ruler guides as shown. If you do not have a power paste option with offset control or an align and distribute option, set the following additional horizontal guides (all distances are measured from the top margin of the *document,* not the top of the page): 3 5/8", 3 7/8", 4 7/8", 5 1/8", 6 1/8", and 6 3/8".
3. Draw an 8-point rectangle to frame the margins.
4. Draw a 1" square with a 2-point line for the first picture and place it as shown.

   If you have a power paste option, copy the square and paste three copies with a horizontal offset of 0 and a vertical offset of 1.25".

   Alternatively, if you have an align option, copy the square and paste three copies of it aligned roughly vertically underneath. Then align the squares on their left sides with a vertical distribution of 1.25".

   If you have neither of these options, copy the square and place each copy, using the ruler guides you added in Step 2.
5. Create the document shown at the right. If you do not have a masking option, try using the cropping option for the graphics. You will have to write new copy to match the graphics you have, of course!
6. Save the document as **ZOO.**
7. Using all printer defaults, print one copy.
8. Close the file.

EXERCISE 41

Exercise 41

ruler guide at 1/2" from the *document* left margin

ruler guide at 1 1/4" from the *document* top margin

What's waiting for *you* at the Essex County Zoo?

serif typeface, 40/auto, bold, two separate lines

ruler guide at 2 5/8" from the *document* top margin

This quadruped wears striped pajamas.

Think pink.

Metamorphosis is a way of life.

Got any eucalyptus leaves on ya?

18-point sans serif typeface. Adjust the leading so each line is even with the midpoint of the graphic to which it refers. This example uses 92-point leading.

The text, objects, and spacing in this exercise have been reduced because of space constraints.

ruler guide at 7 5/8" from the *document* top margin

Location: Route 62, Danvers (Exit 14 off Route 128). Just 35 minutes from Boston. Follow the pawprint signs to the Essex County Zoo.
Hours: 9 a.m.-5 p.m. daily. Call for holiday schedule.
Telephone: 617-555-0312
Admission: $7.95 for adults; $4.95 for children 4 and under and senior citizens.

serif typeface, 13/auto, 1/2" left and right indents

EXERCISE 42

Learning Objectives

Rotate objects

Place inline graphics

Terms

- Rotate
- Inline graphic
- Ellipsis marks

Concepts

Some desktop publishing software has a **rotate** option that allows you to rotate text, graphics, and/or groups. Rotating is accomplished with a rotating tool from the toolbox or through the control palette. You will learn about control palette graphics functions in the next exercise.

Many desktop publishing programs enable you to attach an imported or drawn graphic to text as an **inline graphic.** Inline graphics function much like text characters, moving along with the text they are anchored to when the text is repositioned. In some software, you can place an imported graphic as an inline graphic by clicking an insertion point in the text and selecting an inline graphic option in the place dialog box. In other software, you can copy a graphic object to the clipboard, click an insertion point in the text, and then place the object. In either instance, you may need to re-size the graphic to fit the text.

When you are using inline graphics, you will probably want to fix the leading yourself rather than use the auto option. Auto leading is set to accommodate the largest character in a paragraph. When an inline graphic is larger than the surrounding text, auto leading can make the text look too "gappy."

In the exercise, note that the "Instead of" sentence ends with **ellipsis marks,** three dots separated by spaces. Ellipsis marks generally serve to represent omitted material. In this instance, the ellipsis marks show that the text is intended to trail off and is not a grammatically complete sentence.

INSTRUCTIONS

1. Start a new document. Use the default page settings.
2. Set horizontal ruler guides at 3.5" and 7.5" from the top margin of the document, not the top of the page.
3. Draw a patterned rectangle to frame the margins.
4. Create the document as shown. Edit the text to fit the number of graphics you are using.
   - The first line of the "Instead of" text block should sit on the horizontal ruler guide at 3.5".
   - The text "try this:" is in the same text block as the two lines above.
   - In the example, the computer disk is a separate element, not an inline graphic. The period after the disk is a separate text block.
   - All the text at the bottom of the page (from "The Roberts" on) is one text block. The first line of that text block should sit on the horizontal ruler guide at 7.5".
5. Save the document as **PIM.**
6. Using all printer defaults, print one copy.
7. Close the file.

EXERCISE

42

Exercise 42

36/40, grouped and rotated

Use a serif typeface for all type.

18/60, .5" left and right indent

Instead of this , and this 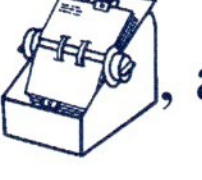, and this , and this , and this , and this . . .

The text, objects, and spacing in this exercise have been reduced because of space constraints.

24/60, bold

try this:

.

24/auto, bold

18/24, .25" left and right indent, center-aligned

The Roberts Personal Information Management System.
One piece of software. Schedule conferences and appointments. Keep phone lists and information logs. Send e-mail. Manage your schedule, your work, and your life. Now at office and computer stores everywhere.

Break the text from this point down line for line.

Insert .085" after this paragraph.

*For the latest in business and productivity software, visit our Web site at **wxx.rob.com.***

12/24, italic, center-aligned

EXERCISE 43

Learning Objectives

Skew objects
Reflect objects
Use the graphics control palette

Terms

- Skew
- Reflect
- Negative leading

Concepts

In Exercise 20, you learned to use the control palette to edit text. In some desktop publishing programs, the control palette also has a graphics version that enables you to resize, rotate, crop, and otherwise edit graphics.

Two functions that are often performed through the control palette are **skew** and **reflect.** The skew option enables you to skew objects such as text blocks, drawn or imported graphics, and groups. The reflect option lets you make an object into a mirror image of itself.

In this exercise, you will need a copyright symbol. Many desktop publishing programs have keyboard combinations for producing copyright symbols and other special characters. Special characters are also available in symbol typefaces.

For the address information in the second coupon, you will set 12-point leading even though the telephone number is 14-point type. Leading that is less than the point size of the type is called **negative leading.** You may need to use negative leading when a paragraph includes type of different sizes and the leading looks too "gappy."

INSTRUCTIONS

1. Start a new document. Use the default margin settings.
2. Draw a rectangle with a 2-point line that measures 6" by 2.5". The rectangle can be anywhere on the page.
3. Copy the rectangle, and paste the copy on the page.
4. Create the two coupons as shown. For the second coupon, use any graphic relating to sports. Edit the "CAPRUS ATBs" text to match the graphic you have.
5. Save the document as **COUPONS.**
6. Using all printer defaults, print one copy.
7. Close the file.

The PageMaker 6.0 Windows Control Palette—Graphics View

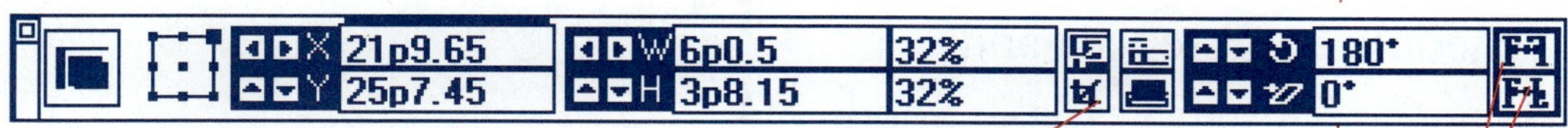

EXERCISE
43

Exercise 43 Use a sans serif typeface for all type.

• Glasses in 1 hour or less
9/auto, .083" after selected paragraphs
• Fashion and designer eyewear
• Contact lenses—all types
• Sports eyewear
• Free adjustments
• Expert frame repairs
• Low, low prices
• Hundreds of styles
• Open 7 days a week
All Major Credit Cards Welcome
9/auto, bold
24/auto, bold, skewed
Optical Express
$15 off all designer frames
Expires October 31, ----
12/auto, bold, center-aligned
$20 off all contact lenses
Expires October 31, ----
5/auto
24/auto, bold
555-2407
2 Mesquito Court
Kissimmee, FL 34741-5987
10/auto, bold
6/auto
Make an impact on customers with IMPACT Advertising
© IMPACT Advertising

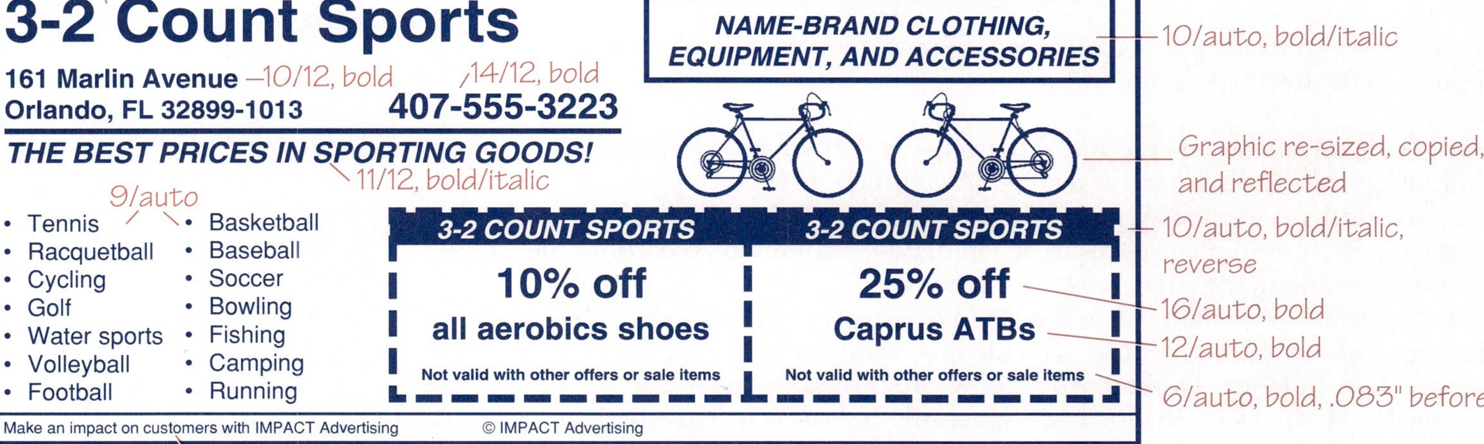

24/auto, bold
3-2 Count Sports
161 Marlin Avenue
Orlando, FL 32899-1013
10/12, bold
14/12, bold
407-555-3223
NAME-BRAND CLOTHING, EQUIPMENT, AND ACCESSORIES
10/auto, bold/italic
THE BEST PRICES IN SPORTING GOODS!
11/12, bold/italic
Graphic re-sized, copied, and reflected
9/auto
• Tennis
• Racquetball
• Cycling
• Golf
• Water sports
• Volleyball
• Football
• Basketball
• Baseball
• Soccer
• Bowling
• Fishing
• Camping
• Running
3-2 COUNT SPORTS
10% off
all aerobics shoes
Not valid with other offers or sale items
3-2 COUNT SPORTS
25% off
Caprus ATBs
Not valid with other offers or sale items
10/auto, bold/italic, reverse
16/auto, bold
12/auto, bold
6/auto, bold, .083" before
Make an impact on customers with IMPACT Advertising
© IMPACT Advertising
6/auto

Learning Objectives

Create a table using desktop publishing software

Terms

- Table editor
- Keyline
- Monospace
- Proportional

Concepts

Tables are text art that can add interest to a document and present data clearly. Many desktop publishing programs have a **table editor** feature that enables you to create tables with relative ease. The finished table can be placed in the desktop-published document like a text or graphic file. Tables can also be created in any desktop publishing program using tab and alignment features. In this exercise, you will create a table in your desktop publishing software. In the next exercise, you will create a table using the table editor feature, if available.

Tables in a document should be separated from the text above and below by a double space. Tables on a separate page can begin a standard distance from the top margin (2", for example) or can be centered vertically. Tables should always be centered horizontally on the page.

The main heading of a table should be in capital letters. If the table has a secondary heading, it should appear in capital and lowercase letters.

Column headings should be either blocked at left or centered over the columns. Generally, they are underlined. The text of a table is usually double-spaced but may be single-spaced.

Words in columns are aligned at the left. Figures are usually aligned at the right or at the decimal point.

Approximately an equal amount of space (.4" to 1.6", or 4 to 16 spaces) should separate the columns of a table. A common method of figuring column widths is to choose center alignment and key a **keyline** (the longest item in each column plus spaces to be left between columns), recording the starting position of the first character in each column and setting tabs at those locations. You then delete the keyline. The keyline method assumes the use of **monospace** typefaces, in which the same amount of space is allotted to each letter. Desktop publishing programs generally use **proportional** typefaces, in which the space allotted to each character is proportional to the width of the character. In desktop publishing, the keyline method is a good starting point, but you will need to check your work visually after creating your table and adjust tabs as necessary so that the table is centered and the space between columns is about equal.

Source lines are single-spaced, with a double-space above. If the table has a divider rule, it should be about 1.5" long, and you should double-space above and below it. If a table has a "Totals" line, you double-space above it.

INSTRUCTIONS

1. Start a new document. Use 1" margins.
2. To create a keyline for the table on the right, drag with the text tool from the left margin to the right and down; choose a sans serif typeface, 12/24; choose center alignment; and key the longest item in each column, followed, for the first three columns, by 10 spaces.
3. Set tabs where the first character in each column falls.
4. Delete the keyline.
5. Choose left alignment, and key the body of the table. Do not double-space between lines; the 24-point leading will have the effect of double spacing.
6. Format the first three lines as shown.
7. Draw or format as a paragraph rule the divider rule.
8. Make sure the table is centered horizontally and that approximately an equal amount of space appears between columns. You may need to adjust tabs or move the table text block.
9. Center the table vertically.
10. Draw a rectangle with an attractive border around the margins.
11. Save the document as **TABLE1.**
12. Using all printer defaults, print one copy.
13. Close the file.

Exercise 44

Bold and larger type are optional in tables.

Make these two lines 14-point bold and centered.

WEST PASADENA HIGH SCHOOL

DS

Home Basketball Schedule*

DS

Column headings can be blocked or centered.

Make this line bold and underlined.

Date	Day	Opponent	Time
November 27	Friday	Harris	8:00 p.m.
December 11	Friday	Wilson	7:30 p.m.
December 23	Wednesday	Lincoln	7:30 p.m.
January 22	Friday	Westlake	4:40 p.m.
January 28	Thursday	Kennedy	4:30 p.m.
February 5	Friday	Hamilton	8:00 p.m.
February 20	Saturday	East Beverly	1:30 p.m.
March 6	Saturday	Carter	8:00 p.m.

DS (between each row)

1.5"

DS

*All games will be held in the Webbley Field House.

Tables should be centered horizontally. When tables appear on a separate page, they may be centered vertically or may begin a standard distance from the top margin. When a table appears within a document, double-space above and below the table.

Table

EXERCISE 45

Learning Objectives

Create a table using the table editor

Concepts

In this exercise, you will create a table using a table editor. Table editors offer many features that make creating a table easier. Chief among these is the ability to set the gutter, or space between columns, automatically; you do not have to figure the space between columns. You can center column headings over a column automatically. Text formatting features, borders, and fills can be applied within the table program.

If you do not have access to table editor software, you can generally follow the steps for Exercise 44 to create this table. To center the column headings over the columns in desktop publishing software, set up the columns using the keyline method as usual. Then, for each heading, from the column starting point, space forward once for each two strokes in the longest entry. From this point, backspace once for each two strokes in the column heading. Then key the heading. Check your work visually and adjust tabs as necessary.

INSTRUCTIONS

1. Load your table editor software and start a new table. Choose 7 rows and 4 columns. Choose a .4" vertical gutter (space between columns).
2. Select the entire table and choose a sans serif typeface, 12/24.
3. Select the cells in the first row and group them. Do the same for the cells in the second row.
4. Select the first two rows and choose bold and center alignment.
5. Select the third row and choose bold, underline, and center alignment.
6. Key the table. Do not be concerned if text in a cell wraps to the next line. You will adjust table columns in the next step.
7. Beginning with the left column, drag to adjust the size of each column so that all the text of each column entry is on one line. Each finished column should be sized so that, if you dragged inward even a little, text would bump to the next line. Sizing like this helps you to ensure that the space between columns is approximately equal.
8. Remove any internal borders on the cells.
9. Format the outside border with a 2-point line.
10. Save the file as **TABLE2.**
11. Close the file.
12. Exit from your table editor software and load your desktop publishing program.
13. Start a new publication with 1" margins.
14. Follow a method appropriate for your software for importing the table into the document.
15. Center the table horizontally and vertically on the page.
16. Using all printer defaults, print one copy.
17. Save the document as **HEARINGT** and close it.

Exercise 45

SAYBROOK PLANNING BOARD

Public Hearings on Zoning and Land Usage

Date	City	Location	Time
August 1	Fenwick	Brookline High School	7:00-9:00 p.m.
August 2	Madison	Riverside Community Center	7:00-8:30 p.m.
August 3	Clinton	Main Street Sea Club	6:00-7:30 p.m.
August 4	Westbrook	Westbrook College	7:00-8:30 p.m.

Adobe Table 2.5

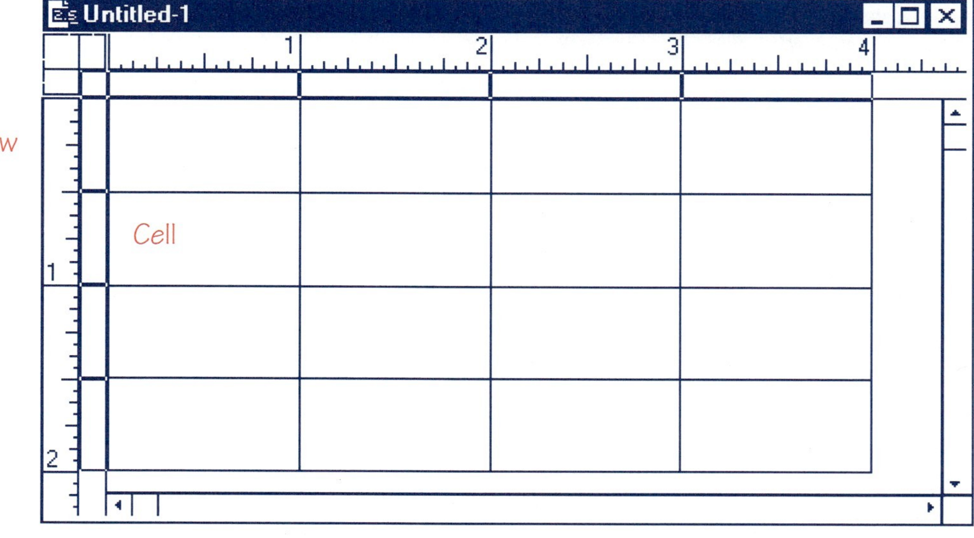

Learning Objectives

Use the image control feature

Learn modified block business letter format

Terms

- Modified block letter

Concepts

On some software, it is possible to control the brightness and contrast of a graphic image. Scanned photo images often require such adjustment. Text may also be changed to appear in shades of gray (or color). A grayed graphic image can be used under text to create an interesting visual effect.

In this exercise, you will create a modified block letter. A **modified block letter** is the same as a block letter except that the date and the closing lines (complimentary close, writer's name, and writer's job title or department) start near the horizontal center of the paper instead of at the left margin. Body text paragraphs may be indented, or they may be blocked at the left margin.

INSTRUCTIONS

1. Open the data file **TEAM2.**
2. Change the letter to a modified block letter with mixed punctuation.
3. Import an appropriate graphic. Place it attractively. Re-size it, if necessary.
4. Lighten the image to a shadow (75% lightness; 50% contrast) and send it to the back.
5. Re-save the file.
6. Using all printer defaults, print one copy.
7. Close the file.

EXERCISE

46

Exercise 46

Business Letter in Modified Block Format

Letterhead

West Pasadena High School
Athletics Department

Date

Set a tab at the horizontal center of the page. Begin text at 2" (or center the letter vertically).

October 19, ——

QS

Letter address

Mr. Bill Javenski
Head Coach
Western University
234 Belleflower Boulevard
Pasadena, CA 90246-8272

DS

Salutation

Body text paragraphs may be blocked at left or indented.

Dear Mr. Javenski:

DS

Body

Attached to this letter is West Pasadena High School's home basketball schedule for this season. I sincerely hope that you will have an opportunity to come to West Pasadena High to observe some of our team members' playing ability.

DS

Two seniors on our team merit particular attention. I have detailed the attributes of two of our most valuable senior players: **Pete Johnson** and **Brian Wilcox.** Knowing the type of team you have, I feel that Pete and Brian will adapt well to your team's style of play.

DS

1" or software default

1" or software default

Pete Johnson has averaged 23 points per game, with 10 rebounds and 6 assists. Clara Martinez of the *Pasadena Herald* recently said, "Pete Johnson's ability to lead the fast break and hit the open man makes him invaluable to the team's success."

DS

Brian Wilcox has averaged 18 points per game and is our best defensive player, blocking 6 shots a game and keeping the opponent's offensive threat down to scoring well below his per-game average.

DS

I look forward to having you or your scouts attend one or more of our games. I know you will not be disappointed with our team members' playing ability. You will be impressed with what you will see. If you have any questions, please phone me at **213-555-7474.**

DS

Complimentary close

Sincerely,

QS

Writer

Alan H. Savoy
Athletic Director

The text, objects, and spacing in this exercise have been reduced because of space constraints.

DS

Reference initials

bcd

DS

Attachment notation

Attachment

1841 Shasta Highway   Pasadena, CA 90246-8272   213-555-7474

At least 1" (but footer may appear below 1" margin)

Learning Objectives

Work with multiple open publications

Copy objects between publications

Use the image control feature

Concepts

In this exercise, you will copy a graphic from one publication to another. Some software allows you to open more than one publication at a time and to drag objects from one publication to another to copy them. Even if your software does not have that option, you can still copy graphics from one publication to another by opening and closing publications and using the clipboard. For objects that consist of multiple parts, grouping the parts before copying will make copying easier.

INSTRUCTIONS

1. Open **DESSERT.**
2. Change the page orientation to landscape.
3. Set all margins at .75".
4. Create two columns with a .25" gutter, to make two pages of the one page.
5. Position vertical ruler guides at 2", 4", 7", 9", and 9 3/16". Place horizontal ruler guides at 1 1/2" and 4".
6. Draw 12-point horizontal lines across the top and bottom margins between the 2" and 4" ruler guides on the "first page" and between the left and right margins on the "second page."
7. Import a graphic that relates to desserts. Lighten the image to a shadow (80% lightness; 50% contrast). Place and size it to fit between the 7" and 9" ruler guides and the top and bottom rules.
8. Drag the second text block to the "second page" and place it so it begins just under the 1 1/2" horizontal ruler guide.
9. Set the second text block in a sans serif typeface, 12/auto, bold, with a decimal tab with leaders for the price information. The decimal point should appear at the horizontal ruler guide at 9 3/16". The example uses a 2.156" tab.
10. Drag the third text block to the "second page." Place and size it so that it appears between the 7" and 9" vertical ruler guides as shown.
11. Set the third text block to sans serif 12/14 bold, center-aligned; set "$2.95" (above the desserts) to 15-point with .125" of space after. Some of the desserts will take two lines, as shown.
12. Drag the first text block to the "first page" below the 4" horizontal ruler guide. Shorten the text block to fit between the 2" and 4" vertical ruler guides.
13. Set the text to 38/50 sans serif bold, force-justified.
14. Re-save the file.
15. Open **OBJECTS** and copy the coffee cup and plate. Center them vertically and horizontally as shown.
16. Re-save the file.
17. Using all printer defaults, print one copy.
18. Close the file.

EXERCISE
47

Exercise 47

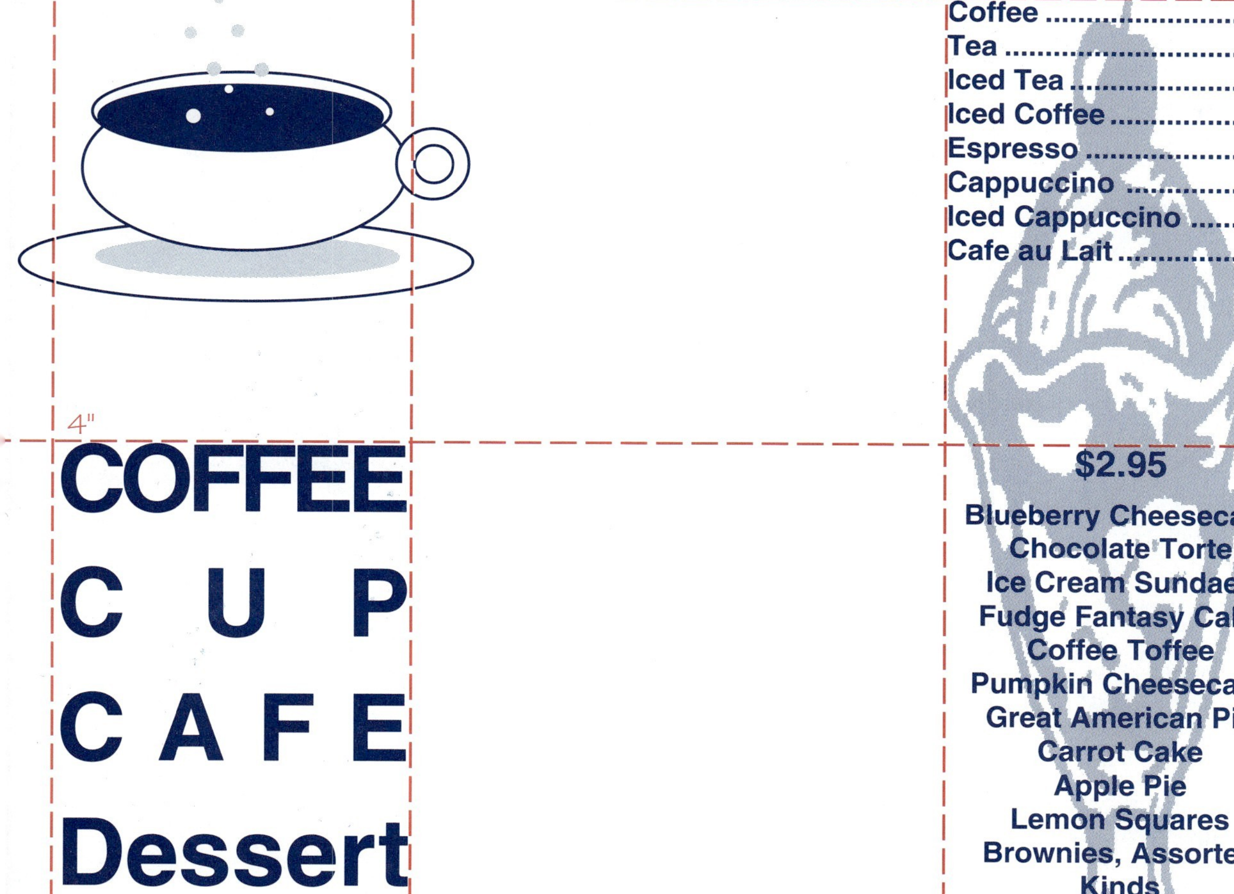

2" 4" 1 1/2" 4"

COFFEE
C U P
C A F E
Dessert
M e n u

7" 9"

Coffee $1.00
Tea $1.00
Iced Tea $1.25
Iced Coffee $1.25
Espresso $1.25
Cappuccino $1.50
Iced Cappuccino $2.00
Cafe au Lait $1.10

$2.95

Blueberry Cheesecake
Chocolate Torte
Ice Cream Sundaes
Fudge Fantasy Cake
Coffee Toffee
Pumpkin Cheesecake
Great American Pie
Carrot Cake
Apple Pie
Lemon Squares
Brownies, Assorted Kinds
Fudge Fantasy
Chocolate Mousse Cake
Strawberries with Lemon Sorbet

The text, objects, and spacing in this exercise have been reduced because of space constraints.

EXERCISE 48

Learning Objectives

Perform a custom wrap
Set indents and tabs
Rotate a graphic
Use en spaces

INSTRUCTIONS

1. Start a new publication. Use the default settings. Set a ruler guide as shown.
2. Import the template file **WONDO.**
3. Format the title as shown.
4. Format the body text in a serif typeface, 12/15, with a .25" left indent and .185" space after.
5. Import a graphic relating to music and wrap text around it. You may need to change the flyer copy to match the graphic.
6. Set the address text in 13-point type. Set the space after so that the coupon appears at the bottom of the page as shown.
7. Format the coupon with a dashed line at the top and half-point rules (drawn or set as paragraph rules). Use a graphic or a symbol typeface (36-point) for the scissors. If you do not have a scissors graphic or symbol, omit the scissors.
8. For the last two lines, set tabs to distribute the check box text as shown. The example uses tabs at 1.9", 3.75", and 5.44". Use an en space between the boxes and the words. If you do not have check boxes, you can draw a box and place copies as inline graphics or use underlining.
9. Save the file as **WONDO.**
10. Using all printer defaults, print one copy.
11. Close the file.

Exercise 48

Add an attractive border around the margins.

ruler guide at .75" from the top margin (not the top of the page)

36-point bold, center alignment, .5" of space after

FREE TRIAL CLASS

Thinking about music lessons? What's been holding you back—the expense? Your busy schedule? The thought that learning the piano, cello, violin, or guitar might not be right for you?

Set those doubts aside. The Wondo Music School is extending you a winning offer.

A free trial lesson with one of our certified music instructors. We'll even provide the instrument.

The Wondo Music School offers contemporary and traditional study for children and adults. Beginning, intermediate, and advanced classes in piano and string instruments are taught. Our conservatory-trained instructors use the highly successful Suzuki method. Easy terms available.

The Wondo Music School
840 Palm Tree Drive
Orlando, FL 32810-8895
407-555-2028

You may need to rotate the scissors.

Name ______________________
Address ______________________
City, State, ZIP ______________________
Telephone ______________________

Add .185" of space after here.

Please enroll me in a free trial class (check the appropriate instrument and level)

❒ Piano ❒ Violin ❒ Cello ❒ Guitar
❒ Beginning ❒ Intermediate ❒ Advanced

The text, objects, and spacing in this exercise have been reduced because of space constraints.

Learning Objectives

Use the library feature
Create a personal library

Terms

- Library feature

Concepts

Many desktop publishing programs offer a **library feature** that you can use to store frequently used text and graphic objects. You can place these items in one or more library files, organize them, view them, search for them, and retrieve them easily into a publication.

INSTRUCTIONS

1. Create a new library file.
2. Place half a dozen text and graphics files that you use frequently in the library.
3. Open a publication in your desktop publishing software.
4. Add two items from the library to the document.
5. Using all printer defaults, print one copy.
6. Save and close the publication.

As you work through this text, continue to add text and graphic objects that you anticipate using frequently to your library.

Learning Objectives

Use spacing techniques to adjust text

Terms

- Kerning
- Tracking
- Set width

Concepts

Desktop publishing programs make adjustments in spacing automatically. Occasionally, however, you may need to adjust text spacing to improve the look of the text or to achieve a special effect. Headlines and other text set in large type may need adjustment more often than body text. Desktop publishing software offers several ways of making adjustments in spacing.

Kerning is the process of adjusting the space between characters to "fine-tune" spacing. On some software, you can manually kern type by increasing or decreasing the space between letters in fractions of an inch. You may wish to kern letter pairs such as *Wo*, *Ya*, and *Tu*, which sometimes appear too far apart. Other pairs, such as *Mi* and *Il*, may look too close together. You may also wish to kern to achieve a special effect. In the word "Outstanding" below, the word, except for the *O*, was set as superscript 24-point and kerned into the *O*. The *O* was set to 48-point.

Most software sets a default for the amount of space left between letters and words. This default may be changed for entire paragraphs or for the publication. Changes are made in percentage increments.

While letter spacing applies to entire paragraphs, **tracking** allows you to adjust the relative space between characters for selected text. Some software offers specific track settings.

On some software, it is possible to expand or condense type by **setting the width** of the characters. While this is not a spacing function, it does affect spacing. The width of text is set in percentage increments.

Kerning Text

Worsen automatic kerning

Worsen automatic plus manual kerning

Outstanding

Settings for Tracking

Tracking	No track
Tracking	Very loose
Tracking	Loose
Tracking	Normal
Tracking	Tight
Tracking	Very tight

INSTRUCTIONS

1. Start a new publication. Use the default settings.
2. Import the template file **PF.**
3. Experiment with the kerning, tracking, set width, and word and letter spacing options in your software.
4. Using all printer defaults, print one copy.
5. Close the file without saving.

Setting the Width

Set width	70%
Set width	Normal
Set width	130%

Setting the Word Spacing

Most software sets a default for the amount of space left between letters and words.

Most software sets a default for the amount of space left between letters and words.

Most software sets a default for the amount of space left between letters and words.

Learning Objectives

Create drop caps and raised caps
Insert a page
Kern text

Terms

- Raised cap
- Drop cap

Concepts

A very effective technique is to enlarge the first character of the first word in a paragraph. Enlarging the initial capital will draw the reader's attention to that paragraph.

A **raised cap** sits on the same baseline as the surrounding text but is much larger. To set a raised cap, you simply select the character and increase the point size for it (you may wish to apply bold as well). You may wish to increase the space before the paragraph to accommodate the enlarged letter.

A **drop cap** is embedded in the paragraph text. The top of the cap is roughly even with the top of the text that follows. The base of the initial cap aligns with the baseline of the last line of text that falls opposite it. There are several ways to create a drop cap. Some software has a feature for creating drop caps automatically. You can also set the character as a separate text block, drag it into place, and set a left indent for the lines that fall opposite it. Still another method is to set the letter as a graphic and use text wrap.

Most software permits you to add pages after creating a publication through a menu option.

INSTRUCTIONS

1. Open the data file **FUN1** (or open a copy of **FUN1** if your software has that option).
2. Save the file as **FUN2.**
3. Copy the entire page, add a page, and paste the copy onto it.
4. On page 1, add .185" of space after the title. Add .35" of space after the rest of the text paragraphs.
5. On page 1, create 36-point bold raised caps for the first character of each of the body text paragraphs. You may need to kern the following text so the space between the raised cap and the subsequent text is not excessive.
6. On page 1, center the text block vertically between the two 8-point lines.
7. On page 2, add .25" of space after all body text paragraphs. Delete the tabs so each paragraph begins flush left.
8. Create drop caps for the initial letter of each paragraph.
9. Center the text block vertically between the two 8-point lines.
10. Re-save the file.
11. Using all printer defaults, print one copy.
12. Close the publication.

You would never use this many raised and drop caps in a short document like this. In this exercise, they are added for practice.

Learning Objectives

Use color to enhance documents

Terms

- Colors palette
- Spot color
- Color matching system
- Process color
- Color separations
- Registration
- Registration marks

Concepts

Color can enhance any desktop-published document. With desktop publishing software, you can apply color to text, graphics, and drawn objects. You can use primary colors, use color mixes supported by commercial printers, or define your own colors. You can print your work on a desktop color printer or take it to a commercial printer for output.

In many programs, color is applied through a **colors palette,** displayed on-screen like the toolbox. You click on a drawn or imported object, or select text, and click on the color in the palette. You may be able to apply color to text in the type dialog box and to paragraph rules in the paragraph dialog box. Color can also be part of a style (see Exercise 56).

Desktop publishing software allows you to use spot color and/or process color. **Spot color** is the assignment of color to selected page elements such as background shapes, portions of text, headings, and rules. Desktop publishing software generally supports standard **color matching systems** for spot color, so that the color you select can be matched exactly by the commercial printer. **Process color** is derived from the basic four inks—cyan, magenta, yellow, and black—printed in patterns of tiny dots to create color blends that are seen as an unlimited range of colors. If you have full-color images like color photographs, you will need to use process color.

Most desktop publishing software supports commercial color printing by printing **color separations.** If a page contains blue and red, the software can produce two copies of the page, one containing just the blue elements, and one just the red. The commercial printer makes a separate printing plate from each of these color separations. When the page goes through the press, it is printed once with the blue-inked plate and a second time with the red-inked plate.

Since the same piece of paper is printed twice separately, once with each color, you can see that the two color separations must align exactly. **Registration** is the alignment of two or more elements. **Registration marks,** marks placed in the same location on every color separation of a publication page, are used to position the color separations precisely so colors print in the proper location. The commercial printer removes the registration marks before printing, or they are printed in an area that will be trimmed.

Most desktop publishing software produces registration marks automatically through an option in the print dialog box. If your software does not have this feature, you can draw registration marks and apply the registration color to them. They will then appear on every color separation.

INSTRUCTIONS

1. Open **COUPONS.**
2. Apply spot color to text and graphic elements as shown. Note that the base color is blue, not black (you should be applying color to every element in every coupon).
3. Add registration marks and print color separations of your work.
4. If you have a color printer, print a composite (not color-separated) version of your work.
5. Save and close the file.

EXERCISE
52

Exercise 52

Glasses in 1 hour or less
Fashion and designer eyewear
Contact lenses—all types
Sports eyewear
Free adjustments
Expert frame repairs
Low, low prices
Hundreds of styles
Open 7 days a week
All Major Credit Cards Welcome
Optical Express
$15 off all designer frames
Expires October 31, ----
$20 off all contact lenses
Expires October 31, ----
555-2407
2 Mesquito Court
Kissimmee, FL 34741-5987
Make an impact on customers with IMPACT Advertising
© IMPACT Advertising

3-2 Count Sports
161 Marlin Avenue
Orlando, FL 32899-1013
407-555-3223
THE BEST PRICES IN SPORTING GOODS!
NAME-BRAND CLOTHING, EQUIPMENT, AND ACCESSORIES
Tennis
Racquetball
Cycling
Golf
Water sports
Volleyball
Football
Basketball
Baseball
Soccer
Bowling
Fishing
Camping
Running
3-2 COUNT SPORTS
10% off
all aerobics shoes
Not valid with other offers or sale items
3-2 COUNT SPORTS
25% off
Caprus ATBs
Not valid with other offers or sale items
Make an impact on customers with IMPACT Advertising
© IMPACT Advertising

Two Color Separations and the Final Page

Neighbor to Neighbor
Race Against Diabetes
Wednesday, August 22
Community Center
2 p.m.

Neighbor to Neighbor
Race Against Diabetes
Wednesday, August 22
Community Center
2 p.m.

↑ Registration mark

Learning Objectives

Use color to enhance documents

Concepts

Like other design elements, color should be used with thought and care. You can use color to emphasize or draw attention to certain parts of a document. Color applied consistently to the same elements throughout a publication can help make it look unified and improve reader comprehension.

Do not pick a color simply because you like it; pick colors that will add to the message you are trying to impart. Choose colors that work well together. Generally, you should use a maximum of four. Just two colors plus black is better.

Logos, rules, and headings are good places to add color. Background color can add interest to drop caps or shadow boxes.

The most important consideration in choosing a color for text is legibility. Make sure the color you have chosen is readable. Set it against a strongly contrasting background.

INSTRUCTIONS

1. Open either **ZOO** or **PIM.**
2. Choose and apply spot color to text and/or graphic elements. You can use the basic colors or colors from a color matching system.
3. Add registration marks and print color separations of your work.
4. If you have a color printer, print a composite (not color-separated) version of your work.
5. Save and close the file.

Learning Objectives

Use templates

Terms

- Template

Concepts

Templates are a timesaving feature of desktop publishing programs. A **template** is a document that has already been designed for you. You simply open the document, replace the text and graphics with your own, and print the document. Most desktop publishing software comes with templates for a variety of commonly used documents, such as letters, memos, reports, brochures, and newsletters. Templates can also be purchased separately.

Templates are especially useful for publications that are produced more than once; a newsletter, for example. Instead of creating each new issue from the beginning, you can simply open the template and place your new text and art in it. Templates are also helpful when you are new at creating a certain type of publication and need some help on design.

When you open a template, a copy, not the original, is opened automatically. That way, the original template is not altered and is always available for your use. You can modify an original template if you want to, however.

Besides using and modifying the templates provided by your desktop publishing software, you can create your own templates easily as well. You will create a template in Exercise 55.

When you are working with templates, you will want to replace the text and graphics placeholders in the template with text and graphics of your own. Most desktop publishing software contains options in the print dialog box for replacing current text or graphics with new items. With these options, new text replaces the old text; new graphics not only replace the old graphics but also are resized automatically to fit the space available.

PageMaker 6.0 (Windows) Templates

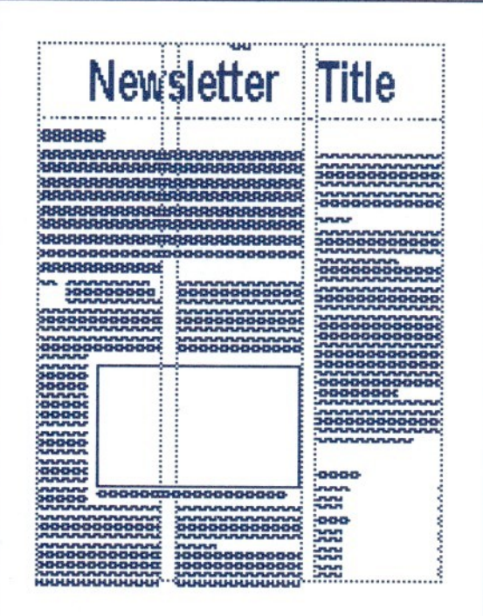

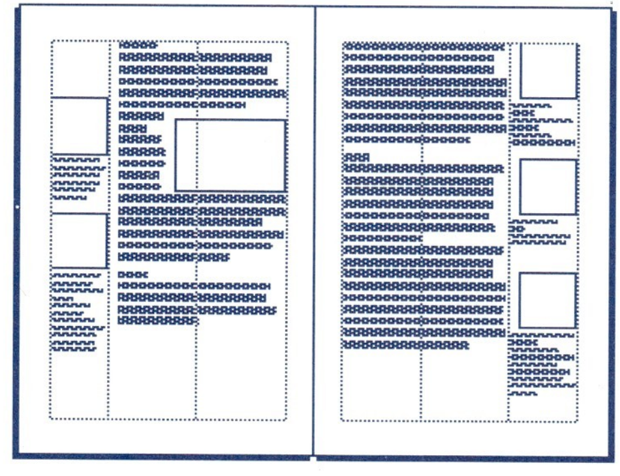

INSTRUCTIONS

1. Open several of the templates in your desktop publishing software. Examine them, and close each without saving.
2. Choose a template that contains both text and placeholders for graphics.
3. Replace a story with the template file **PF1.** You may need to delete text at the end of the story, depending on the template you have chosen.
4. Replace two or three of the graphics placeholders with graphics of your own.
5. Using an appropriate filename, save your document.
6. Using all printer defaults, print one copy.
7. Close the file.

Learning Objectives

Create a template

Concepts

You may often want to use the same document format more than once. Letterheads, newsletters, reports, and news releases are examples of documents that look the same from use to use. To employ a document format more than once, you can save it as a template. Each time you open the template, you will open a copy, rather than the original. You can then place new text and graphics as needed. Of course, you can modify the template as you require. If your desktop publishing software does not support created templates, you can use a document as a template by deleting the old text and graphics and adding new ones on each use.

INSTRUCTIONS

1. Open the data file **YARDFILL.**
2. Save the publication as a template, and close it.
3. Open the **YARDFILL** template you just created.
4. Create the letter at the right as shown.
5. Save the file as a publication, not a template, called **YARDFIL1**.
6. Using all printer defaults, print one copy.
7. Close the file.

Exercise 55

5 Magnolia Lane
Maplewood, NJ 09875-1813
Phone: 201-555-7676
Fax: 201-555-0816

January 14, ----

Mr. Joseph Westbrook
16 Cross Street
Maplewood, NJ 09875-2123

Dear Mr. Westbrook

As a longtime customer of Yardfill Nurseries, you will be interested in our new line of certified 100% organically grown seeds for the flower, vegetable, and herb gardens. These seeds include 50 heirloom and traditional varieties. From asters to zinnias, from bush beans to turnips, and from basil to tarragon, you can grow a garden that is more beautiful and flavorful than ever before, and environmentally sound as well.

Please give us a call or stop by if we can help you with questions or gardening advice. Bring this letter with you and receive 25% off your first order from our new enclosed catalog.

Sincerely

Peter Moss

eg

Enclosure

Peter Moss, Proprietor

Set the body text to a serif typeface, 12/auto. Center the letter vertically.

The text, objects, and spacing in this exercise have been reduced because of space constraints.

Learning Objectives

Use styles to format documents

Terms

- Styles feature
- Style
- Styles palette
- Style sheet

Concepts

In the next few exercises, you will learn to use features of desktop publishing software to facilitate the production of long documents.

Most desktop publishing programs offer a **styles feature.** A **style** is a set of formatting characteristics that can be applied to a paragraph (meaning any unit of text that ends with a hard return) or selected text. (Only some desktop publishing programs offer the latter option.) A style can contain information such as the font, alignment, indents, tabs, hyphenation, spacing, and even the color of the text.

Styles save time and effort, and they promote consistency. For example, suppose you set up a style for headings consisting of Helvetica 12-point bold with center alignment. Instead of having to make four individual format changes to each heading, you can simply click on each head. All the formatting will be applied automatically. What is more, if you decide later that all headings should be Times Roman 11-point italic, flush left, you can simply change the style, and all the headings will be reformatted by the program automatically.

Styles are usually applied by (1) clicking an insertion point in the paragraph or selecting the text and (2) choosing the style name from the style menu option. Some programs offer a **styles palette** that can be displayed like the color palette, making application easier. Styles can also be applied through the control palette in paragraph view.

Most desktop publishing programs come with default styles; you can use them, modify them, and create new styles. A **style sheet** is the set of styles used in a particular document. The style sheet is stored with the document. Changes made to styles, even default styles, do not affect styles by the same name in other documents. You can copy individual styles or a style sheet from other documents and make modifications as needed.

Most desktop publishing software allows you to import styles created in word processing programs. Check your software manuals.

INSTRUCTIONS

1. Start a new document. Use the default settings.
2. Define a style for body text of a serif typeface, 12/18, fully justified, with a tab set at .35".
3. Define a style for headings of a sans serif typeface, 14/18, bold, flush left, with .25" before and .125" after.
4. Import the template file **PF1.** Delete the last paragraph.
5. Select all the text and apply the body text style to it.
6. Insert the heads shown. Apply the heading style to each head.
7. Save the document as **PF9.**
8. Using all printer defaults, print one copy.
9. Save the document as **PF10.**
10. Change the body text style to serif 11/13, flush left, with .185" of space after and a tab at .3".
11. Change the heading style to sans serif 13/13 bold, red, small caps, with .1" of space before and after and a paragraph rule.
12. Using all printer defaults, print one copy.
13. Save and close the file.

EXERCISE

56

Exercise 56

Using Practice Text

This is practice or "dummy" text that you can use for importing, placing, and playing purposes. Desktop publishers often use dummy text. When you are first designing a publication, you can flow a dummy text file in to see how your design will look with type. Desktop publishers also use dummy text for publications that will be produced periodically, such as a monthly newsletter. The dummy text serves as a placeholder for the different articles that will appear in each issue. You will learn more about using dummy text in this way in later exercises.

Some desktop publishing programs give you practice or "dummy" text that looks like Latin (but it's not). It is called a *lorem ipsum* file. Really, any file can serve as dummy text. The more it looks like the kind of text you will be using in your final publication, the better. You can manipulate and move sections of practice text as you desire. You can experiment with different elements such as typefaces, type styles, type sizes, and leading.

Planning Your Work

Later in this book, you will be given the opportunity to create your own projects. Before you tackle them, you will learn to plan your publication ahead by drawing a "thumbnail" sketch on a piece of blank paper. Drawing a thumbnail will give you direction in creating your page layout on the computer. The sketch should define the approximate positions of all the text and graphic elements that will appear on each page. Of course, the design may be changed as you are working on your project in the desktop publishing program.

Designing a Document

There are countless ways to design a document. Professional designing requires education and skill, but you do not have to be a professional designer to create simple, attractive publications in your desktop publishing software. The exercises in this book will give you the general guidelines you need for document design, as well as ideas to consider and examples to follow. Looking at different publications will give you other ideas to try.

Desktop publishing software often comes with sample documents, or *templates*, already designed and formatted for you. Your software may provide templates for letters, memos, newsletters, reports, and other common documents. Templates can be used as is or modified as needed. You will learn more about templates later in this text.

When you begin to design a publication, try different typefaces, type styles, type sizes, and leading options. Change the margins, and vary the space between columns. Stretch your text boxes to varying lengths. Don't be afraid to experiment! If you are not happy with your work, delete the story, or close your desktop publishing file without saving it and place the file again. You can place files as many times as you like without altering them.

USING PRACTICE TEXT

This is practice or "dummy" text that you can use for importing, placing, and playing purposes. Desktop publishers often use dummy text. When you are first designing a publication, you can flow a dummy text file in to see how your design will look with type. Desktop publishers also use dummy text for publications that will be produced periodically, such as a monthly newsletter. The dummy text serves as a placeholder for the different articles that will appear in each issue. You will learn more about using dummy text in this way in later exercises.

Some desktop publishing programs give you practice or "dummy" text that looks like Latin (but it's not). It is called a lorem ipsum file. Really, any file can serve as dummy text. The more it looks like the kind of text you will be using in your final publication, the better. You can manipulate and move sections of practice text as you desire. You can experiment with different elements such as typefaces, type styles, type sizes, and leading.

PLANNING YOUR WORK

Later in this book, you will be given the opportunity to create your own projects. Before you tackle them, you will learn to plan your publication ahead by drawing a "thumbnail" sketch on a piece of blank paper. Drawing a thumbnail will give you direction in creating your page layout on the computer. The sketch should define the approximate positions of all the text and graphic elements that will appear on each page. Of course, the design may be changed as you are working on your project in the desktop publishing program.

DESIGNING A DOCUMENT

There are countless ways to design a document. Professional designing requires education and skill, but you do not have to be a professional designer to create simple, attractive publications in your desktop publishing software. The exercises in this book will give you the general guidelines you need for document design, as well as ideas to consider and examples to follow. Looking at different publications will give you other ideas to try.

Desktop publishing software often comes with sample documents, or templates, already designed and formatted for you. Your software may provide templates for letters, memos, newsletters, reports, and other common documents. Templates can be used as is or modified as needed. You will learn more about templates later in this text.

When you begin to design a publication, try different typefaces, type styles, type sizes, and leading options. Change the margins, and vary the space between columns. Stretch your text boxes to varying lengths. Don't be afraid to experiment! If you are not happy with your work, delete the story, or close your desktop publishing file without saving it and place the file again. You can place files as many times as you like without altering them.

The text and spacing in this exercise have been reduced because of space constraints.

EXERCISE 57

Learning Objectives

Learn unbound report format
Learn about feasibility reports
Format a long document
Format text with styles
Use top of caps leading
Use the keep with next option

Terms

- Unbound reports
- Textual citation
- Top of caps leading
- Keep with option
- Feasibility report
- Analysis

Concepts

In this exercise, you will use a master page and styles to format an unbound report. **Unbound reports** are generally short reports that are fastened together in the upper left corner by a staple or paper clip. They have the following formatting features:

- The top margin of an unbound report is 1", except for the first page, which has a top margin of 2". The bottom margin is at least 1". The side margins are 1" or the default setting.
- Body text is usually double-spaced, but it may be single-spaced. The first line of body text paragraphs is indented .5".
- The title is in capital letters and centered. Quadruple-space after the title.
- Page numbers appear at the top and right margins, except for the first page, which has no page number. Double-space between the page number and the body text.
- Side headings may be in bold or underlined. The first letters of important words in side headings are capitalized. Side headings are double-spaced like the rest of the body text.
- Enumerated text is indented .5" and single-spaced, with double spacing between entries, above the first entry, and below the last entry.
- A popular method of formatting references is **textual citation.** In this method, the name(s) of the author(s), the year of publication, and the page number are cited in parentheses following the text to which the citation refers. If the name of the author is mentioned in the sentence that precedes the reference, his or her name is omitted from the reference, which then contains only the date and page number.
- All references cited in a report are listed alphabetically by the last name of the author(s) at the end of the report, under the title "REFERENCES," "BIBLIOGRAPHY," or "WORKS CITED." References are single-spaced, with double spacing between individual references. References have a hanging indent of .5". Quadruple-space between the references title and the first reference.
- If references appear on a separate page, the reference page has the same margins as the first page. If references appear immediately after the body text on the same page, quadruple-space between the body text and the references title.

The traditional unbound report format uses line spacing (double, single, and so forth) for different report parts. This format sometimes does not translate well into desktop publishing, which uses leading measured in points and space after paragraphs. If you can choose leading options for

continued on page 102

INSTRUCTIONS

1. Start a new document. Set the top and bottom margins at 1"; use the default side margins. Set the number of pages at 4.
2. Go to the master page. Set up automatic page numbering in a serif typeface, 12/auto, at the top and right margins as shown. Place a horizontal ruler guide slightly above 1.25".
3. Define a style for body text of a serif typeface, 12/24, flush left, with top of caps leading, hyphenation on, widow/orphan protect on, and a first indent of .5".
4. Define a title style of a serif typeface, 12/24, centered, with top of caps leading.
5. Define a style for enumerated text of a serif typeface, 12/12, with top of caps leading and a left indent of .5".
6. Define a style for side headings of a serif typeface, 12/24, bold, with top of caps leading and the keep with next feature on (set for the next 2 lines).
7. Define a style for references of a serif typeface, 12/12, with top of caps leading and a hanging indent of .5".

continued on page 102

EXERCISE 57

Exercise 57

2"

Title CAFETERIA MENU CHANGES

QS

.5" In September 19—, a group of employees approached management with a request that the current cafeteria menu be thoroughly revamped to what they considered a more healthy bill of fare: generally, lower in calories, protein, sugar, and fat, and higher in carbohydrates and fiber. President Josephine Costanza appointed a committee to research and consider such a change and to make recommendations.

The following recommendations are submitted: Enumerated text

1" or default

.5" 1. Costanza and Associates should make all cafeteria menu offerings health-conscious.

1" or default

2. A chief catering manager should be appointed to work out a comprehensive plan of menu offerings for all plant catering managers.

3. Plant catering managers should continue to compose their own menus, but from the comprehensive plan.

4. Any savings in costs resulting from the menu change should be passed on to employees in the form of decreased cafeteria prices.

Current Policies and Procedures Side heading

Costanza and Associates operates 13 plant facilities in separate locations. Each facility houses a partially subsidized employee cafeteria that offers breakfast, lunch, and dinner service to some 250 employees. The menu for each cafeteria is developed by the cafeteria manager.

Of the 13 cafeteria managers, seven are registered nutritionists. Three were previously managers in commercial restaurants. Three are graduates of cooking programs.

The committee examined whether the type of menu requested by the employee group is currently being offered at any of our locations. Members interviewed each catering manager and analyzed menu offerings for the past year. The committee found that two cafeterias offered a standard health-conscious alternative on the menu daily. The remainder sporadically offered health-conscious fare.

at least 1"

1"

2

DS

Employee Preferences Side heading

Interviews conducted with cafeteria employees failed to yield more than anecdoctal observations as to whether employees purchase health-conscious food as much as or more than traditional fare. Neither could employee preferences be determined by analyzing purchases or discarding of leftover food; records at that level of specificity are not kept. Instead, the committee conducted out-of-house research on other company cafeterias, in-house focus groups at each location, and a written survey of all employees.

Out-of-house research shows that implementing a health-conscious menu would not result in any significant change in employee cafeteria patronage. Employees are as likely to purchase health-conscious food as traditional fare. (West, 1992, 143) In a study of 150 companies that implemented a health-conscious menu, the National Nutrition Council found that, overall, a slight initial decrease in sales (3 percent) was compensated for within six months by an increase of 5 percent. (1994, 16)

1" or default

1" or default

In the written in-house survey of all employees, 60 percent said that they would regularly purchase a health-conscious offering, and 51 percent said that all menu offerings should be health-conscious. These figures rose to 79 percent and 65 percent respectively in the focus groups, which sampled six health-conscious meals prepared by Catering Manager Kim Cheung of the Langley plant.

textual citation

Health Benefits of a Health-Conscious Menu Side heading

textual citation

The benefits of a health-conscious diet are incontrovertible and have been widely reported. (National Institutes of Health, 1995, 14) Persons who regularly consume a health-conscious bill of fare are at less risk for many diseases and conditions, including heart disease, high blood pressure, stroke, diabetes, osteoporosis, obesity, and cancer. (National Research Council, 1997, 3) — textual citation

Research showing direct benefits to employees deriving solely from a health-conscious cafeteria menu is less conclusive, because of the lack of control factors. For example, employees may consume other types of food outside of work and may or may not exercise.

at least 1"

continued on page 103

Unbound Report

The text and spacing in this exercise have been reduced because of space constraints.

EXERCISE

57

Concepts continued from page 100

your software, choose **top of caps leading** as specified in the exercise. Otherwise, you may need to adjust the spacing to emulate the traditional spacing of an unbound report.

This exercise calls for applying the body text style to the entire document first and then applying other styles to particular text. This method is more efficient than applying each style individually to each paragraph.

In this exercise, you will format the side heading style using the **keep with option,** to keep the side headings with the next two lines of body text, so they will not appear alone at the bottom of the page. This option, which is often set in the paragraph dialog box, is similar to widow/orphan protect.

This exercise uses a **feasibility report.** This type of report explains actions that must be taken and barriers that must be surmounted to make a change. The change could be a new policy or product. Feasibility reports are generally directed to someone with the power to make decisions. The report explains how feasible, or how likely or suitable, an idea is.

A feasibility report is an **analysis.** It clearly states a problem, question, or issue; examines it; and proposes a solution. The solution is supported by other documents, expert opinion, and other reliable resources. You can use these guidelines for writing an analysis:

1. **Know your subject.** Thoroughly research your subject before you begin to write. Your analysis will help you understand all sides of the issue.
2. **Identify your assumptions.** Once you identify your own views, try to set them aside and look at the issue objectively. Determine the most reasonable position on the issue.
3. **Gather information.** Sources of information might include books, newspaper or magazine articles, reference books or software, the Internet, and people.
4. **Collect, organize, and analyze evidence.** Make an outline of your position. For each point you make, cite at least one supporting reference.
5. **Draft and revise your analysis.** Read your draft critically to make sure your analysis is thorough. Proofread carefully, and revise as needed.[1]

[1]This discussion of feasibility reports was adapted from Christine LaRocco and Elaine Johnson, *British & World Literature for Life and Work* (Cincinnati: South-Western Educational Publishing, 1996), pp. 294-295.

INSTRUCTIONS

continued from page 100

8. Go to page 1, and either turn off the display of master page items or cover the page number with a paper-filled, no-line box.
9. Import the template file **HEALTH.**
10. Save the file as **HEALTH1.**
11. Select all the text. Format it with the body text style.
12. On page 1, adjust the top windowshade handle so that the text begins just under the 2" mark on the vertical ruler.
13. Format the title with the title style.
14. Format the enumerated text with the appropriate style. *HINT:* Apply the style to the *entire* line preceding "Current Policies and Procedures."
15. Format the side headings with the appropriate style.
16. As you go through the document, make sure that, for pages 2-4, the first line of body text on the page sits on the horizontal ruler guide just above 1.25".
17. Format the references title with the title style.
18. Format the references with the appropriate style.
19. Go through the text and check for violations of the rules for hyphenation.
20. Re-save the file.
21. Using all printer defaults, print one copy.
22. Close the file.

EXERCISE 57

Exercise 57 continued from page 101

1"

3

DS

Implementing a Health-Conscious Menu Side heading

The committee researched fees that outside consulting services would charge for creating a health-conscious menu. Costs were significant, ranging in eight quotes from $5,000 to $15,000. The committee also interviewed executives at five companies that have made such a change and discussed the topic with Costanza and Associates catering managers. Creating a chief catering manager position, at a recommended increase from the current catering manager's salary of $4,500, was the least expensive alternative. The committee concluded that it was also a practical and popular alternative. Our current staff of catering managers includes individuals who are well-qualified to develop such a dietary plan. These catering managers have the additional advantage of being thoroughly familiar with Costanza and Associates' methods.

1" or default

1" or default

The next question was whether all catering managers should strictly follow the menu plan to be developed by the chief catering manager, or should continue to develop their own menus, but using the comprehensive plan. The committee recommends the latter. Catering managers are accustomed to working independently, and they do their own purchasing. Changing these procedures would result in a significant increase in administrative costs and would require hiring new personnel and reassigning responsibilities.

Costs of a Health-Conscious Menu Side heading

Although not a prime consideration in whether to implement a health-conscious menu, costs are a factor. Out-of-house research shows that cafeterias that switched to a totally health-conscious menu decreased overall annual costs by 15 percent. (Scott, 1996, 25) The largest reduction in costs came from a decrease in purchases of meat and an increase in purchases of fruits and vegetables, which are generally less expensive. As reported above, after a slight initial decrease, sales rose slightly and remained constant.

A related consideration is whether to pass on all or a portion of the decrease in costs to employees. Fourteen companies that passed on all or part of purchase savings to employees through a reduction in cafeteria prices reported an increase in cafeteria sales of 7 percent. (O'Quindo, 1994,

at least 1"

1"

4

DS

23) The committee recommends passing on all or part of the food purchase savings to employees in the form of decreased cafeteria prices.

QS

REFERENCES

QS

National Institutes of Health. *Food for Life.* Washington: Government Printing Office, 1995.

National Nutrition Council. *America's Choice: Employers and Good Food.* Washington: National
.5" Academy, 1994.

National Research Council. *Diet and Disease Prevention.* Washington: Government Printing Office, 1997.

Fior O'Quindo. "Sell More—Buy Less." *Responsible Management,* November 1994, 23-27.

L. Anthony Scott. "Reducing Costs and Promoting Good Health." *Responsible Management,* April 1996, 22-28.

Joanna C. West. "Healthy Eating on the Job." *Cafeteria Quarterly*, Spring 1992, 140-145.

1" or default

1" or default

at least 1"

Unbound Report

The text and spacing in this exercise have been reduced because of space constraints.

EXERCISE 58

Learning Objectives

Edit a style
Use the table of contents feature
Format a table of contents

Terms

- Table of contents
- Paragraph headings

Concepts

Many reports have a **table of contents.** The table of contents has the same margins as the first page of the report. The title, "TABLE OF CONTENTS," is centered. Quadruple-space between the title and the first contents entry.

Contents entries consist of the side headings and paragraph headings used in the report. (**Paragraph headings** are subheadings that you will use in a later exercise.) Side headings are double-spaced and begin at the left margin. Paragraph headings are indented and single-spaced, with a double space above and below them. The page number of each entry appears at the right margin and is preceded by dot leaders. The table of contents page itself is not numbered.

Many desktop publishing programs have a feature for generating a table of contents automatically. Such a feature might not be very useful in a short report, but in a long report, it could save considerable time and effort and reduce the chance of inaccuracies. You can generate a table of contents not only for one document, but also for several related documents that can be linked, generally through an option in the File menu.

The option for including a paragraph as a table of contents entry generally appears in the paragraph dialog box. It can also be specified as part of a style. For long documents, this is the most efficient method. In this exercise, you will edit the side heading style you created in Exercise 57, adding the option for including the paragraph in the table of contents. You must be careful when editing styles. If you created styles based on other styles, a change to one style could be carried automatically to others. It is best not to base styles on one another unless you are certain that you want any change you make to one style to be passed on to others.

Tables of contents can generally be created either as separate documents or in the same document. In this exercise, you will create the table of contents in the **HEALTH1** data file.

Tables of contents do not adjust automatically if you make changes to the text. If you generate a table of contents and then revise your work so that the pagination changes, you will need to generate a new table of contents.

The formatting of the table of contents in your software may not match the traditional table of contents format described above. You may need to adjust the formatting of the finished table of contents to match the model.

INSTRUCTIONS

1. Open the data file **HEALTH1.**
2. Edit the side headings style to include side headings in the table of contents.
3. Check the other styles to ensure the table of contents option is not selected.
4. On page 4, format "REFERENCES" for inclusion in the table of contents. Choose the option for just this paragraph, not for the title style.
5. Insert a page at the end of the document, and go to that page (page 5).
6. On page 5, either turn off the display of master page items or cover the page number with a paper-filled, no-line box.
7. Choose the option to generate a table of contents. If your software lets you key the title, key "TABLE OF CONTENTS." If your software lets you format page numbers of table of contents entries, set the page number at the right margin with dot leaders, if possible.
8. Select all the text in the table of contents; format it in a 12/24 serif typeface with top of caps leading.
9. Set the title in the title style.
10. Make any changes necessary so your work matches the model.
11. Re-save the document.
12. Using all printer defaults, print one copy of the table of contents only.
13. Close the file.

EXERCISE

58

Exercise 58

Use the same margins
as for the first page of the report.

TABLE OF CONTENTS

QS

Table of Contents

The text and spacing in this exercise have been reduced because of space constraints.

EXERCISE 59

Learning Objectives

Compose an index
Use the index feature

Terms

- Index

Concepts

Long documents sometimes have an **index** that lists topics and the pages on which they are discussed. A carefully considered index gives the reader instant access to any pertinent topic.

Many desktop publishing programs have a feature for generating an index automatically. You can generate an index not only for one document, but also for several linked documents.

Index entries generally consist of two parts, a topic and a page number or cross-reference. Topics can be set at different levels, so that some are subtopics of others. Formatting of indices varies widely. Indices can generally be created either as separate documents or in the same document. In this exercise, you will create the index in the **HEALTH1** data file.

Indices do not adjust automatically if you make changes to the text. If you generate an index and then revise your work so that the pagination changes, you will need to generate a new index.

Some guidelines for preparing an index follow.

- Read the work and consider it carefully as a whole. Try to anticipate the needs of the reader.
- Main headings are often a good starting point for index entries.
- Headings are usually nouns or noun phrases (names of persons, places, and things).
- Subheadings should be logically and grammatically related to headings.
- Choose and compose subheadings that will be useful to the reader.
- Index proper names.
- Do not index preliminary material (e.g., the table of contents) or back matter (except appendices containing new material).
- Avoid following an index entry with a long string of page numbers. Where practical, break such topics into subtopics.
- Use "See also" references when additional information can be found in another entry.
- Use "See," or cross-reference, entries when you anticipate the reader may look up information under a title other than the one you have used (for example, the reader may look up *feline*, when the appropriate entries are under *cat*). An alternative, if you can afford the space, is to list all entries under both topics.

INSTRUCTIONS

1. Open and print the data file **HEALTH1.**
2. Read the document carefully, marking index entries. *Your entries do not need to match those in the example on the right.* Create your own index.
3. Using your marked-up copy as a guide, code text for inclusion in the index.
4. Insert a page before the table of contents (a new page 5) for the index.
5. Choose the option to generate an index. If your software lets you key the title, key "INDEX."
6. Format your index attractively and consistently with the rest of the document. *Your index does not need to match the example on the right.*
7. Read through your index carefully. Correct any inconsistencies and errors.
8. Re-save the document.
9. Using all printer defaults, print one copy of the index only.
10. Close the file.

EXERCISE 59

Exercise 59

5

INDEX

Index

The text and spacing in this exercise have been reduced because of space constraints.

EXERCISE 60

Learning Objectives

Learn title page format

Terms

- Cover or title page

Concepts

Many reports have a **cover** or **title page.** The title page uses the same side margins as the first page of the report. Each line is centered horizontally. The report title is in capital letters and appears 2" from the top. The author's name appears 5" from the top, with the company name or school a double space below. The date appears 9" from the top.

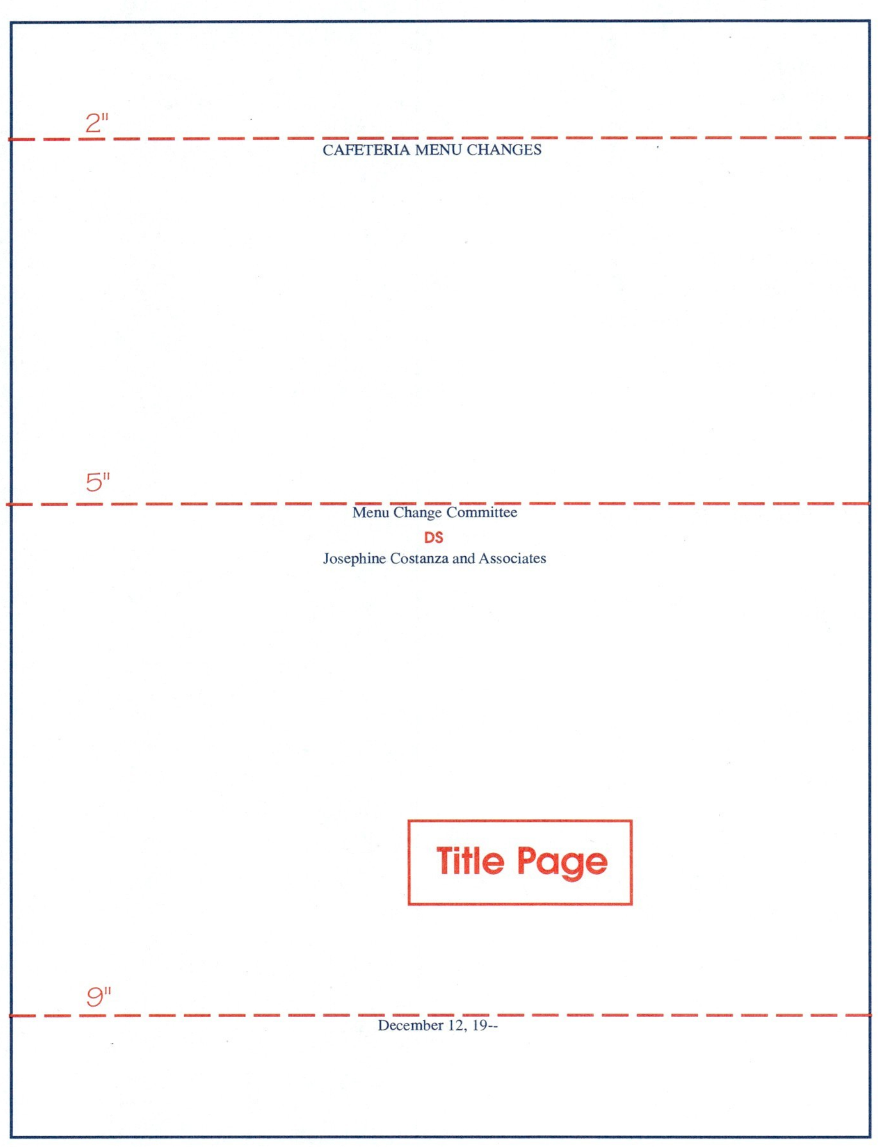

2"
CAFETERIA MENU CHANGES
5"
Menu Change Committee
DS
Josephine Costanza and Associates
Title Page
9"
December 12, 19--

INSTRUCTIONS

1. Start a new document. Set the top and bottom margins at 1". Use the default side margins.
2. Place horizontal ruler guides at 2", 5", and 9".
3. Key the copy as shown in the model at the left in a serif typeface, centered, 12/24.
4. Save the document as **HEALTH2**.
5. Using all printer defaults, print one copy.
6. Close the file.

The text and spacing in this exercise have been reduced because of space constraints.

PART 

CREATING PRESENTATION DOCUMENTS

In Part I of this text, you learned how to use desktop publishing techniques to enhance documents. In Part II, you will use what you have learned to produce professional-looking publications. You will learn a variety of new document formats, such as memos, brochures, and newsletters. You will learn design strategies for making your documents look good. The objective of desktop publishing is to present information and communications attractively and clearly, thus creating a stronger communication that is more appealing to the reader.

At the end of Part II, you will have the opportunity to complete several projects on your own, with little or no direction. These "on your own" projects will be followed by a capstone simulation exercise, which will allow you to practice your desktop publishing skills in a realistic business setting, producing your own professional publications.

Learning Objectives

Create a letterhead

Desktop Techniques Applied

Use different fonts
Use different alignments
Choose a bullet style
Use em spaces
Import a graphic

INSTRUCTIONS

1. Start a new document with .75" margins.
2. Place vertical ruler guides at 2.5" and 6" and a horizontal ruler guide at 1.75".
3. Drag a text block at the top margin from the left ruler guide to the right ruler guide and down about an inch.
4. Key "VOYAGES" in serif 14-point, force-justified, with .185" of space after. The text should extend from one ruler guide to the other.
5. Key "Travel Consultants, Inc." in serif 10-point, center-aligned, with no space after.
6. Key the address information as a separate text block in serif 10-point italic, flush left. The information should begin just below the horizontal ruler guide.
7. At the bottom of the page, key the names of the cities in serif 10-point italic, center-aligned, so that the text sits on the bottom margin guide. For the bullet, use a character from a symbol typeface (you may choose a different symbol), the bullet character from your desktop publishing program, or a drawn, filled square placed as an inline graphic. Key an em space on either side of the bullet. The example uses a Zapf Dingbat character in 8-point.
8. Import an appropriate graphic. Place it as shown; re-size it, if necessary.
9. Save the file as a **template;** name it **VOYAGES.**
10. Using all printer defaults, print one copy.
11. Close the file.

Design Pointers/Hints

- A **logo** is a symbol, picture, or saying that creates an image of a company. The logo in the example is a ship.

EXERCISE 61

Exercise 61

V O Y A G E S

Travel Consultants, Inc.

46 South Street
Columbus, Ohio 43215-3406
Phone: 614-555-9544 or 1-800-555-9995
Fax: 614-555-4321
Internet: wxx.vyg.com

Columbus ■ *New York* ■ *Boston* ■ *Los Angeles*

The text, objects, and spacing in this exercise have been reduced because of space constraints.

Learning Objectives

Create a letterhead

Adjust type and spacing for readability and attractiveness

Desktop Techniques Applied

Draw a filled rectangle

Use different fonts

Use em spaces and en spaces

Save a file as a template

INSTRUCTIONS

1. Start a new document with .5" top and bottom margins and 1" side margins.
2. Place vertical ruler guides at 2.5" and 6". Place horizontal ruler guides at .75", 1", and 10.25".
3. Create a solid black rectangle to fit in the space created by the top margin, vertical ruler guides, and horizontal ruler guide at .75".
4. Copy the rectangle to the bottom of the page, so that it sits on the bottom margin guide and fits between the vertical ruler guides.
5. Drag a text block at the 1" horizontal ruler guide from one vertical ruler guide to the other and down about an inch.
6. Key "VISIONIMAGE" in sans serif 18-point, force-justified, with .35" of space after. The text should begin just under the horizontal ruler guide at 1".
7. Key the address information in sans serif 9-point, force-justified, with an en space between the street address and the city and between the ZIP Code and the telephone number. You may need to change the type size and/or the spacing to fit the text attractively on one line and to ensure it can be read easily.
8. Drag a text block at the 10.25" horizontal ruler guide from one vertical ruler guide to the other and down about half an inch.
9. Key the footer text in sans serif 9-point, force-justified, with an em space plus an en space between each element. You may need to adjust the type size and/or the spacing to fit the text attractively on one line and to ensure it can be read easily. The text should sit on the ruler guide.
10. Save the file as a **template;** name it **IMAGE**.
11. Using all printer defaults, print one copy.
12. Close the file.

Design Pointers/Hints

- Rules or boxes can enhance, organize, and complete a design.
- Letterheads do not have to be elaborate. The letterhead in this exercise has a very simple design; yet it is effective and attractive.

EXERCISE
62

Exercise 62

VISIONIMAGE

245 Lamberts Lane Chicago, IL 60630-1215 (312) 555-0267

Corporate Identity Programs Advertising Graphic Design

The text, objects, and spacing in this exercise have been reduced because of space constraints.

Learning Objectives

Create a letterhead

Desktop Techniques Applied

Draw a filled circle and rule
Use different fonts
Use different alignments
Add space to paragraphs
Save a file as a template

INSTRUCTIONS

1. Start a new document with .75" left and right margins and 1" top and bottom margins.
2. Key the name and address text just inside the top and left margins.
3. Set all the name and address text in a 9/auto bold sans serif font.
4. Set "CIRCLE ARTS MUSEUM" in 18-point with .35" after.
5. Create a solid black circle around the word "CIRCLE," and set the word to reverse. You may need to bring the text to the front to see it. The circle will extend above the top margin.
6. Add .125" of space after the telephone number.
7. Set the director's name in italic.
8. Key the sponsors and patrons text flush right at the right margin, in 9/13.5 sans serif italic.
9. Make "Sponsors" 10-point and bold; add .125" of space after it.
10. Make "Patrons" 10-point and bold; add .25" of space before and .125" of space after it.
11. If necessary, move the sponsors and patrons text block so that the block ends just above the bottom margin.
12. Draw a 1-point vertical line to the left of the sponsors and patrons text as shown, starting above the word "Sponsors" and ending at the bottom margin
13. Save the file as a **template;** name it **CIRCLE**.
14. Using all printer defaults, print one copy.
15. Close the file.

Design Pointers/Hints

- In this letterhead, the drawing tools and some changes in alignment and type style make for a simple, yet attractive, design.

EXERCISE 63

Exercise 63

35 Canvas Lane
New York, NY 10012-2786
(212) 555-5600

Richard Warren, Director

Sponsors

Dr. & Mr. Alexander
Louis Arrone, Jr.
Granite Foundation
J. Harris, Inc.
Oscar Jones
Sang Joy
Mohammed Khair
Janet Lawrence

Patrons

Allied Industries
Armond Fund
Ferris Flowers, Inc.
William French, III
Phillip Gomez
Sarah Kamph
Lorus Group
Donna L. McKinney
Martin Mortimer
Roberta Torres
Salvatore Vitale
Wall Street Foundation
Norma Winter
Zeon Corporation

The text, objects, and spacing in this exercise have been reduced because of space constraints.

Learning Objectives

Create a letterhead

Desktop Techniques Applied

Draw a box border
Import a graphic
Use different fonts
Add space to paragraphs
Add a paragraph rule

INSTRUCTIONS

1. Start a new document with 1" left and right margins and .75" top and bottom margins.
2. Draw a 1-point box to frame the margins.
3. Import a graphic suitable as the logo for the lodge. Place it in the upper left corner as shown. The graphic should be 1 1/8" from the left edge of the page and 7/8" from the top of the page. The graphic should not be wider than 3 inches. Re-size the graphic, if necessary.
4. Drag to create a text box beginning at 3" on the horizontal ruler and extending to 7 3/8". The box should be about 1 1/2" deep.
5. Key the text shown in an 11-point bold sans serif font, right-aligned.
6. Change the first line to 18-point with .1" after.
7. Add .08" after the line that contains the city, state, and ZIP Code. For the same line, add a 1-point paragraph rule that appears .12" below the baseline. If a paragraph rule feature is not available, draw the line 1/8" below the telephone number baseline.
8. Move the text block straight up or down so that it is vertically centered opposite the graphic.
9. Save the file as a **template;** name it **LODGE.**
10. Using all printer defaults, print one copy.
11. Close the file.

Design Pointers/Hints

- This simple design leaves a lot of room for writing the message.

EXERCISE 64

Exercise 64

THE HOLIDAY MOUNTAIN LODGE

459 Ski Mountain Road
Gatlinburg, TN 37738-1016

615/555-4669

The text, objects, and spacing in this exercise have been reduced because of space constraints.

Learning Objectives

Learn guidelines for the content of a job application letter

Format a personal-business letter

Desktop Techniques Applied

Save a file as a template

Import a text file

Change the font of text

Concepts

When you are applying for a job, you will send a job application letter along with a resume. Some guidelines for what to include in a job application letter, and in what order, follow.[1]

The first paragraph of a job application letter should state the position for which you are applying. It should mention how you learned of the position. If you can, say something positive that you know about the company or someone who works for the company.

In the next one or two paragraphs, make sure the reader knows that you understand the requirements for the position. Explain how your background qualifies you for the position. You can elaborate on some of the information in your resume, such as courses taken or skills achieved that are particularly relevant to the position for which you are applying. At the end of the last paragraph in this section, refer the reader to your resume for additional information.

In the last paragraph, request an interview. Provide the reader with an easy way to contact you to schedule the interview.

INSTRUCTIONS

1. Open the data file **ECOLOG.**
2. Delete all the text except the letterhead.
3. Save the document as a **template;** name it **JAMES.**
4. Import the template file **CHIMERA.**
5. Save the document as a document; name it **CHIMERA1.**
6. Set all the letter text in a serif typeface, 10/12.
7. Center the letter vertically on the page.
8. Re-save the file.
9. Using all printer defaults, print one copy.
10. Close the file.

[1]This discussion of job application letters was adapted from Jerry Robinson et al., *Century 21 Keyboarding & Information Processing* (Cincinnati: South-Western Publishing Co., 1997), p. 323.

EXERCISE 65

Exercise 65

James Constantino
43 Beacon Street   Amesbury, MA 01984-2234   (508) 555-8990

July 15, 19—

Mr. Alberto Sanchez
Personnel Director
Chimera Publishing
52 Beacon Street
Boston, MA 02111-3384

Dear Mr. Sanchez:

Christy Peters, a Senior Production Editor in your College Division, has informed me of the Production Editor I position that will be available at Chimera Publishing on August 20. In her capacity as a mentor for students at Glover College, she has shown me some of the award-winning magazines and catalogs produced by Chimera Publishing. Please consider me as an applicant for the Production Editor I position.

I received my A.A. in Graphic Design from Glover College in June. My course work included two advanced classes in desktop publishing, one entirely on Quark XPress, which Ms. Peters tells me is the software used by production editors at Chimera Publishing. In college, I worked as an intern at Olivera Publishing in Salem, designing and producing technical manuals and a sales catalog. For detailed information about my educational background and work experience, please refer to the attached resume.

I would welcome the opportunity to discuss the production editor position with you in a personal interview. Please call me at (508) 555-8990 to arrange a mutually convenient time.

Sincerely,

James Constantino

Attachment

The text, objects, and spacing in this exercise have been reduced because of space constraints.

Learning Objectives

Format a block business letter

Desktop Techniques Applied

Drag-place a text file
Change the font of text

INSTRUCTIONS

1. Open **CIRCLE,** the template you created in Exercise 63.
2. Import the template file **HOLIDAY.** Drag-place the file so that it extends from the left margin to the 6" mark on the horizontal ruler.
3. Save the file as a document; name it **CIRCLE1.**
4. Set the letter text to a 12/14 serif font, and justify it.
5. Center the letter vertically.
6. Re-save the document.
7. Using all printer defaults, print one copy.
8. Close the file.

EXERCISE

66

Exercise 66

35 Canvas Lane
New York, NY 10012-2786
(212) 555-5600

Richard Warren, Director

December 1, 19—

Ms. Roberta Torres
655 Fifth Avenue
New York, NY 10022-3495

Dear Ms. Torres

The Circle Arts Museum will hold its annual tree lighting ceremony and caroling party on Monday, December 12, at 4:40 p.m. on the Fountain Plaza. George Talbot will throw the switch to light the 40-foot blue spruce and open the Circle Arts Museum holiday season.

The Chamber Brass Quintet and soprano Tamara Damon will perform. The Chamber Singers will lead the singing of holiday songs.

We invite you as a special patron of Circle Arts to join us at this exciting holiday event.

Sincerely

Barbara Chung
Program Director

yrs

Sponsors

Dr. & Mr. Alexander
Louis Arrone, Jr.
Granite Foundation
J. Harris, Inc.
Oscar Jones
Sang Joy
Mohammed Khair
Janet Lawrence

Patrons

Allied Industries
Armond Fund
Ferris Flowers, Inc.
William French, III
Phillip Gomez
Sarah Kamph
Lorus Group
Donna L. McKinney
Martin Mortimer
Roberta Torres
Salvatore Vitale
Wall Street Foundation
Norma Winter
Zeon Corporation

The text, objects, and spacing in this exercise have been reduced because of space constraints.

EXERCISE 67

Learning Objectives

Learn about special letter parts
Format a block business letter

Desktop Techniques Applied

Change the font of text
Choose a bullet style
Insert bullets
Space text attractively

Concepts

Letters sometimes have special features. You have already used several special features in the letters you have prepared in this text. The letter in this exercise illustrates a variety of special features. (Of course, all these features ordinarily would not appear in one letter.) Special features and their formatting are described below.

Attention line. An attention line is used when you want to write to someone in a specific position in a company, but you do not know the name of the person. Always make every attempt to obtain the name of the recipient of your letter. The attention line is the first line of the letter and envelope address. When you use an attention line, use the salutation "Ladies and Gentlemen."

Subject line. The subject line states the subject of the letter. It appears in capital letters a double space below the salutation. If the body text is blocked, the subject line is blocked as well. If the body paragraphs are indented, the subject line should be indented the same amount.

Company name. When you use a company name, place it a double space below the complimentary close, and key it in capital letters. Quadruple-space to the writer's name.

Reference initials. If someone other than the author of the letter keyed it, that person's initials appear in lowercase letters a double space below the signer's name, title, or department, whichever comes last.

Enclosure/Attachment notation. Place this notation a double space below the reference initials. Use "Attachment" if the additional pages are attached to the letter; use "Enclosure" if they are not. If there is more than one enclosure or attachment, add to "Enclosures" or "Attachments" a colon and two spaces; then list each enclosure or attachment.

Copy notation. A copy notation shows that a copy of the letter is being sent to someone other than the addressee. Use "c" followed by the name(s) of the person(s) who will receive the copy (each name appears on a separate line and flush with the preceding name). The copy notation appears a double space below the last line of the enclosure/attachment notation or the reference initials if there is no enclosure/attachment.

Postscript. A postscript is the last line in the letter. It may read like an afterthought, although often it has been composed as carefully as the rest of the letter. The postscript may be used to emphasize all or part of the text of the letter, to set off information, or to convey a personal message.

INSTRUCTIONS

1. Open **IMAGE,** the template you created in Exercise 62.
2. Import the template file **DESIGN**.
3. Save the file as a document; name it **VISION.**
4. Set all the text to an 11/13 serif font.
5. *If you have a symbol typeface,* use an appropriate character as a bullet for the three services, with a visually appealing amount of space between the bullet and the text. The example uses an en space. The bullet is sized at 13/13.

   Alternatively, you can use the desktop publishing software bullet, draw a bullet such as a filled square using the drawing tools, or use a graphic. Use the inline graphic and power paste or align and distribute feature, if appropriate.
6. Center the letter vertically.
7. Re-save the file.
8. Using all printer defaults, print one copy.
9. Close the file.

EXERCISE 67

Exercise 67

VISIONIMAGE

245 Lamberts Lane Chicago, IL 60630-1215 (312) 555-0267

March 20, 19—

QS

The text, objects, and spacing in this exercise have been reduced because of space constraints.

Attention line Attention Art Director
Air, Land, and Sea Magazine
5417 West Higgins
Chicago, IL 60630-1215
DS
Ladies and Gentlemen:
DS
Subject line SERVICES OF VISIONIMAGE
DS
VisionImage has just opened on Lake Shore Drive in the Chicago area. We would like to introduce our services. The enclosed brochure details the graphic design and desktop expertise we offer our clients. Below is a summary of some of our services.

- **VisionImage** creates state-of-the-art computer graphics and page layouts for businesses.
- **VisionImage** will find a solution to any design problem.
- **VisionImage** will consult with you or representatives of your company to create corporate designs.

Zachary Westgate, our Chicago representative, will phone you sometime next week. Mr. Westgate would like to set up an appointment to show you our award-winning designs.

Cordially,
DS
Company name VISIONIMAGE

QS

Martin Pilsner
President
DS
Reference initials yrs
DS
Enclosure notation Enclosure
DS
Copy notation c Zachary Westgate
DS
Postscript You can view our work at the upcoming Design Show on April 1.

Corporate Identity Programs Advertising Graphic Design

Learning Objectives

Format a modified block business letter with special parts

Desktop Techniques Applied

Import text and graphics files
Change the font of text

INSTRUCTIONS

1. Open **LODGE,** the template you created in Exercise 64.
2. Import the template file **GETAWAY**.
3. Save the file as a document; name it **LODGE1.**
4. Set all the text to an 11/13 serif font.
5. If either or both tab settings did not import correctly, select all the text and reset the tabs so that the first is indented a half-inch and the second is at the midpoint of the page. In the example, tabs are set at .5" and 3.25".
6. Center the list as shown.
7. Import four appropriate graphics. Place two to the left and two to the right of the centered items. Re-size the graphics, if necessary. You may have to edit the list, depending on the graphics you have available.
8. Center the letter vertically on the page.
9. Re-save the file.
10. Using all printer defaults, print one copy.
11. Close the file.

Design Pointers/Hints

- Bold and graphics may be used more liberally in promotional letters than in other business letters. In this letter, they draw attention to the activities the Lodge offers and its name and telephone number.

EXERCISE 68

Exercise 68

THE HOLIDAY MOUNTAIN LODGE

459 Ski Mountain Road
Gatlinburg,TN 37738-1016

615/555-4669

January 14, 19—

Dr. Chandra Reddy
87 Waverly Circle
Staten Island, NY 10302-4787

Dear Dr. Reddy

YOUR GREAT SMOKIES GETAWAY

Thank you for your inquiry about our accommodations and rates at the **Holiday Mountain Lodge.** We are enclosing a brochure that details our winter room rates and special attractions.

We are located in the Great Smoky Mountains, where we can offer you and your family:

skating
indoor swimming and tennis
racquetball
cross-country skiing
archery
basketball
volleyball

The Holiday Mountain Lodge offers very reasonably priced two- or three-meals-per-day packages. We also provide an outstanding nursery and day camp.

If you have any questions or if you would like to make a reservation, please phone me at **615-555-4669.**

THE HOLIDAY MOUNTAIN LODGE

Pamela Tricia Blaine
Reservations Manager

yrs

Enclosure

The text, objects, and spacing in this exercise have been reduced because of space constraints.

EXERCISE 69

Learning Objectives

Create a letterhead
Format a modified block business letter with special parts
Insert a table into a letter

Desktop Techniques Applied

Format text in different fonts
Rotate text
Draw rules and boxes
Reset tabs
Create a table

Concepts

For letters that consist of more than one page, a standard page heading is used for subsequent pages. This consists of the recipient's name, the date, and the page number (e.g., "Page 2") keyed at 1" from the top of subsequent pages. A double space separates the subsequent-page heading from the text of the letter.

If you had a very long letter, you could set up the heading on the master page with automatic page numbering and suppress or hide it on the first page.

In this exercise, you will insert a table into a letter. Tables in letters are centered horizontally between the left and the right margins. A double space traditionally separates the text above and below from the table.

INSTRUCTIONS

1. Start a new two-page publication with .75" left and top margins and 1" right and bottom margins.
2. On page 1, place a vertical ruler guide at 2".
3. Key "The EarthOne Social Investment Fund" in a 39-point serif font.
4. If you have an appropriate graphic or symbol from a symbol typeface, place it in the text, as shown.
5. Rotate the text block as shown. It should fit just inside the top, left, and bottom margins. The graphic may extend slightly outside the left margin.
6. Draw a 1-point rule at 1 5/8" on the horizontal ruler extending from the top to the bottom margin.
7. Set the address text to a serif typeface, 12/auto, flush right, at the top and right margins. Use your desktop publishing software bullet, with an en space on either side, between the street and city and between the two telephone numbers.
8. Draw a 1-point rule at the 1.25" mark on the vertical ruler from the rule you drew in Step 6 to the right margin.
9. Save the document as a **template;** name it **INVEST.**
10. Import the template file **EARTH.**
11. Save the file as a document; name it **INVEST1.**
12. Set the letter text in a 12/14 serif font. Reset the tabs, if necessary. You will probably need to set different midpoint tabs on pages 1 and 2, since the text has different margins. The example uses 2.25" and 3" respectively. For the enclosures, reset the tab, if necessary, to emulate an indent of two spaces after the colon. The example uses a tab at .906".
13. Adjust the text on page 1 so it begins just under the 2" mark on the vertical ruler.
14. On page 2, add a heading in a 12/14 serif font as shown. The heading should begin just under the 1" mark on the horizontal ruler. Adjust the following text so that it begins approximately the equivalent of two line returns below.
15. Create the table in your desktop publishing software or table editor. For help, see pages 80-83. Use an 11/22 sans serif font (the first two lines are 12/22). If you are using a keyline, key ten spaces between the columns. Center the table horizontally between the margins. Separate it from the text above and below by a double space. Block column heads. The "Returns" figures should be right-aligned. The example uses a tab at 1.47" for Column 1, a right-aligned tab at 5.28" for the Column 2 figures, and a left-aligned tab at 4.7" for the Column 2 heading. Add a shadow box with a 2-point border.
16. Re-save the file.
17. Using all printer defaults, print one copy.
18. Close the file.

EXERCISE 69

Exercise 69

The EarthOne Social Investment Fund

1437 Stratford Place • Arlington, VA 22216-1115
(703) 555-9789 • 1-800-555-3421

December 15, 19—

Mr. Curtis Capeta
14 Church St.
Greenfield, MA 01301-9595

Dear Mr. Capeta:

Thank you for your inquiry about the EarthOne Social Investment Fund. We offer investors a managed-growth portfolio (mutual fund) as well as a money market portfolio invested solely in socially responsible organizations. This letter gives an overview of our history, investment philosophy, current holdings, and past and present returns.

The EarthOne Social Investment Fund was founded in 1968 by a group of 15 shareholders who wanted to put their savings into companies with socially responsible goals, policies, and practices. In the past 30 years, the fund has grown, as of last June, from initial assets of $50,000 to assets of $300,000,000 invested by more than 35,000 shareholders.

The investment philosophy of our fund has changed little over time. We do not invest in nuclear power, the tobacco industry, companies that test their products on animals, or companies doing business in countries with poor records on human rights. Our investments support organizations with a participatory management philosophy and companies that negotiate fairly with employees. We invest in companies that advocate equal opportunities for women and members of minority groups. Organizations that make worker safety a priority receive favorable consideration from EarthOne. Good community relations is another factor in our decision to invest. Finally, we support companies that manufacture safe products and services in a manner that is protective of the environment.

Some of the organizations in which we invest include the PathFinder Corporation, the Gorin Company, the World Energy Corporation, Renewable Resources, Inc., Northwest Recycling, and New Data, Inc. We hold 25 different issues of government bonds, primarily from the Federal National Mortgage Association, Federal Farm Credit Banks Consolidated, and the Federal Home Loan Bank System. The fund also holds current investments in 25 local housing cooperatives, credit unions, and community loan funds. The enclosed

Mr. Curtis Capeta
December 15, 19--
Page 2

semi-annual report lists all our investments, the number of shares, market value, percent of net assets, and so forth.

EARTHONE

Total Returns

Period	Returns
June 30, 1998 - September 30, 1998	7.84%
September 30, 1997 - September 30, 1998	30.42%
September 30, 1993 - September 30, 1998	91.87%
September 30, 1988 - September 30, 1998	351.76%

Critics of socially responsible investing argue that screening companies for social factors must result in lower yields and lesser earnings. To such critics, our emphatic response is, "Not so!" In the past 30 years, our fund has equaled and even exceeded the rate of return of comparable funds that do not use a social investment philosophy.

Please look over the enclosed report and call us if we can answer any questions for you. Thank you for considering investment in EarthOne.

Sincerely,

J. Scott Harris
President

ev

Enclosures: Semi-Annual Report
Disclosure Statement
Prospectus and Application

The text, objects, and spacing in this exercise have been reduced because of space constraints.

Learning Objectives

Learn standard memo format
Create a memo form
Format a memo

Desktop Techniques Applied

Save a file as a template
Import text and graphics files
Change the font of text

Concepts

Memorandums, or **memos,** are used to communicate messages to individuals within a company. Companies create memorandums on blank paper or on letterhead. Some use preprinted forms, while others create the memo form.

Standard memos have a top margin of 2", side margins of 1" or the software default, and a bottom margin of at least 1". All lines begin at the left margin. Memos are single-spaced, with a double space between parts.

The headings TO, FROM, DATE, and SUBJECT begin a standard memo. Tabs are keyed between the memo headings and the appropriate text.

TO: <tab><tab> Linda Petrosino

FROM: <tab> John Chavez

DATE: <tab> February 28, 19--

SUBJECT:<tab>NEW MEMO FORMAT

The subject line of a memo may be in capital letters. Alternatively, you can use initial capital letters for important words.

Memos use some of the same special parts as letters. Reference initials, attachment/enclosure notations, copy notations, and subsequent-page headings are formatted in memos as they are in letters.

INSTRUCTIONS

1. Open **CIRCLE,** the template you created in Exercise 63.
2. As shown, delete all text except the CIRCLE ARTS MUSEUM logo (employees communicating within a company do not need the deleted information). Delete the rule as well.
3. Save the file as a **template;** name it **CIRCLEM.**
4. Import the template file **CAMMEMO** so that the text begins just under the 2" mark on the vertical ruler.
5. Save the file as a document; name it **CIRCLEM1.**
6. Set the memo in a 12/auto serif font.
7. Make sure the text after the headings is aligned. You may need to add an extra tab after "DATE:".
8. Import some appropriate graphics. Arrange them attractively; re-size them, if necessary.
9. Re-save the file.
10. Using all printer defaults, print one copy.
11. Close the file.

EXERCISE
70

Exercise 70

Standard Memorandum

CIRCLE ARTS MUSEUM

2"

TO: **Tab Tab** All Staff
DS
FROM: **Tab** Richard Warren, Director
DS
DATE: **Tab** December 20, 199-
DS
SUBJECT: **Tab** Holiday Party
DS **The subject line may be all caps or initial caps.**

On behalf of the officers of the CIRCLE ARTS MUSEUM, I wish you all a happy holiday season and a joyous New Year. In keeping with the spirit of the season, please join us for our annual Holiday Party on Friday, December 23, at 4 p.m. in the main gallery on the second floor. The gallery will be closing early that day to accommodate our employees and their guests.

1" or default   1" or default

DS

Once again, we will enjoy a holiday banquet of festive food from different cultures, prepared and served by One World Caterers. The Carta Ensemble will offer us holiday music from many times and many places as we enjoy our dinner. Finally, our own Yuletide Caroleers will sing some popular carols of the holiday season. You are cordially invited to sing along.

DS

CIRCLE ARTS takes pride in its family of dedicated employees. We look forward to seeing you on December 23. If you will be attending, please fill out the attached form and send it to Barbara Takei in Human Relations. Be sure to indicate the number of guests who will accompany you.

DS
yrs
DS
Attachment

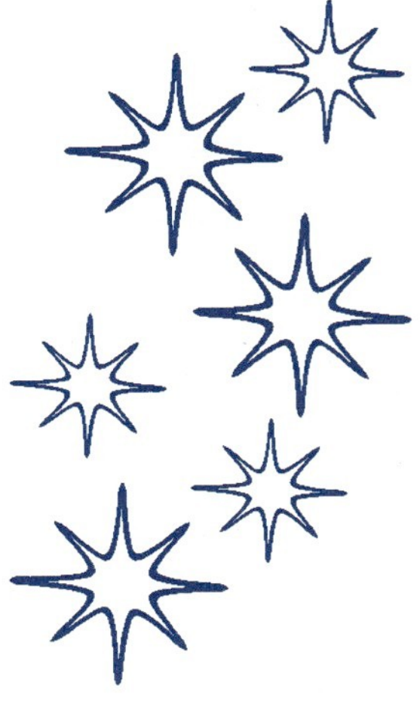

at least 1"

The text, objects, and spacing in this exercise have been reduced because of space constraints.

Learning Objectives

Create a memo form
Format a memo

Desktop Techniques Applied

Save a file as a template
Import a text file
Change the font of text
Create a table

INSTRUCTIONS

1. Open **VOYAGES,** the template you created in Exercise 61.
2. Change the bottom margin to 1".
3. Delete the address information and the text and graphic at the bottom of the page, as shown.
4. Save the file as a **TEMPLATE;** name it **VOYAGEM.**
5. Import the template file **AIR** so that the text begins just under the 2" mark on the vertical ruler.
6. Save the file as a document; name it **VOYAGEM1.**
7. Set the memo in a 12/14 serif font.
8. Make sure the text after the headings is aligned. You may need to add an extra tab after "DATE:".
9. Create the table in your desktop publishing software or table editor. Refer to pages 80-83 if you need help. Use a serif 12/12 font. Note that the column headings are longer than the column text. If you are creating the table in your desktop publishing software, choose center alignment for the column heading line, and key the column headings with 16 spaces between them (you do not need to set tabs). In either desktop publishing software or a table editor, you will need to set tabs for the column text to be centered under the column headings. With proportional typefaces, the only method to do this is trial and error: setting a tab for the longest column entry, deciding whether the tab centers the text under the column heading, and adjusting the tab as needed. The example uses tabs set at 2.78" and 4.02".
10. Give the table a border with a 1-point line. In desktop publishing software, draw a box with solid fill over the table title. In a table editor, give the grouped cells a solid fill. Set the text of the title to reverse.
11. Re-save the file.
12. Using all printer defaults, print one copy.
13. Close the file.

EXERCISE 71

Exercise 71

V O Y A G E S

Travel Consultants, Inc.

TO: All Travel Agents

FROM: Rena Dodd, Director

DATE: August 1, 19—

SUBJECT: Special Promotion—AeroLift Airlines

For the next three months, AeroLift Airlines is offering travel agents a 12 percent commission for each flight booked to any location they serve on the West Coast and in Hawaii. AeroLift will pay an additional bonus of from 1 to 6 percent on the number of tickets an agent sells monthly.

AEROLIFT AIRLINES PROMOTION

Monthly Bonus Commission Levels

Tickets	Bonus
20-30	1%
31-40	2%
51-70	3%
71-90	4%
91-99	5%
100+	6%

During this special promotion, let's use AeroLift for our West Coast and Hawaii bookings when possible. We should see a satisfying increase in our personal and company earnings.

The text, objects, and spacing in this exercise have been reduced because of space constraints.

EXERCISE 72

Learning Objectives

Learn simplified memo format
Format a memo

Desktop Techniques Applied

Import a text file
Change the font of text

Concepts

An alternative to the standard memorandum is the **simplified memorandum.** Like standard memos, simplified memorandums have a top margin of 2", side margins of 1" or the software default, and a bottom margin of at least 1". All lines begin at the left margin, unless the memo contains some special part, such as an internal title, which is centered. Simplified memos are single-spaced, with a double space between parts. A quadruple space separates the date from the name of the addressee and the last paragraph of the memo from the writer's name.

Simplified memos do not use the traditional memo headings TO, FROM, DATE, and SUBJECT. The first line is the date. The second is the name of the addressee. The third is the subject line. The writer's name appears at the end of the memo, as in a letter.

In simplified memos, names are not preceded by personal titles. Names may be followed by an official title or department name.

INSTRUCTIONS

1. Start a new publication. Set a 1" bottom margin.
2. Just below the 1" mark on the vertical ruler, key "INTER-OFFICE MEMORANDUM" in a 14-point bold sans serif font, centered.
3. Import the template file **FAX** so that the text begins just under the 2" mark on the vertical ruler.
4. Save the file; name it **FAXM.**
5. Set the text in an 11/13 serif font.
6. Re-save the file.
7. Using all printer defaults, print one copy.
8. Close the file.

EXERCISE
72

Exercise 72

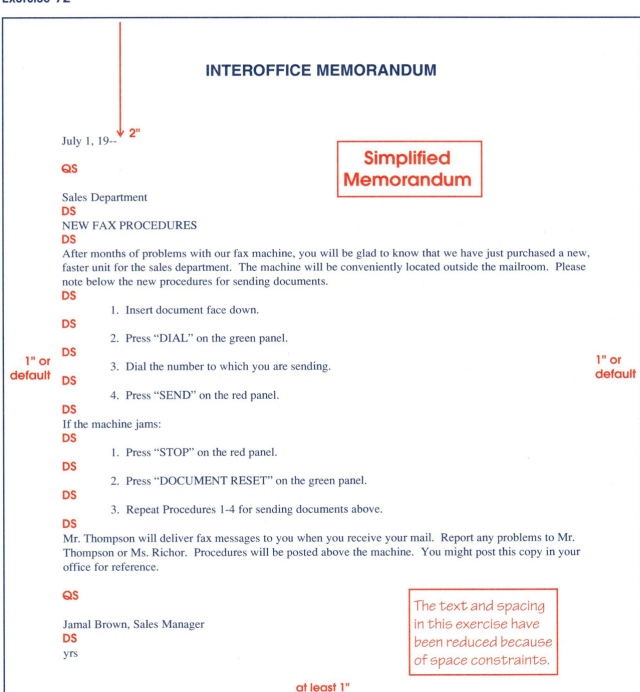

INTEROFFICE MEMORANDUM

2"

July 1, 19--

QS

Simplified Memorandum

Sales Department
DS
NEW FAX PROCEDURES
DS
After months of problems with our fax machine, you will be glad to know that we have just purchased a new, faster unit for the sales department. The machine will be conveniently located outside the mailroom. Please note below the new procedures for sending documents.
DS

1. Insert document face down.

DS

2. Press "DIAL" on the green panel.

DS

3. Dial the number to which you are sending.

DS

4. Press "SEND" on the red panel.

DS
If the machine jams:
DS

1. Press "STOP" on the red panel.

DS

2. Press "DOCUMENT RESET" on the green panel.

DS

3. Repeat Procedures 1-4 for sending documents above.

DS
Mr. Thompson will deliver fax messages to you when you receive your mail. Report any problems to Mr. Thompson or Ms. Richor. Procedures will be posted above the machine. You might post this copy in your office for reference.

QS

Jamal Brown, Sales Manager
DS
yrs

1" or default (left margin)

1" or default (right margin)

at least 1"

The text and spacing in this exercise have been reduced because of space constraints.

EXERCISE 73

Learning Objectives

Format a memo

Desktop Techniques Applied

Draw filled rectangles
Add bullets and en spaces
Add space to paragraphs
Drag-place text
Set text in columns
Adjust text blocks

INSTRUCTIONS

1. Start a new publication with margins of .75" (top) and 1" (all others).
2. Set a horizontal ruler guide at 1.25".
3. Key "NEW LISTINGS" just inside the top and left margins in sans serif 30-point, bold and reverse, with a .125" left indent.
4. Create a rectangle with solid fill around the text you just keyed, extending from the top margin to the horizontal ruler guide at 1.25" and horizontally to 1/8" past the last letter of the text. Move the text up or down until it is centered inside the rectangle.
5. Import the template file **HOUSE** so that the text begins just under the 2" mark on the vertical ruler.
6. Save the file; name it **HOUSEM.**
7. Set all letter text to sans serif 12/auto.
8. Set all the house description text, including the city and state, to 10/auto with a left indent of .125".
9. Set the city and state text to 14/auto.
10. Add .05" before "CHAPPAQUA" and after each house price, "Greenhouse," and "5 1/2 baths." Add .135" after the two states.
11. Add a desktop publishing software bullet followed by an en space before "Master bedroom." Copy the bullet and en space to the other listings details as shown.
12. Set two columns with a .75" gutter.
13. Move the bottom windowshade handle up so that all text from "GREENWICH, CONNECTICUT" down is hidden.
14. Re-place the hidden text, dragging across the *right* column, beginning opposite "CHAPPAQUA" and ending opposite "Sarah Alicia, Sales Agent." You will have more text to place.
15. Set a ruler guide on the baseline of "CHAPPAQUA." Adjust the text block in the right column so that "GREENWICH" sits on the same line.
16. Adjust the bottom windowshade handle of the text in the right column as necessary so that all the descriptive text for the Greenwich, Connecticut, property is in the right column. The last body text paragraph and closing lines should be hidden.
17. Drag-place the rest of the text *from margin to margin* as shown. Adjust the text block so that approximately a double space is left between the description text and the last text block.
18. Create a rectangle with solid fill around "CHAPPAQUA, NEW YORK." Set the city and state text to reverse. Adjust the rectangle so that the text is centered horizontally and vertically within it.
19. Copy the rectangle to the other city and state; re-size it, if necessary.
20. Re-save the file.
21. Using all printer defaults, print one copy.
22. Close the file.

EXERCISE

73

Exercise 73

NEW LISTINGS

July 1, 19--

Sales Agents

NEW LISTINGS

The following luxury houses have just come on the market. You should send the listings and descriptions below to those clients who have shown an interest in similar properties:

CHAPPAQUA, NEW YORK

2-3 Bedroom Contemporary
$650,000

- Master bedroom with deck overlooking pool
- Living room with fireplace
- Library
- Greenhouse

Contact: Sarah Alicia, Sales Agent

GREENWICH, CONNECTICUT

7-8 Bedroom Tudor
$1,200,000

- Slate roof
- Designer kitchen
- Circular stairway
- Guest house, pool, and tennis court
- 5 1/2 baths

Contact: Kenisha Williams, Sales Agent

We plan to place these advertisements in this Sunday's newspapers. If Sarah or Kenisha is unavailable to answer questions from callers, all other agents should be prepared to take calls. Everyone should be familiar with the specifics about these properties.

Cathy O'Connor

yrs

The text, objects, and spacing in this exercise have been reduced because of space constraints.

Learning Objectives

Create a bar or pie chart
Format a report

Desktop Techniques Applied

Use a master page
Create styles
Kern text
Draw rules and filled boxes
Cut and paste text and objects
Drag-place text

Concepts

In Exercise 57, you set up a report in traditional unbound report format. In this exercise, you will format the same report with a different design. You will use the features of your desktop publishing software to enhance the look of the report. You will also create a bar chart or pie chart to illustrate some of the statistical data.

You will use the **hanging indent style** for enumerated items. In this style, numbers are indented to the first default tab. The text following the numbers is aligned at the next default tab. If you prefer less space after the numbers, you can set a tab about .25" to the right of the period.

You will use the **endnotes** method of referencing sources. In this method, each reference in the body of the report has a superscript number.[1] An endnotes page and a separate references page appear at the end of the report. The traditional endnotes page has essentially the same formatting as the references page (see page 100). The first line of each reference is indented .5". References appear in numerical order, with their reference numbers. As you can see on page 139, the text of endnotes has a slightly different arrangement and punctuation than that of references.

continued on page 138

INSTRUCTIONS

1. Start a new six-page publication with .75" margins.
2. On the master page, draw a 2-point rule along the top margin guide from the left margin to the right margin.
3. On the master page, set 2 columns with a .35" gutter. Drag the column guides so the *right* column begins at 3".
4. On the master page, set automatic page numbering .25" below the bottom margin at the left margin. Use a 10-point bold sans serif font.
5. Position a horizontal ruler guide at 1 3/8".
6. Define a style for side headings of a 12/14 bold sans serif font.
7. If you can create character styles, define a style for raised caps of a 22/14 bold serif font.
8. Define a style for enumerated text of an 11/14 serif font with a left indent of .594", a first indent of -.244", .125" after, and a tab at .594".
9. Define a style for references of an 11/14 serif font with a .35" hanging indent, .125" after, and hyphenation off.
10. Define a style for the ENDNOTES and REFERENCES heads of an 18/auto bold sans serif font.
11. Go to page 1, mask the page number, and import the template file **HEALTH** in the *right* column.
12. Save the file; name it **HEALTH3.**
13. Cut the title, adjust the body text to begin at 1.75" on the vertical ruler, and drag-place the title above the text across both columns.
14. Set the title to a 24-point bold sans serif font. Adjust its text block so that it begins at 1" on the vertical ruler.
15. Select all the body text and set it to an 11/14 serif font with a .35" first indent, .125" after, hyphenation on, and widow/orphan protect on.
16. As you go through the body text, apply styles and edit text as follows (but see Step 17 about creating the chart before you format text below the chart):
    - If you created a style for the raised caps, apply it; otherwise, set each to 22-point bold. You may need to kern between the raised cap and the following character.
    - Apply the appropriate style to the enumerated text. Delete the extra line returns between items. Bold the numbers and periods.
    - Cut the side headings, drag-place them in the left column, and apply the appropriate style. Align the headings with the first line of the section baseline to baseline as shown. Use two line returns before each section; insert an extra return when appropriate.

continued on page 138

EXERCISE 74

Exercise 74

CAFETERIA MENU CHANGES

In September 19—, a group of employees approached management with a request that the current cafeteria menu be thoroughly revamped to what they considered a more healthy bill of fare: generally, lower in calories, protein, sugar, and fat, and higher in carbohydrates and fiber. President Josephine Costanza appointed a committee to research and consider such a change and to make recommendations.

The following recommendations are submitted:

1. Costanza and Associates should make all cafeteria menu offerings health-conscious.
2. A chief catering manager should be appointed to work out a comprehensive plan of menu offerings for all plant catering managers.
3. Plant catering managers should continue to compose their own menus, but from the comprehensive plan.
4. Any savings in costs resulting from the menu change should be passed on to employees in the form of decreased cafeteria prices.

Current Policies and Procedures

Costanza and Associates operates 13 plant facilities in separate locations. Each facility houses a partially subsidized employee cafeteria that offers breakfast, lunch, and dinner service to some 250 employees. The menu for each cafeteria is developed by the cafeteria manager.

Of the 13 cafeteria managers, seven are registered nutritionists. Three were previously managers in commercial restaurants. Three are graduates of cooking programs.

The committee examined whether the type of menu requested by the employee group is currently being offered at any of our locations. Members interviewed each catering manager and analyzed menu offerings for the past year. The committee found that two cafeterias offered a standard health-conscious alternative on the menu daily. The remainder sporadically offered health-conscious fare.

Employee Preferences

Interviews conducted with cafeteria employees failed to yield more than anecdotal observations as to whether employees purchase health-conscious food as much as or more than traditional fare. Neither could employee preferences be determined by analyzing purchases or discarding of leftover food; records at that level of specificity are not kept. Instead, the committee conducted out-of-house research on other company cafeterias, in-house focus groups at each location, and a written survey of all employees.

Out-of-house research shows that implementing a health-conscious menu would not result in any significant change in employee cafeteria patronage. Employees are as likely to purchase health-conscious food as traditional fare.[1] In a study of 150 companies that implemented a health-conscious menu, the National Nutrition Council found that, overall, a slight initial decrease in sales (3 percent) was compensated for within six months by an increase of 5 percent.[2]

In the written in-house survey of all employees, 60 percent said that they would regularly purchase a health-conscious offering, and 51 percent said that all menu offerings should be health-conscious. These figures rose to 79 percent and 65 percent respectively in the focus groups, which sampled six health-conscious meals prepared by Catering Manager Kim Cheung of the Langley plant.

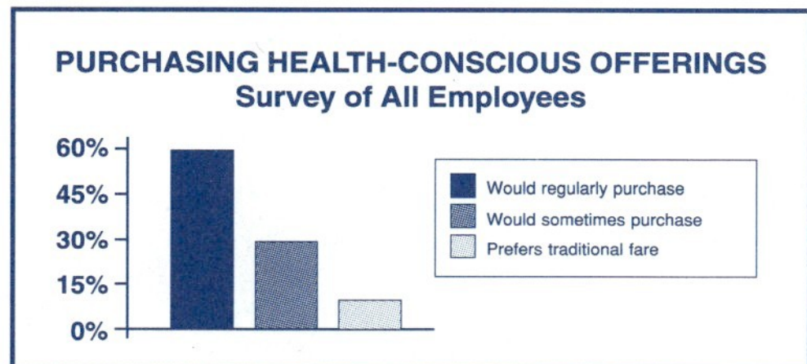

Health Benefits of a Health-Conscious Menu

The benefits of a health-conscious diet are incontrovertible and have been widely reported.[3] Persons who regularly consume a health-conscious bill of fare are at less risk for many diseases and conditions, including heart disease, high blood pressure, stroke, diabetes, osteoporosis, obesity, and cancer.[4]

Research showing direct benefits to employees deriving solely from a health-conscious cafeteria menu is less conclusive, because of the lack of control factors. For example, employees may consume other types of food outside of work and may or may not exercise.

Implementing a Health-Conscious Menu

The committee researched fees that outside consulting services would charge for creating a health-conscious menu. Costs were significant, ranging in eight quotes from $5,000 to $15,000. The committee also interviewed

2

continued on page 139

EXERCISE

74

Concepts continued from page 136

Graphs and charts present numeric information in a readily comprehensible format. They also serve as good illustrations. You can create graphs and charts in a separate program, such as a spreadsheet, and import them into your desktop-published document. Alternatively, you can create some types of graphs or charts in your desktop publishing software.

Bar graphs are used to show quantities of the same item at different times, quantities of different items for the same time, or quantities of the different parts of an item that make up the whole.

Line graphs show the relationship between two sets of numbers by means of points plotted in relation to the horizontal and vertical axes. The points are connected to form a continuous line. The vertical axis usually represents amounts; the horizontal axis, increments of time.

Pie charts present the different parts of a whole as wedges of a pie, or circle.

Many graphs have an **X-axis** (a horizontal axis) and a **Y-axis** (a vertical axis). In the bar chart on page 137, the three rectangles sit on the X-axis; the "0-60" axis is the Y-axis. That chart also has a **legend:** a key that tells you what certain elements of the chart mean. On page 137, the legend is the boxed text that explains the shading used.

INSTRUCTIONS continued from page 136

- Delete the textual citations and insert superscript page numbers as appropriate.
- Copy the references. Insert the copy as part of the same text story immediately after. In subsequent steps, the first copy of the references will become the endnotes; the latter will be the references.

17. Create a bar chart or pie chart as on page 2. The employee percentages are 60%, 30%, and 10%. The example, which was created in desktop publishing software, uses the following parameters: a 2-point bordering box, all other lines 1-point except the legend and filled-box borders (which are .5-point), all text sans serif, title and subtitle 12-point bold, numbers 10/20 bold, legend text 9/12, and filled rectangles 100%, 50%, and 10%. The first rectangle, which is 3/8" wide, was copied and the copies pasted with a horizontal offset of .5" (on each copy, the fill was then changed and the height adjusted). The tick marks were created by drawing one and pasting copies with a vertical offset of .278". A legend square, 5/16", was copied and the copies pasted with a vertical offset of .19" (on each copy, the fill was then changed).
18. Set text wrap around the chart; use the jump over option.
19. Arrange the endnotes and references text so that each set of references appears on a separate page (pages 4 and 5).
20. On page 4, create an ENDNOTES head in the left column and apply the appropriate style to it. Both the ENDNOTES head and the first line of endnotes text should sit on the horizontal ruler guide at 1 3/8".
21. Arrange, number, and format the endnotes as shown.
22. On page 5, cut the REFERENCES head, drag-place it in the left column, and apply the appropriate style to it. The head and the first line of references text should sit on the horizontal ruler guide at 1 3/8".
23. Go to page 6 and hide master page items. You will create the title page on this page.
24. At the 2" mark on the vertical ruler, key the title in a 30-point bold sans serif font.
25. At 2 5/8" on the vertical ruler, draw a 4-point line under the title.
26. At 8 1/8" on the vertical ruler, key the author/date text in a 15/auto bold sans serif font, double-spaced and aligned at the right margin.
27. At 8" on the vertical ruler, draw a 2-point line extending from the beginning of the text below to the right margin.
28. Check the report for violations of the rules for hyphenation.
29. Using all printer defaults, print one copy.
30. Save and close the file.

EXERCISE

74

Exercise 74 continued from page 137

executives at five companies that have made such a change and discussed the topic with Costanza and Associates catering managers. Creating a chief catering manager position, at a recommended increase from the current catering manager's salary of $4,500, was the least expensive alternative. The committee concluded that it was also a practical and popular alternative. Our current staff of catering managers includes individuals who are well-qualified to develop such a dietary plan. These catering managers have the additional advantage of being thoroughly familiar with Costanza and Associates' methods.

The next question was whether all catering managers should strictly follow the menu plan to be developed by the chief catering manager, or should continue to develop their own menus, but using the comprehensive plan. The committee recommends the latter. Catering managers are accustomed to working independently, and they do their own purchasing. Changing these procedures would result in a significant increase in administrative costs and would require hiring new personnel and reassigning responsibilities.

Costs of a Health-Conscious Menu

Although not a prime consideration in whether to implement a health-conscious menu, costs are a factor. Out-of-house research shows that cafeterias that switched to a totally health-conscious menu decreased overall annual costs by 15 percent.[5] The largest reduction in costs came from a decrease in purchases of meat and an increase in purchases of fruits and vegetables, which are generally less expensive. As reported above, after a slight initial decrease, sales rose slightly and remained constant.

A related consideration is whether to pass on all or a portion of the decrease in costs to employees. Fourteen companies that passed on all or part of purchase savings to employees through a reduction in cafeteria prices reported an increase in cafeteria sales of 7 percent.[6] The committee recommends passing on all or part of the food purchase savings to employees in the form of decreased cafeteria prices.

Cafeteria Menu Changes

Menu Change Committee

Josephine Costanza and Associates

December 19, 19--

ENDNOTES

[1]Joanna C. West, "Healthy Eating on the Job," *Cafeteria Quarterly*, Spring 1992, pp. 140-145.

[2]National Nutrition Council, *America's Choice: Employers and Good Food* (Washington: National Academy, 1994), p. 16.

[3]National Institutes of Health, *Food for Life* (Washington: Government Printing Office, 1995), p. 14.

[4]National Research Council, *Diet and Disease Prevention* (Washington: Government Printing Office, 1997), p. 3.

[5]L. Anthony Scott, "Reducing Costs and Promoting Good Health," *Responsible Management,* April 1996, pp. 22-28.

[6]Fior O'Quindo, "Sell More—Buy Less," *Responsible Management,* November 1994, pp. 23-27.

REFERENCES

National Institutes of Health. *Food for Life*. Washington: Government Printing Office, 1995.

National Nutrition Council. *America's Choice: Employers and Good Food.* Washington: National Academy, 1994.

National Research Council. *Diet and Disease Prevention.* Washington: Government Printing Office, 1997.

Fior O'Quindo. "Sell More—Buy Less." *Responsible Management,* November 1994, 23-27.

L. Anthony Scott. "Reducing Costs and Promoting Good Health." *Responsible Management,* April 1996, 22-28.

Joanna C. West. "Healthy Eating on the Job." *Cafeteria Quarterly*, Spring 1992, 140-145.

EXERCISE 75

Learning Objectives

Create a bar or pie chart
Format paragraph styles
Format a report

Desktop Techniques Applied

Use a master page
Create styles
Draw rules, ovals, and boxes
Generate a table of contents
Generate an index

Concepts

In this exercise, you will format a longer report, which will include paragraph headings. **Paragraph headings** are subheadings of side headings. They are indented .5" from the left margin. Only the first letter of the first word is capitalized. In traditional unbound report format, a paragraph heading is underlined and followed with a period.

Use subheadings only when you can divide a topic into more than one section. In other words, do not use only one paragraph heading under a side heading.

INSTRUCTIONS

1. Start a new 11-page publication with 1" margins.
2. Go to the master page and create the header shown at the top and right margins. Use a 10-point sans serif typeface with an em space between "Report" and the page number. Make the header italic, except for the page number; and bold to "CASAO". Add a half-point rule (paragraph or drawn) below the text extending from the left margin to the right. The rule should sit on the top margin guide.

   Draw a 1-point bordering box .5" outside all the margins as shown.

   Position a horizontal ruler guide at 1.5" on the vertical ruler. The text on the first page, table of contents, references page, and index will begin just under the guide. For the rest of the body text pages, the first line of text will sit on the guide.
3. Define a style for body text of a 12/15 serif font with a 1" left indent and widow/orphan protect on.
4. Define a style for side headings of a 14/auto bold/italic sans serif font with a .35" left indent, .125" before and after, keep with next 2 lines on, and inclusion in a table of contents.
5. Define a style for bulleted text of a 12/15 serif font with a hanging indent. Text should begin at 1.25". Use your desktop publishing software bullet or a symbol of your choice. Increase the hanging indent space if necessary to accommodate your symbol.
6. If you can create character styles, create a style for paragraph headings of a 12/15 sans serif bold/italic font. If you cannot create such a style, you will need to apply this formatting manually to the three paragraph headings.
7. Create a style based on the body text style for references. Give it a hanging indent of .5" (the second and subsequent lines of a reference should be indented .5" past the 1" left indent for body text).
8. Create a style based on the body text style for table of contents entries. Change the leading to 24-point, and set a right-aligned tab with leaders at 6.5".
9. Go to page 1 and import the template file **CASA.**
10. Save the file; name it **CASARPT.**
11. Select all the text and format it with the body text style.

continued on page 142

EXERCISE
75

Exercise 75

On page 4 of the report, create a bar or pie chart using the data shown.

The text, objects, and spacing in this exercise have been reduced because of space constraints.

The Center Against Substance Abuse
19— Annual Report

Statement of Mission

The Center Against Substance Abuse (CASA) provides a wide variety of treatment and prevention programs for women, men, elderly people, teenagers, and young children whose lives are affected by the abuse of alcohol and other substances. We are dedicated to providing quality care and prevention services to help people improve their lives. At CASA, clients are afforded the respect and dignity they deserve as human beings. With both state-of-the-art and proven intervention methods, we work with individuals, families, businesses, and communities to prevent substance abuse and to help addicted persons achieve a healthy, drug-free, and productive existence.

Looking Back

For the past 20 years, CASA has helped local communities handle problems associated with alcohol and other drug addiction. With the help of an experienced, enthusiastic, and dedicated staff, we have developed innovative programs and services to meet the needs of diverse clients. Despite dramatic cuts in governmental funding for substance abuse programs, CASA has continued to provide both traditional and innovative services. This past year saw the implementation of three grant-funded pilot programs: the Northland Youth Alliance Project, the Senior Citizen Assistance Initiative, and the Workplace Intervention Series. In

The Year in Brief
Tobacco Control Community Project
The New Horizons Center (planned)
Just for Women Health Fair
Fall Silent Auction
Expanded Senior Citizen Services
The Senior Citizen Assistance Initiative
The Northland Youth Alliance Project
The Workplace Intervention Series

19—, we also started fund-raising for the planned New Horizons Center, which will offer residential and outpatient services to some 350 clients. Combined with a variety of other special activities and our ongoing services, in 19— we provided direct assistance to some 4,500 people and education and drug awareness services to many more.

Despite decreased funding from state and federal government sources, we have maintained and even increased services offered, with the help of an innovative private funding program created and implemented by Southland Community Bank and a committee of patrons. The table below describes current sources of funding.

SOURCES OF FUNDING	
Federal Grants and Contracts	31%
State Grants and Contracts	10%
Insurance and Client Fees	37%
Private Grants and Contributions	20%
Cooperative Way	1%
Miscellaneous	1%

Youth Services

Both national and local studies show that experimentation with alcohol and drugs by young people is a significant problem. (Jones, 1994, 213) Study after study proves the importance of educating and working with young people so they will not make poor choices about alcohol and drugs. (Arroyo, 1996, 3) On a community-wide basis, CASA offers school drug education programs, conducted by experienced social workers and popular volunteer speakers such as local sports figures. We also assist schools in planning activities that promote a drug-free lifestyle.

Our programs for young people include assessment, recovery, structured outpatient services, and counseling. Since substance abuse affects not only the addicted person but also his or her family, we offer parenting and family counseling programs that emphasize opening the channels of communication, taking active therapeutic measures, making good decisions, and reinforcing positive behavior.

Women's Programs

At CASA, we offer a variety of programs to help women affected by substance abuse. For pregnant and postpartum women, we offer a program in collaboration with local community health centers and obstetricians to educate against substance abuse, to assess substance abuse problems, and to intervene with effective recuperative therapy.

With the help of an experienced, enthusiastic, and dedicated staff, we have developed innovative programs and services to meet the needs of diverse clients.

Support groups for recovering substance abusers and co-dependency groups are open to all women—and all men—affected by substance abuse. Led by trained counselors, these groups instruct participants on proven methods for staying drug-free, educate them on the long-term effects of substance abuse on the abuser and the family, and provide a forum for the interchange of ideas and the support of others.

We offer several residential resource services for women affected by substance abuse who have children. Hathaway House, our residential center, offers child care as well as therapeutic services. We also operate the Haven, a shelter for families of addicted persons.

Services for the Elderly

The new Senior Citizen Assistance Initiative, funded by several public and private agencies, is a two-year pilot project designed to help senior citizens access needed services. The Initiative provides an educational outreach program, targeted support groups, peer and counselor telephone contact services, and transportation to activities.

Prevention Programs

Studies have shown that educational, public awareness, and other drug prevention programs have a significant, dramatic, and far-reaching effect in deterring substance use and abuse. (Waters, 1997, 13) At CASA, we offer a comprehensive range of programs designed to service the prevention needs of schools, individuals, families businesses, and communities.

- Our school drug education programs are conducted by experienced social workers and popular volunteer speakers such as local sports figures. We also offer schools assistance in planning activities that promote a drug-free lifestyle.
- For businesses, we offer consultative and technical assistance in training and education programs.
- For all citizens, our counselors can interpret and help change behaviors and conditions that put a person at risk for substance abuse.
- For the public, we offer public education programs on alcohol and other drugs, tobacco, and other substance abuse concerns.
- For the concerned, our library includes journals, books, videos, and on-line services relating to substance abuse available to anyone free of charge.

SERVICES PROVIDED
Residential (15.00%)
Community-Based (19.00%)
Alcoholism (13.00%)
Shelter (6.00%)
Research (5.00%)
Detox (23.00%)
Prevention (19.00%)

Under a grant from the federal Agency of Substance Abuse Prevention, CASA is managing the Northland Youth Alliance Project, a five-year model prevention program for young people. The goal of the program is to develop a coordinated, broad-based plan to prevent substance abuse through education, mentor programs, incentives, drug-free activities, and school and workplace counseling.

continued on page 143

EXERCISE 75

INSTRUCTIONS continued from page 140

12. Select the title and format it in a sans serif bold typeface, 20/auto for the first line and 18/auto for the second. Mark the title for inclusion in the table of contents. Remove the left indent.

13. As you go through the report, apply styles appropriately to text.

14. To create the chart at the bottom of page 1, draw the top left oval as shown; use a 1-point line, and make the oval 1.5" by .75". Use the multiple paste/offset feature, align and distribute option, or ruler guides to position copies of the ovals as shown. In the rows containing three ovals, the ovals are .25" apart. In the row containing two ovals, the ovals are at the left and right margins. The text in the center is in a 14/auto bold serif font; the lines radiating from the center are 1-point. Use a 9/auto sans serif font for the text in the ovals. Use ruler guides to align the text of ovals in the same row baseline to baseline. Adjust the bottom windowshade handle of the text to leave an attractive amount of space above the chart.

15. Create the table as shown in your desktop publishing software or a table editor feature. See pages 80-83 if you need assistance. Use a 12/22 bold sans serif font for the table title and an 11/22 sans serif font for the table text. The line at the top of the table is 2-point, the line at the bottom is 1-point, and the fill is 20%. Add space before the heading below the table, if necessary. The example, which was created in desktop publishing software, has a left tab at 1.64" and a right tab at 4.875".

16. Pull quotes should be in an 18/22 serif italic font, with a .35" left indent. Use a 2-point line above and a 1-point line below. *Hint:* Create one pull quote and copy and paste it for the others. Then highlight the text on the copies and change it. You may need to adjust the size of text blocks and line lengths to achieve attractive pull quotes.

17. At the end of the report, cut the list of funding contributors. On page 7, create 2 columns with a .167" gutter. Paste the list at the bottom of Column 1 on page 7 as an independent text block. Cut the board of directors list and paste it in the right column as shown.

18. Format the two headings in sans serif bold 11/13. Format the rest of the text in the independent text blocks in serif 11/13 with a .25" left indent.

continued on page 144

EXERCISE 75

Exercise 75 continued from page 141

Individualized Services

Through CASA, individuals affected by substance abuse have access to a wide variety of outpatient and inpatient programs and client management services.

Inpatient. Individuals requiring inpatient treatment can be entered in programs with the goal of medically supervised withdrawal from alcohol and other drugs. Private units are available. Pregnant women can be treated through delivery. The CASA staff includes physicians, nurses, psychiatrists, and clinicians who are certified drug and alcohol counselors.

At CASA, clients are afforded the respect and dignity they deserve as human beings.

Residential. We operate three transition shelters that provide temporary residence in a supportive environment for recovering addicted persons. These shelters combine a homelike atmosphere with active, supportive counseling and an employment program. In, addition, CASA coordinates a Roommate Program that pairs recovering clients in local apartments. Our residential program includes individual and group counseling, substance abuse education, and planning and referral services.

Outpatient. Outpatient services at CASA include assessment, education, treatment, and follow-up programs. Our clients are self-referred or enter into treatment through the workplace, the courts, social services, or other community programs. Our licensed social workers provide diagnostic assessment, treatment planning and management, and individual and group therapy.

Outpatient services also include counseling for persons whose lives are affected by the addiction of a family member. Children, spouses, families, and co-dependents can receive individual counseling or participate in supportive group counseling sessions.

Services for Businesses

Problems associated with the abuse of alcohol and other drugs cost U.S. businesses billions of dollars each year. (Chitose, 1997, 24) At CASA, we offer businesses assistance in developing a substance abuse policy and drug-free workplace programs. We have developed an Employee Aid Program that helps employers and employees recognize and conquer chemical dependency. Our Employee Aid Program, now in place in 25 local businesses, has proven supportive, successful, and cost-effective.

The CASA Care Management Program helps employers control the cost of chemical dependency insurance. Because payment is certified prior to treatment, this program ensures that employees receive appropriate and high-quality therapy while costs are controlled for them and their employers.

Our Employee Aid Program, now in place in 25 local businesses, has proven supportive, successful, and cost-effective.

The Workplace Intervention Series, funded by the National Business Alliance, is a three-year pilot program for the management of substance abuse problems that can impair productivity in the workplace. This program, which is being conducted at five area businesses, offers a coordinated and managed approach to the problem of substance abuse, including education of employees and supervisors and confidential access to innovative therapeutic services.

Professional Growth Series

Physicians, social workers, and others whose professions put them in contact with substance abuse have a powerful resource in CASA. We offer a comprehensive research library, including journals, on-line services, and an up-to-date bank of information on treatment methods, from well-established to state-of-the-art. We also operate a referral service of specialists.

The text, objects, and spacing in this exercise have been reduced because of space constraints.

Crisis Hotline

At CASA, we operate a 24-hour crisis hotline at 555-HELP. Staffed by counselors and trained volunteers, the hotline offers immediate access to needed services.

The New Horizons Center

In these days of declining governmental funding for substance abuse programs, CASA is turning to the public to help us fund this facility. New Horizons will provide inpatient services for some 100 recovering clients, as well as state-of-the-art outpatient services for 250 more. The Center will be located in the old Delaney Department Store building on Route 14 in Southland, providing central and convenient access for all communities to be serviced by the center. Funding is 40 percent complete as of this writing. Contributions of up to $500 will be matched dollar for dollar by the Komuro Corporation. To contribute to the New Horizons Fund, contact Jerry Fox at 555-1234.

We are dedicated to providing quality care and prevention services to help people improve their lives.

FUNDING

The following organizations provide funding support to CASA:

Agency of Substance Abuse Prevention
City of Northland
City of Southland
Cooperative Way
Komuro Corporation
State Department of Education
State Department of Public Health
State Department of Public Welfare
National Business Alliance
National Council Against Drug Dependency
Project Drug-Free
Social Security Administration
Southland Community Bank

CASA BOARD OF DIRECTORS

Erin Altman, Esq.
Ai-lien Chang, M.D.
Richard Dinsmore, Jr.
Alexandra S. Jones
John W. Silva
Michael J. West, Ed.D.

References

Jose Arroyo. "Education Against Drug Abuse." *Psychology Monthly*, March 1996, 2-9.

Alex Chitose. "Drug Abuse and the Nation." *Economic Vistas*, January 1997, 24-29.

Anthea Jones. *Alcohol and Drug Use and Abuse*. New York: Hathaway Publishing, 1994.

Beth Waters. *Winning the Fight Against Substance Abuse*. Washington: Government Printing Office, 1997.

continued on page 145

EXERCISE

75

INSTRUCTIONS continued from page 142

19. Add .05" after the title in each text block and after the first paragraph in the "FUNDING" text block.
20. Draw a box with 20% fill and no line around each text block as shown. If necessary, adjust the text blocks and boxes so text appears attractively.
21. Draw a 2-point line above and a 1-point line below each box as shown.
22. Go to page 8. Apply the side headings style to the references title. Adjust the text if necessary so it begins under the horizontal ruler guide at 1.5".
23. Format the references with the reference style.
24. Prepare an index for the document and place it on page 9.
25. Format the index title with the side headings style. Adjust the text if necessary so it begins under the horizontal ruler guide at 1.5".
26. Use the default format for index entries for your software. If necessary, adjust the font and spacing so that the index does not exceed one page.
27. Go to page 10, mask the running head, and generate a table of contents for your document.
28. Format the table of contents head with the side heading style. Adjust the text if necessary so it begins under the horizontal ruler guide at 1.5".
29. Format the table of contents entries with the appropriate style.
30. Go to page 1 and copy the report title. Go to page 11, mask the running head, and paste the copy of the title. Adjust the text block so that it begins at 2.5" on the vertical ruler. Give it a .25" left indent. Draw a 1-point rule beneath the title extending from 1" to 7.5" as shown.
31. Re-save the file.
32. Using all printer defaults, print one copy.
33. Close the file.

EXERCISE 76

Learning Objectives

Format a form
Learn purchase order format

Desktop Techniques Applied

Key text in different fonts
Draw rules
Use bullets and en spaces
Use symbols or graphics

Concepts

Desktop publishers produce many **forms.** Purchase orders, invoices, expense reports, request forms, surveys, and service records are some of the kinds of forms produced regularly on desktop publishing software. Indeed, desktop publishing programs often have templates for common forms.

When you are designing a form, consider carefully the needs of the person who will fill it out and the equipment that person will be using. Always leave a generous amount of space for text that will be written in or keyed. If a name and address block will show through the window of a window envelope, plan exactly where to place it so that, when the document is folded, the text appears as it should.

In this exercise, you will create a purchase order. Purchase orders are generally numbered and dated. The categories shown in the example on the right are fairly standard. The third and fourth columns are divided so that dollars can appear on one side of the rule and cents on the other.

INSTRUCTIONS

1. Start a new publication; use the default settings.
2. Just inside the top margin, key "Tabitha's" in serif 24/auto italic, center-aligned. Use an appropriate graphic or symbol from a symbol typeface with the title.
3. Key the next line in serif 12/auto small caps. The first two words should be bold. The rest of the line should be right-aligned. Use desktop publishing bullets set off by en spaces as shown.
4. Draw a double line under the address information extending from the left to the right margin.
5. Approximately .5" below the double line and at the left margin, draw a rectangle using a .5-point line. The rectangle should measure approximately 3" wide by 1" long.
6. Key the four lines beginning with "PO No." in sans serif 12/12 bold, right-aligned. Adjust the text block so its top is even with the top border of the rectangle and the left-most word ("Shipped") appears about .75" to the right of the right border of the rectangle.
7. Key "Purchase Order" approximately 3/8" base to base from the bottom line of the double line and approximately .25" to the right of the colons in the right-aligned text below.
8. Approximately .25" below the rectangle, draw a .5-point line extending from margin to margin. Draw another .5-point line (or copy the line you just drew) 3/8" below.
9. Draw (or draw and copy) .5-point vertical rules extending down from the top horizontal rule you drew in Step 8. Rules should be 5" long and should appear at the left margin, 1.25" in from the left margin, at the right margin, 1.25" in from the right margin, and 2.5" in from the right margin.
10. Draw a .5-point horizontal line extending from margin to margin and across the bottom of all the vertical rules you just drew.
11. Key the text beginning "Quantity" as separate, center-aligned text blocks extending from one edge of each column to the other. Use sans serif 12/auto bold. Use a ruler guide to align the column headings baseline to baseline.
12. Draw .5-point rules dividing the last two columns as shown. The rules should be 5/8" in from the left border of the column.
13. Approximately 3/8" below the grid, draw a .5-point line extending 4" from the right margin. Key "By" in sans serif 12-point bold; align the baseline of the text with the line.
14. Save the file; name it **PO.**
15. Using all printer defaults, print one copy.
16. Close the file.

EXERCISE 76

Exercise 76

Tabitha's

ORIGINAL DESIGNS 14 HERON STREET • HARBOR SPRINGS, MI 49740-3453 • (616) 555-8013

Purchase Order

PO No.:
Date:
Terms:
Shipped Via:

Quantity	Description/Stock Number	Price	Total

The text, objects, and spacing in this exercise have been reduced because of space constraints.

Purchase Order

By ____________________

FORM

Format a form

Learn purchase order format

Key text in different fonts

Draw rules

Exercise 76

Concepts

INSTRUCTIONS

Tabitha's

expense reports, request forms, surveys, and service records are some of the kinds of forms produced regularly on desktop publishing software. Indeed, desktop publishing programs often have templates for common forms.

consider carefully the needs of the

amount of space for text that will be written in or keyed. If a name and address block will show through the window of a window

place it so that, when the document is folded, the text appears as it should.

In this exercise, you will create a **purchase order.** Purchase orders are generally numbered and dated.

2. Just inside the top margin, key "Tabitha's" in serif 24/auto italic, center-aligned. Use an appropriate graphic or symbol from a symbol typeface with the title.
3. Key the next line in serif 12/auto small caps. The first two words should be bold. The rest of the line should be right-aligned. Use desktop publishing bullets set off by en spaces as shown.
4. Draw a double line under the address information extending from the left to the right margin.
5. Approximately .5" below the double line and at the left margin, draw approximately 3" wide by 1" long.
6. Key the four lines beginning with "PO No." in sans serif 12/12 bold
7. Key "Purchase Order" approximately 3/8" base to base from the bottom line of the double line and approximately .25" to the right of the colons in the right-aligned text below.
8. copy the line you just drew) 3/8" below.
9. Draw (or draw and copy) .5-point vertical rules extending down from the top horizontal rule you drew in Step 8. Rules should be 5" long and should appear at the left margin, 1.25" in from the left margin, at the right margin, 1.25" in from the right margin, and 2.5" in from the right margin.
10. Draw a .5-point horizontal line extending from margin to margin and
11. blocks extending from one edge of each column to the other. Use should be 5/8" in from the left border of the column.
13. Approximately 3/8" below the grid, draw a .5-point line extending 4"
15. Using all printer defaults, print one copy.
16. Close the file.

Date:

Quantity	Description/Stock Number	Price	Total

The text, objects, and

Purchase Order

By ____________________

EXERCISE 77

Learning Objectives

Format a form
Learn invoice format

Desktop Techniques Applied

Key text to replace existing text
Use copy and paste features
Adjust text blocks and rules
Draw a rectangle with fill

Concepts

In this exercise, you will create an **invoice.** Invoices generally have an order number and a shipping date, as well as the date on which the form was keyed. Invoices often show the means by which the purchase will be shipped and usually detail the terms of payment.

INSTRUCTIONS

1. Open the data file **PO** (or open a copy of the file if your software has that option).
2. Save the document as **INVOICE.**
3. Select "Purchase Order" and key "Invoice" to replace it.
4. In the text block beginning "PO No.," delete the first line and change "Terms" and "Shipped Via" to "Customer" and "Order No."
5. Select the entire column structure and move it to the bottom of the page.
6. Select the column headings and the rules above and below them (you are selecting the column heading row). Copy the row.
7. Paste a copy immediately above the original column headings. Align the copy so that the rule at the bottom of the copy is superimposed on the rule at the top of the original. Delete one of the two superimposed rules.
8. Repeat Step 7 to place a second copy above the first.
9. In the row above the original column headings, delete all the text.
10. Extend upwards as shown the vertical rule at the left margin and the three vertical rules serving as borders for the last two columns.
11. Draw a short vertical rule 1.5" in from the left margin and down through the first two rows to create the "Terms" column as shown.
12. In the first row, key the appropriate headings as replacement text as shown. You will have to adjust the first and second text blocks to center-align correctly, since you changed the width of the columns.
13. Draw a rectangle with 60% fill and no line to frame the first row. Set the column headings in that row to reverse.
14. Select all the columnar material and adjust it so the first row begins .5" below the address rectangle.
15. Re-save the file.
16. Using all printer defaults, print one copy.
17. Close the file.

EXERCISE 77

Exercise 77

Tabitha's

ORIGINAL DESIGNS

14 HERON STREET • HARBOR SPRINGS, MI 49740-3453 • (616) 555-8013

Invoice

Date:
Customer:
Order No.:

Terms	Shipped Via	Our Order No.	Date Shipped

Quantity	Description/Stock Number	Price	Total

The text, objects, and spacing in this exercise have been reduced because of space constraints.

Invoice

By ______________________________

Learning Objectives

Format a form
Learn survey format

Desktop Techniques Applied

Key text in different fonts
Draw rules
Set tabs
Use em spaces
Use symbols or drawn objects

Concepts

Desktop publishers frequently produce **surveys.** Surveys are designed to elicit information about a product, service, procedure, or idea.

You can choose from several different types of survey questions, depending on the information you are seeking:

- **Dual alternative** questions offer only two answer choices: true or false, yes or no.
- **Multiple choice** questions offer three or more choices.
- **Completion** questions ask the person being surveyed to fill in a blank and complete a sentence.
- **Essay** or **open-ended** questions elicit the most information. These questions, which usually begin with terms like *how, in what way*, and *why*, invite more than a yes-or-no response.[1]

INSTRUCTIONS

1. Start a new publication; use the default settings.
2. Just inside the top and left margins, key "Todd's" in sans serif 36/auto bold. Key an em space, and key "ELECTRONICS" in sans serif 14/auto bold.
3. Draw two 4-point lines below the text you just keyed as shown.
4. Approximately .25" below the double line, key the survey. Use sans serif 14/auto bold, center-aligned, for the title. Use 12/auto sans serif for the remainder of the text. Set tabs at .25", .5", and 3" for the numbers, text after the numbers, and second check-box response, respectively. Use an appropriate symbol from a symbol typeface for the check box. If you do not have a symbol, draw a box, copy it, and paste copies of the box for check boxes. Key an em space between the check box and the text that follows. Double-space before and after questions as shown. Use .5-point rules in Questions 4 and 7. In Question 7, use a paragraph rule, if available, with a .5" left indent and 18-point leading. Alternatively, you can use a power paste option with vertical offset of .25". If you have neither of these options, draw one rule and paste six copies .25" apart.
5. Key the last line of text at the bottom margin in sans serif 11/auto, center-aligned. Use an em space between the ZIP Code and the telephone number.
6. Save the file; name it **SURVEY1.**
7. Using all printer defaults, print one copy.
8. Close the file.

[1]This discussion of survey questions was adapted from *Module 3, Communication 2000* (Cincinnati: South-Western Publishing Co., 1996), p. 115.

EXERCISE 78

Exercise 78

Todd's ELECTRONICS

CUSTOMER SATISFACTION SURVEY

1. How would you rate your shopping experience at Todd's today?

   ❒ Highly satisfactory ❒ Satisfactory
   ❒ Unsatisfactory ❒ Highly unsatisfactory

2. Were our salesclerks polite and helpful?

   ❒ Yes ❒ No

3. Did our salesclerks seem informed about the products they were selling?

   ❒ Yes ❒ No

4. Did you purchase anything today at Todd's?

   ❒ Stereo ❒ Television
   ❒ VCR ❒ Radio
   ❒ Cassette tape player ❒ Other ______________________

5. Did you receive prompt service?

   ❒ Yes ❒ No

6. Did you consider our prices competitive with those of other stores?

   ❒ Yes ❒ No

7. How would you describe your shopping experience at Todd's today?

   ____
   ____
   ____
   ____
   ____
   ____
   ____

14 Elliot Street, Beverly, MA 01915-2294 (508) 555-7491

The text, objects, and spacing in this exercise have been reduced because of space constraints.

Survey

EXERCISE 79

Learning Objectives

Format a form

Desktop Techniques Applied

Change the spacing of text
Key text in different fonts
Use paragraph rules or power paste
Use em spaces and en spaces
Use symbols or drawn objects

INSTRUCTIONS

1. Start a new publication; use the default settings.
2. Just inside the top and right margins, key, with a return between the words, "Sushiba Advertising" in sans serif 30/30 bold with 120% spacing. Use an appropriate symbol as part of the logo.
3. Draw a line below the text extending from margin to margin as shown.
4. Approximately 3/8" below the line, key the survey. Use sans serif 16/auto bold, center-aligned, for the title. Double-space where extra space is shown. Body text will be keyed in sans serif 12/24.
5. Use .5-point rules throughout. For the first seven lines, rules should begin .25" after the word "Number" and should extend to the right margin. For the numbered items, rules should begin .25" in from the left margin and should extend to the right margin. Use a paragraph rule feature, if available. Alternatively, you can use a power paste feature with a vertical offset of approximately .33". If you do not have either of these features, you can place ruler guides on the baselines of each line of text and draw (or draw and copy) lines.
6. Center the subtitles; make them 13/24 sans serif bold.
7. Key an en space after each check box and an em space before all check boxes except the first.
8. Quadruple-space before the last two lines. Make them 12/auto.
9. Save the file; name it **SURVEY2.**
10. Using all printer defaults, print one copy.
11. Close the file.

EXERCISE
79

Exercise 79

Tushiba
Advertising

CLIENT QUESTIONNAIRE

Company Name ____________________

Address ____________________

City, State, ZIP ____________________

Telephone Number ____________________

Contact Person ____________________

Product or Service ____________________

____

CURRENT ADVERTISING METHODS (CHECK ALL THAT APPLY.)

❒ Newspaper ❒ Television ❒ Radio ❒ Direct Mail ❒ Other ____________________

____

CUSTOMER PROFILE

List the three most common characteristics of the potential customers you wish to reach.

1. ____________________
2. ____________________
3. ____________________

Please return your questionnaire today so we can help you reach new customers. Use the enclosed postage-paid reply envelope or mail or FAX your form to 407-555-1245.

The text, objects, and spacing in this exercise have been reduced because of space constraints.

Learning Objectives

Learn agenda format
Format an agenda

Desktop Techniques Applied

Draw rectangles and rules
Import a text file
Format text in different fonts
Reset a tab

Concepts

An **agenda** is a plan, a program, a schedule, an outline, a calendar, or a list of things to be done, events to occur, or matters to be brought before a committee, council, or board. The format of an agenda will vary (a traditional format is shown below), but the agenda will always include the date and time of the planned activities.

Agenda (Traditional Format)

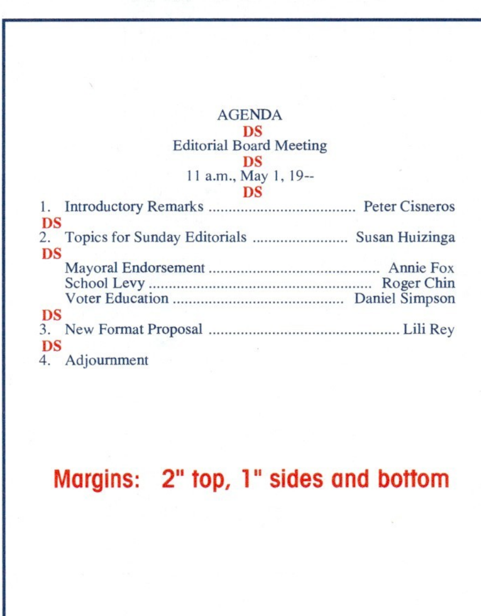

AGENDA
DS
Editorial Board Meeting
DS
11 a.m., May 1, 19--
DS
1. Introductory Remarks .... Peter Cisneros
DS
2. Topics for Sunday Editorials .... Susan Huizinga
DS
Mayoral Endorsement .... Annie Fox
School Levy .... Roger Chin
Voter Education .... Daniel Simpson
DS
3. New Format Proposal .... Lili Rey
DS
4. Adjournment

Margins: 2" top, 1" sides and bottom

INSTRUCTIONS

1. Start a new publication with a 1" top margin and the other margins set at .5".
2. Position horizontal ruler guides at 1.5", 2", 2.25", and 10.25". Position vertical ruler guides at .75" and 7.75".
3. Place the template file **AGENDA** at the top margin.
4. Save the file; name it **AGENDA1.**
5. Set all text to a sans serif typeface with auto leading.
6. Set "TOTTENVILLE HIGH SCHOOL" to 34-point with .75" after.
7. Draw a rectangle around "TOTTENVILLE HIGH SCHOOL" extending from the left to the right margin and from the top margin to the 1.5" horizontal ruler guide; give it a solid fill.
8. Set "TOTTENVILLE HIGH SCHOOL" to reverse. Move the text block straight down so that "TOTTENVILLE HIGH SCHOOL" is centered in the rectangle.
9. Set "PROGRAM" to 18-point. Use 14-point for the rest of the heading through the time and for "LUNCHEON TO FOLLOW."
10. Draw an 8-point line under "PROGRAM" and another 8-point line under "Model Office Classroom" as shown.
11. Set the body text to 10-point with a .5" left indent. Reset the tab to 3.75".
12. Draw a box to frame the program, using a 4-point line, extending from the left to the right margin and from the horizontal ruler guide at 2" to the bottom margin.
13. Draw another box using an 8-point line, extending from the vertical ruler guide at .75" to the vertical ruler guide at 7.75" and from the horizontal ruler guide at 2.25" to the horizontal ruler guide at 10.25".
14. Re-save the file.
15. Using all printer defaults, print one copy.
16. Close the file.

EXERCISE 80

Exercise 80

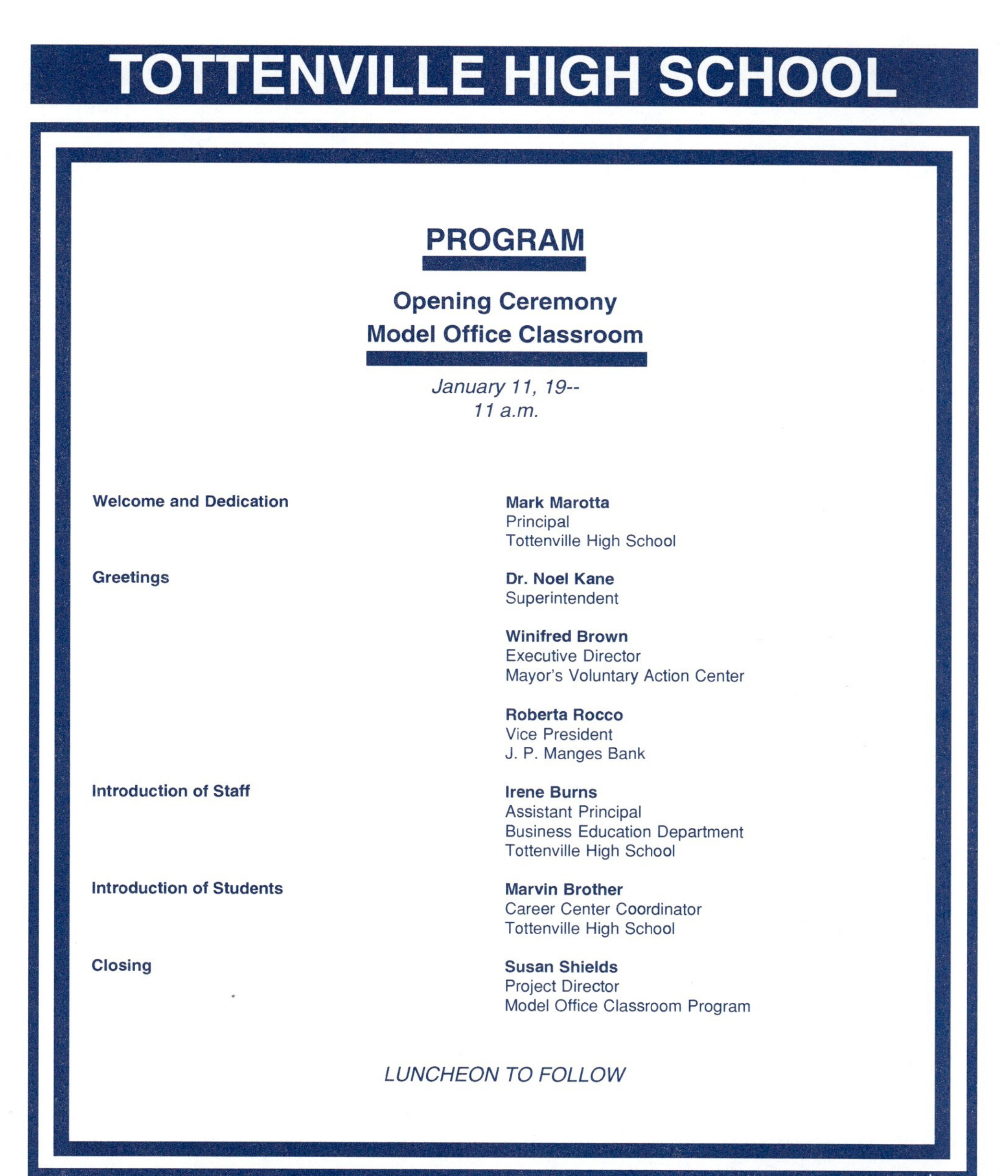

TOTTENVILLE HIGH SCHOOL

PROGRAM

Opening Ceremony
Model Office Classroom

January 11, 19--
11 a.m.

Welcome and Dedication	**Mark Marotta** Principal Tottenville High School
Greetings	**Dr. Noel Kane** Superintendent
	Winifred Brown Executive Director Mayor's Voluntary Action Center
	Roberta Rocco Vice President J. P. Manges Bank
Introduction of Staff	**Irene Burns** Assistant Principal Business Education Department Tottenville High School
Introduction of Students	**Marvin Brother** Career Center Coordinator Tottenville High School
Closing	**Susan Shields** Project Director Model Office Classroom Program

LUNCHEON TO FOLLOW

Agenda

The text, objects, and spacing in this exercise have been reduced because of space constraints.

Learning Objectives

Format an agenda

Desktop Techniques Applied

Create custom columns
Format text in different fonts
Set a hanging indent
Set tracking and character width
Create a style based on text

INSTRUCTIONS

1. Start a new publication with .5" margins.
2. Create 2 columns with .167" between columns.
3. Move the column guides so that the right border of the first column is at 2.5".
4. Import the template file **MEET** into the second column, at just below 1" on the vertical ruler.
5. Save the file; name it **MEET1.**
6. Select all the text and set it to a 10/auto serif font.
7. If any of the Objectives runs more than one line, set a hanging indent of 1" for that text so the text in the second line will align with the first. If more than one Objective runs multiple lines, you may want to create a style.
8. Cut the title to the clipboard.
9. Set "Session One" and "Session Two" to 24-point. Use very tight tracking. Set the width of the characters to 70% (if available).
10. Set the time of each session to 12-point. Replace the space between the session number and the time with an em space.
11. Add a .5-point paragraph rule below the first topic. Create a style based on the text and apply it to all the other topics. If your software does not have a paragraph rule feature, draw a line, copy it, and paste multiple copies (use the multiple paste feature with offset, or the align and distribute feature, if available).
12. Draw a rectangle with solid fill to frame the first column.
13. Paste the title on the pasteboard (the area outside the document).
14. Insert a return between each pair of words, placing each word on its own line. Insert one additional return between "FOUNDATION" and "SECTIONAL." Right-align the text.
15. Set the heading text to 24-point reverse. Use very tight tracking, and set the width of the characters to 70% (if available).
16. Drag the title text block into the black column to begin 4" down from the top of the page. Adjust a right windowshade handle so that the text block ends 1/8" short of the right edge of the column.
17. Draw a 1-point horizontal line, set to reverse, between "FOUNDATION" and "SECTIONAL."
18. Re-save the file.
19. Using all printer defaults, print one copy.
20. Close the file.

Design Pointers/Hints

- When you need to place large amounts of text on a page, use lines to help organize the text.
- Where possible, use large amounts of white space to aid in the readability of the text.

EXERCISE 81

Exercise 81

NATIONAL BUSINESS EDUCATION FOUNDATION

SECTIONAL MEETINGS

Session One 8:15-9:30 a.m.

TECHNIQUES OF PROMOTING YOUR BUSINESS PROGRAM

Kay's Pier South

Presenter: Ralph Johnson, Business Education Consultant
Objective: *To provide innovative techniques in promoting business programs.*

INTERNATIONAL BUSINESS: THE NEW FOCUS

Glass Room

Presenter: Leslie Day, Ph.D.
Objective: *To identify international business topics to be integrated into business courses.*

NETWORKING IN BUSINESS EDUCATION

Seaview North

Presenter: Kareem Brown, Educational Specialist
Objective: *To understand the power of networking with state-of-the-art software.*

Session Two 10:15-11:30 a.m.

MAKING THE TRANSITION FROM WORD PROCESSING TO DESKTOP PUBLISHING

Kay's Pier South

Presenter: Shirley Dembo, Graphic Design Consultant
Objective: *To present strategies for creating desktop designs from ordinary business documents.*

USING THE INTERNET

Glass Room

Presenter: Donna Newman, Programmer
Objective: *To present strategies and tips for getting the most out of the Internet.*

TOOLS IN OFFICE TECHNOLOGY

Seaview North

Presenter: Jaime Leigh, Technology Consultant
Objective: *To provide an overview of productivity tools in the office.*

The text, objects, and spacing in this exercise have been reduced because of space constraints.

Learning Objectives

Learn news release format

Format a news release

Desktop Techniques Applied

Import a text file

Right-align text

Change the font of text

Set a first indent

Concepts

A **news release** is a document sent to newspapers, magazines, or other publications announcing a new product, a development, or an item of special interest. A news release is also referred to as a *press release,* since the document is sent to the press (newspaper).

News releases are written in the traditional journalistic format of putting the most important information first, for the convenience of both the reader, whose time is often at a premium, and the editor, who may need to shorten the release because of space constraints. The *who, what, when, where,* and *why* of the story should appear in the first sentences. Information is arranged from most to least important. As in all writing, clarity and concision are essential.

News releases are often sent out on letterhead. Side margins are 1"; the bottom margin is at least 1". The first line of the release appears 2" from the top of the page. This line may include the words "News Release," flush left; it always includes the "For Release" information, flush right. The "For Release" information tells the editor when the release may be used. The next line, which tells the editor who to contact for more information, begins flush right. A quadruple space separates the contact line from the body of the release.

The first paragraph of the body of the news release begins with the place (city and state, using the two-letter postal state abbreviation) and date of the release. The body is double-spaced. Paragraphs are indented .5" from the left margin. The end of a story is indicated by the symbols "###," which are center-aligned a double space below the last line of text.

INSTRUCTIONS

1. Open **IMAGE,** the template file you created in Exercise 62.
2. Save the file as a document; name it **SHOW.**
3. Import the template file **NEWS1.**
4. Right-align "For Release: Immediately" and "Contact: Zachary Westgate."
5. Set all the text to serif 12/24.
6. Set the first two lines and the three blank lines after them to 12/12.
7. Give the rest of the copy except the last line a .5" first indent.
8. Re-save the file.
9. Using all printer defaults, print one copy.
10. Close the file.

EXERCISE 82

Exercise 83

VISIONIMAGE

top margin 2"

245 Lamberts Lane Chicago, IL 60630-1215 (312) 555-0267

News Release

For Release: Immediately
Contact: Zachary Westgate

QS

.5" CHICAGO, IL, March 1, 19—. Four talented high school students will win an all-expense-paid trip to New York City in this year's Design Show High School Competition, sponsored by VisionImage. The contest, the first of its kind in the area, challenges high school design students to use their imagination, creativity, and skills to devise practical solutions to important societal problems. The theme of this year's competition is "Helping the Homeless."

1" 1"

The contest will be held at the Design Show on April 1. A panel of instructors from the Art Institute will judge the entries, which will be on display at the show.

"Students coming out of our Chicago high schools are very talented designers," said Martin Pilsner, president of VisionImage, a new company specializing in corporate identity programs, advertising, and graphic design. "I believe their talents should be challenged, showcased, and rewarded." Pilsner decided on the theme for this year's competition when he read about some engineering students who devised a simple and lightweight sleeping bag for homeless people. "I feel strongly that designers, like other professionals, have an obligation to use their skills in service to their communities."

###

at least 1"

Corporate Identity Programs Advertising Graphic Design

News Release

The text, objects, and spacing in this exercise have been reduced because of space constraints.

Learning Objectives

Format a news release

Desktop Techniques Applied

Change the margins of a file
Import a text file
Change the font of text
Set a first indent

INSTRUCTIONS

1. Open **CIRCLE,** the template file you created in Exercise 63.
2. Change the side margins to 1".
3. Move the logo at the top of the page (text and circle) so that its left edge is flush with the new left margin.
4. Delete the sponsor and patron information and the vertical rule.
5. Save the file as a document; name it **RODIN.**
6. Import the template file **NEWS2** so that text begins at just under 2.75" on the vertical ruler.
7. Set all the text to serif 11/22.
8. Set the first two lines and the three blank lines after them to 11/11.
9. Give the rest of the copy except the last line a .5" first indent.
10. Re-save the file.
11. Using all printer defaults, print one copy.
12. Close the file.

EXERCISE 83

Exercise 83

35 Canvas Lane
New York, NY 10012-2786
(212) 555-5600

Richard Warren, Director

For Release: March 1, 19—
Contact: Gina Valparaiso

NEW YORK, NY, February 15, 19—. "Rodin: A Retrospective," the largest traveling exhibition ever of the works of Auguste Rodin, will open at the Circle Arts Museum on April 1 for a six-week run. This highly popular exhibition, which has been shown to record-breaking crowds in Los Angeles, Philadelphia, and Boston, is available by special engagement at the Circle Arts Museum.

The Rodin exhibit features 150 of the artist's bronze and marble works, including such well-known masterpieces as *The Age of Bronze, The Walking Man, The Gates of Hell, The Three Shades,* and *The Burghers of Calais.* Many of these works have never been seen outside of their native galleries before.

Auguste Rodin (1840-1917) was a seminal influence in the origins of modern sculpture. His work, known for its naturalism and realism, began in revolt against the sentimentality and idealism of academic artists. His later work became more expressive and impressionist.

"Rodin: A Retrospective" will be at the Circle Arts Museum from April 1 through May 15. Special extended hours for this exhibit are 8:30 a.m.-8 p.m. Monday through Saturday. Entrance to the exhibit can be purchased separately or as part of a general admission. Reservations will be taken for Mondays, Wednesdays, and Fridays and are recommended.

###

The text, objects, and spacing in this exercise have been reduced because of space constraints.

EXERCISE 84

Learning Objectives

Format a resume

Desktop Techniques Applied

Reset tabs

Set tracking and character width

Insert bullets in text

Create and apply a style

Add paragraph rules

INSTRUCTIONS

1. Start a new publication with a 1" left margin and the other margins .75".
2. Position a vertical ruler guide at 3".
3. Place the template file **RESUME2** at the top margin.
4. Save the file; name it **RESUMTB.**
5. Set all the text to sans serif 12/12 with tabs at 2" and 2.5".
6. Change "THOMAS BERGMAN" to 14/12 with very loose tracking and 120% width.
7. Draw a horizontal 1-point line below the name and address text, extending it to the right margin.
8. Create a small square with solid fill below the start of the line as shown.
9. *If your software has a paragraph rule feature,* create a style based on one of the side headings for a 1-point paragraph rule below the heading with a right indent of 4.875". Then apply the style to all the side headings.

   If your software does not have a paragraph rule feature, draw (or draw and copy) a 1-point line below each side heading, extending to slightly short of the 3" ruler guide. Use a vertical ruler guide to ensure that all lines end at the same place.
10. Right-align "New York, NY."
11. Insert (or insert and copy) desktop publishing software bullets as shown.
12. Re-save the file.
13. Using all printer defaults, print one copy.
14. Close the file.

Design Pointers/Hints

- A resume conveys an image to the reader about the sender. The design of a resume should be conservative and somewhat formal. The resume should look professional and should be appropriate for the audience.

EXERCISE

84

Exercise 84

THOMAS BERGMAN
467 Ramblewood Drive
Darien, Connecticut 06820-1459
(203) 555-8238

Education

August 1992-
June 1996

Yale University
New Haven, CT
B.A., History

Work Experience

June 1996-
August 1998

SALMON BROTHERS, INC. New York, NY

Trade Desk Support.
- Supported government and corporate desks.
- Set up new issues on proprietary systems.
- Produced daily KEY ISSUE package.
- Priced corporate issues daily.

Computer Skills

- Lotus, WordPerfect, Excel, Windows
- Mainframe and timesharing systems

Hobbies

Basketball, Volleyball

Personal Data

- Will relocate.
- Innovative.
- Intuitive.
- Highly motivated.

References

Mr. Peter Willins
Vice President
Salmon Brothers, Inc.
45 Wall Street
New York, NY 10006-2345
(718) 555-2354

Abby Quest, Ph.D.
Professor of American History
Yale University
P. O. Box 8843
New Haven, CT 06508-9746
(203) 555-1803

The text, objects, and spacing in this exercise have been reduced because of space constraints.

EXERCISE 85

Learning Objectives

Learn functional resume format
Format a resume

Desktop Techniques Applied

Import a text file
Change the font of text
Set left and right indents
Create and apply a style
Draw rules and boxes

Concepts

The resume format you used in previous exercises is appropriate when your employment history shows steady progress toward the position for which you are applying. If you have little employment experience, or if your strengths can be placed effectively in categories, a **functional resume** may be a desirable alternative.

The functional resume emphasizes experience, skills, and accomplishments, rather than a straight progression of increasingly responsible positions. In a functional resume, you can be selective, including only skills, experiences, and achievements relevant to the position sought.

A functional resume should include dates of employment, school attendance, and activities. Personal information, educational background, and references are formatted as in traditional chronological resumes.[1]

INSTRUCTIONS

1. Start a new publication with .75" left and right margins and .5" top and bottom margins.
2. Position a horizontal ruler guide at .75".
3. Import the template file **RESUME3** so that the text begins just below the .75" horizontal ruler guide.
4. Save the file; name it **RESUMMC.**
5. Set all the text to serif 10-point with a 1" left indent and a .5" right indent.
6. Create and apply a style for the name and address information at the top and the headings of sans serif 10-point with a .5" indent.
7. Create a double-line box (border) to frame the margins.
8. Draw double horizontal lines to the right of each side heading, extending each to the right border. You could set the lines as a paragraph rule but, in this case, drawing them might be easier.
9. Re-save the file.
10. Using all printer defaults, print one copy.
11. Close the file.

[1]This discussion of functional resumes was adapted from Jerry Robinson et al., *Century 21 Keyboarding & Information Processing* (Cincinnati: South-Western Publishing Co., 1997), p. 517.

Exercise 85

Functional Resume

MARY C. CAVALE
87 Pine Street
Washington, DC 20019-0084
(202) 555-8374

SKILLS AND EXPERIENCE SUMMARY

Part-time employment and participation in school activities that enabled me to write for a wide variety of purposes, write individually and as part of a team, manage deadlines and prioritize important tasks, and work with and on behalf of others.

EDUCATION

Will graduate from Georgetown University in June 1997, with a bachelor of arts degree in English.

WRITING SKILLS

Wrote copy for advertisements for print, radio, and television media for 17 corporate clients in an intensive internship and a summer job at major advertising agencies. Worked as a member of a team to write a market research report.

Wrote and edited news releases for three Georgetown University student organizations.

Obtained Gold Key Certificate in Writing from Georgetown University for academic writing.

ORGANIZATIONAL SKILLS

Planned, coordinated, and oversaw the activities of 15 counselors in a camp for preschool children.

Regularly prioritized tasks and wrote important copy under deadline pressure for senior copywriters at two major advertising agencies.

COMPUTER EXPERIENCE

Skilled in operating word processing, page layout, and draw programs.

WORK EXPERIENCE

Bransford Advertising, Summer Intern (Summer 1996)
Henricks Advertising, Copy Assistant (Summer 1995)
Camp Swanee, Senior Counselor (Summer 1994)

EXTRACURRICULAR ACTIVITIES

English Society, President (1996-present)
Sigma Delta Sorority, Member (1994-present)
Symphonic Band, Member (1993-present)

REFERENCES

References available upon request.

The text, objects, and spacing in this exercise have been reduced because of space constraints.

Learning Objectives

Format a resume

Desktop Techniques Applied

Set custom columns
Import a text file
Reset a tab
Cut and paste text
Align text baseline to baseline

INSTRUCTIONS

1. Start a new publication with .75" margins.
2. Set up two columns with a .167" gutter.
3. Adjust the column guides so that the left column is 1.5" wide.
4. Import the template file **RESUME4** in the *right* column at the 2.5" mark on the vertical ruler.
5. Save the file; name it **RESUMMP.**
6. Cut the name and address information, and drag-paste it at the top margin, extending from the left margin to the right.
7. Set "MANUEL ANTONIO PINERO" to sans serif 13-point.
8. Set the first letter of his first, middle, and last names to bold.
9. Set the remaining heading text to sans serif 11/18.
10. Draw (or draw and copy, or set as paragraph rules) 4-point horizontal lines extending from the beginning to the end of the longest line in the heading as shown. The example uses paragraph rules with a 2.23" left and right indent, .125" between the rule and the baseline, and .25" between the top rule and the name baseline.
11. Set all body text to serif 11-point with a tab at 2.5".
12. Cut each heading and paste it in the left column. Align the headings baseline to baseline with the appropriate text as shown.
13. Re-save the file.
14. Using all printer defaults, print one copy.
15. Close the file.

EXERCISE
86

Exercise 86

MANUEL ANTONIO PINERO

46 Hill Tower Road

Morris Plains, NJ 07950

(201) 555-9856

SKILLS AND EXPERIENCE SUMMARY:	Part-time supervisory and sales jobs, as well as leadership positions in school activities, that taught me to interact well with others, communicate effectively in person and on the telephone, and manage money and other resources responsibly.
EDUCATION:	Will graduate from Union High School in June 1997.
INTERPERSONAL SKILLS:	Supervised a staff of ten lifeguards, including evaluating them and working with them on their performance. Persuaded prospective buyers over the telephone to purchase newspapers and other publications. Made sales successfully in both English and Spanish. Was required to make six sales in one three-hour shift. Serve as Representative to the Student Council. Currently working as a member of a team to produce a bilingual welcoming handbook for new students.
ORGANIZATIONAL SKILLS:	Successfully managed school, personal, and work schedule to attain a GPA of 3.94 and a class rank of 9th in a class of 300. Earned membership in the National Honor Society, a National Merit Letter of Commendation, and Garden State Distinguished Scholar status. Was voted Student Athlete of the Year. Participate in three student organizations, including leadership roles in two. Work part-time during the school year.
EMPLOYMENT:	National Newspaper Sales Company, Salesperson (Summer 1996-present) Morris Plains Township, New Jersey, Assistant Pool Manager (Summers, 1994 and 1995)
SPECIAL SKILLS:	Familiar with word processing and database software on both PCs and mainframe computers; fluent in Spanish.
SCHOOL ACTIVITIES:	Swimming Team, Member (1994-present) Student Council, Representative (1995-present) *Guardsman* (school newspaper), Editor (1996-present)
REFERENCES:	Mr. Alan Crenski, Coach Union High School 14 Front Street Morris Plains, NJ 07933-2231 (201) 555-1432 Ms. Valerie Swenson, Principal Union High School 14 Front Street Morris Plains, NJ 07933-2231 (201) 555-1476

The text, objects, and spacing in this exercise have been reduced because of space constraints.

EXERCISE 87

Learning Objectives

Format a resume

Desktop Techniques Applied

Import a text file
Change the font and width of text
Create styles based on text
Format text with a paragraph rule
Draw a filled box

INSTRUCTIONS

1. Start a new publication with 2" left and right margins and .75" top and bottom margins.
2. Position horizontal ruler guides at 1" and 1.25".
3. Import the template file **RESUME5** just below the 1.25" horizontal ruler guide.
4. Save the file; name it **RESUMPB.**
5. Select all the text and change it to sans serif with 120% width.
6. Set the name and address text at the top to 11/14.
7. Set "PAMELA TRICIA BLANE" to 15/14, replace the spaces between the words with em spaces, and force-justify the line.
8. Select all the text below the heading and set it to 10/12.
9. Add a paragraph hairline rule to the first heading, extending from the left to the right margin. Create a style based on the heading, and apply it to the other headings. If you do not have a paragraph rule feature, draw the rules.
10. Indent the first paragraph under "EDUCATION" .5". Then create a style based on the text and apply it to the rest of the resume body text.
11. Create a rectangle with no line and solid fill at the top of the page. Its borders should be the top, left, and right margins and the horizontal ruler guide at 1".
12. Re-save the file.
13. Using all printer defaults, print one copy.
14. Close the file.

Design Pointers/Hints

- Because the design has wide margins, this resume appears "full" despite the student's limited experience.

EXERCISE 87

Exercise 87

PAMELA TRICIA BLANE
201 West 79th Street
New York, NY 10010-8794
(212) 555-8686

EDUCATION

Senior at Stuyvesant High School
High School Diploma, pending graduation
Major: Physics
Grade Point Average: 3.85; upper 10% of class

SCHOOL ACTIVITIES

Editor of *Spectator* (student magazine), 1996-present.

Member of *National Honor Society*, 1997.

Westinghouse Scholarship Participant, national third-place winner, 1995.

Creator of *Connections*, online newsletter connecting specialized science and math high schools nationwide, 1996.

Captain, varsity volleyball team, 1996-present.

WORK EXPERIENCE

Office Assistant, G & G Investments, New York, NY, summer 1996. Managed appointments, correspondence, and special assignments for ten brokers.

Sales Assistant, RPI Sportswear, New York, NY, summer 1995. Sold apparel, worked cash register, and set up displays.

REFERENCES

Ms. Shirley Dembo, Assistant Principal
Stuyvesant High School
West Street
New York, NY 10009-5439
(212) 555-9420

Mr. Alan Carlson, Vice President
G & G Investments
65 Wall Street
New York, NY 10008-2020
(212) 555-4000

The text, objects, and spacing in this exercise have been reduced because of space constraints.

Learning Objectives

Format an invitation

Desktop Techniques Applied

Draw shapes with fills
Draw lines
Key text in different fonts
Import a graphic file
Use ruler guides to align text

INSTRUCTIONS

1. Start a new publication with landscape (wide) orientation, 3.5" left and right margins, and .75" top and bottom margins..
2. Position vertical ruler guides at 1", 3.75", 7.25", and 10". Position horizontal ruler guides at .25, 2", 2.5", 4.5", and 8.25".
3. Create a box with a 1-point line and 20% shade to frame the margins.
4. Create a paper-shaded oval with a 1-point line between the vertical ruler guides at 3.75" and 7.25" and between the horizontal ruler guides at .25" and 8.25".
5. Draw two 4-point lines that extend from the 1" to the 10" vertical ruler guides. Place one on the 2" horizontal ruler guide and one on the 4.5" horizontal ruler guide. Send the rules to the back as shown.
6. Key the "NEW YORK CITY" text in 12/20 serif small caps at the 1" vertical ruler guide and just under the 2.5" horizontal ruler guide. Double-space between the seminar information and the name of the restaurant. Use bold as shown.
7. Key the "WASHINGTON, DC" text right-aligned at the 10" vertical ruler guide, following the same procedures as in Step 6.
8. Place a ruler guide under one line of text in the "NEW YORK CITY" text block so the text sits on it. Move the "WASHINGTON, DC" text block straight up or down until the corresponding line of text sits on the same ruler guide.
9. Key the body of the invitation in serif small caps 14/25, center-aligned. Use italic for the "Food Specialties" line as shown. Double-space before "Invite You" and "Food Specialties." Key six returns where the graphic will appear.
10. Import an appropriate graphic. Re-size it, if necessary, and place it above the R.S.V.P. information. Add or delete returns as needed.
11. Save the file; name it **TASTE.**
12. Using all printer defaults, print one copy.
13. Close the file.

Design Pointers/Hints

- Typefaces have their own personalities. Select a typeface (if you have a variety from which to choose) that best suits the message being communicated.

EXERCISE 88

Exercise 88

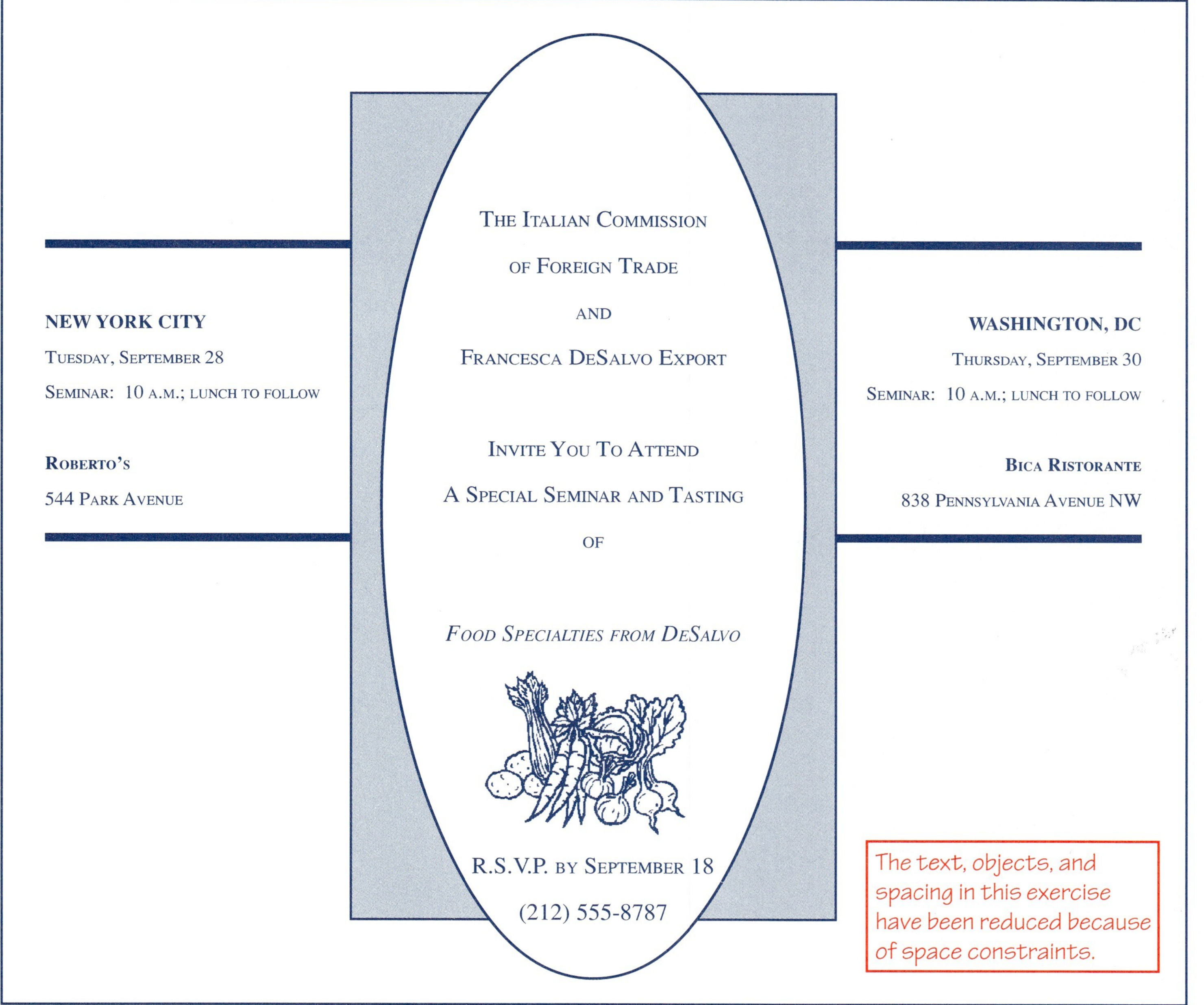

NEW YORK CITY
Tuesday, September 28
Seminar: 10 a.m.; lunch to follow
Roberto's
544 Park Avenue
The Italian Commission
of Foreign Trade
and
Francesca DeSalvo Export
Invite You To Attend
A Special Seminar and Tasting
of
Food Specialties from DeSalvo
R.S.V.P. by September 18
(212) 555-8787
WASHINGTON, DC
Thursday, September 30
Seminar: 10 a.m.; lunch to follow
Bica Ristorante
838 Pennsylvania Avenue NW

The text, objects, and spacing in this exercise have been reduced because of space constraints.

Learning Objectives

Format an invitation

Desktop Techniques Applied

Use a custom page size
Key text in different fonts
Copy objects between files
Re-size drawn objects
Use copy and paste features

INSTRUCTIONS

1. Start a new 5" wide x 7" long publication with .25" margins.
2. Position horizontal ruler guides at 1.75", 3.5," and 5.5".
3. Key the word "PARTY" below the top margin using sans serif 36-point bold with .15" after, and force-justify the text.
4. Key the rest of the invitation text using serif 14/14.5, center-aligned. Return twice between lines of text where shown. For "SIXTEENTH BIRTHDAY," set left and right indents of .5", key an em space between the two words instead of a regular space, and force-justify the text. Note that "SIXTEENTH BIRTHDAY" is bold.
5. Save the file; name it **JAIME.** (Do not exit.)
6. Open the data file **PAUL** and copy one of the candles. Place it at the left and bottom margins. Change the base of the candle to 20% gray with no line. Re-size the candle to be .25" wide and to reach to the horizontal ruler guide at 1.75" as shown. You may want to re-size the candle as a group, if you have that option; or you may want to adjust the parts separately.
7. *If you have a multiple paste feature with offset,* paste one copy of the candle at the right margin (the example uses a horizontal offset of 4.25"). Paste another copy of the first candle .5" to the right of the first candle (the example uses a horizontal offset of .75"). Re-size that copy as shown. Then paste a copy of the second, re-sized candle 2.5" to its right (the example uses a horizontal offset of 2.75"). Finally, paste another copy of the second candle 1" to its right (the example uses a horizontal offset of 1.25"). Re-size that candle as shown.

   If you do not have these features, draw vertical ruler guides at .5", 1.25", 2.5" and 4". Copy the first candle, and paste two copies, one whose right side is aligned with the vertical ruler guide at 1.25", and one whose right side is aligned with the right margin (the base of all candles should be flush with the bottom margin). Re-size the second candle as shown. Copy that candle, and paste two copies whose right sides are aligned with the vertical ruler guides at 2.5" and 4". Re-size the third candle as shown.
8. Re-save the file.
9. Using all printer defaults, print one copy.
10. Close the file.

EXERCISE 89

Exercise 89

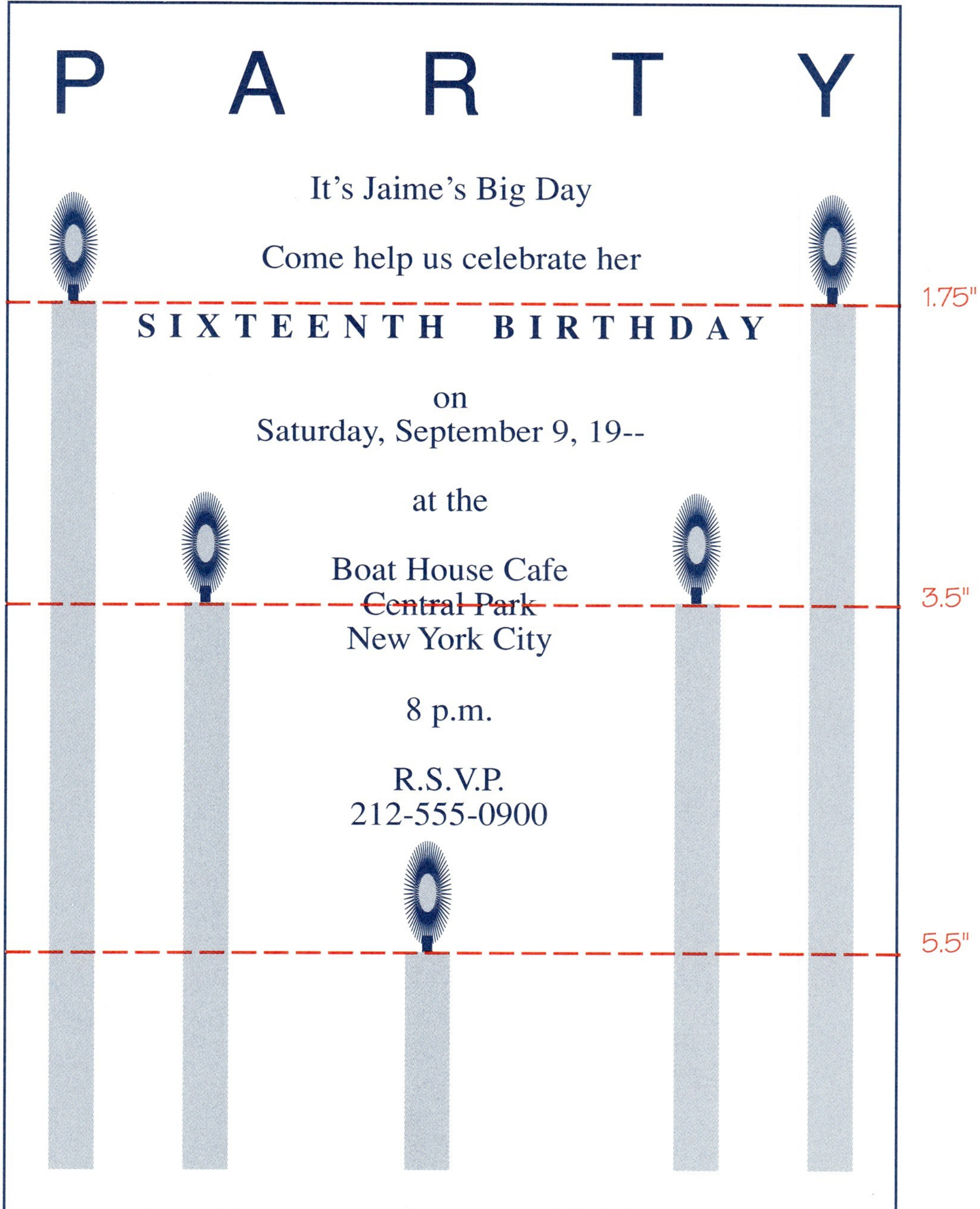

P A R T Y
It's Jaime's Big Day
Come help us celebrate her
SIXTEENTH BIRTHDAY
on
Saturday, September 9, 19--
at the
Boat House Cafe
Central Park
New York City
8 p.m.
R.S.V.P.
212-555-0900
1.75"
3.5"
5.5"

Learning Objectives

Format an invitation

Desktop Techniques Applied

Use a custom page size
Use landscape orientation
Set tracking and character width
Create raised caps
Force-justify text

INSTRUCTIONS

1. Start a new one-page publication, 7" wide x 6" long, with landscape (wide) orientation and .25" margins.
2. Position vertical ruler guides at 1", 3.75", and 4.25" and horizontal ruler guides at 1.75" and 2.5".
3. Create a double-line box to frame the margins.
4. Key "Voyages" just below the top margin in serif 72/74 bold, with very loose tracking and a character width of 130%, if available.
5. Draw a 1-point line at 1.5" on the vertical ruler, extending from the left to the right margin. The line should not cross through the double line border you created in Step 3, but should stop at the inside border.
6. Key the invitation text to the right of the 4.25" vertical ruler guide and just below the 1.75" horizontal ruler guide in a 9/22 script or serif italic font.
7. Import an appropriate graphic. Re-size it, if necessary, and place it between the ruler guides as shown.
8. Just below the graphic and between the ruler guides at 1" and 3.75", key "Travel Consultants, Inc." Use a 14/21 serif font, with en spaces rather than spaces between the words.
9. Set the initial capitals in "Travel Consultants, Inc." to 18-point bold.
10. Force-justify "Travel Consultants, Inc."
11. Save the file; name it **SAIL.**
12. Using all printer defaults, print one copy.
13. Close the file.

EXERCISE

90

Exercise 90

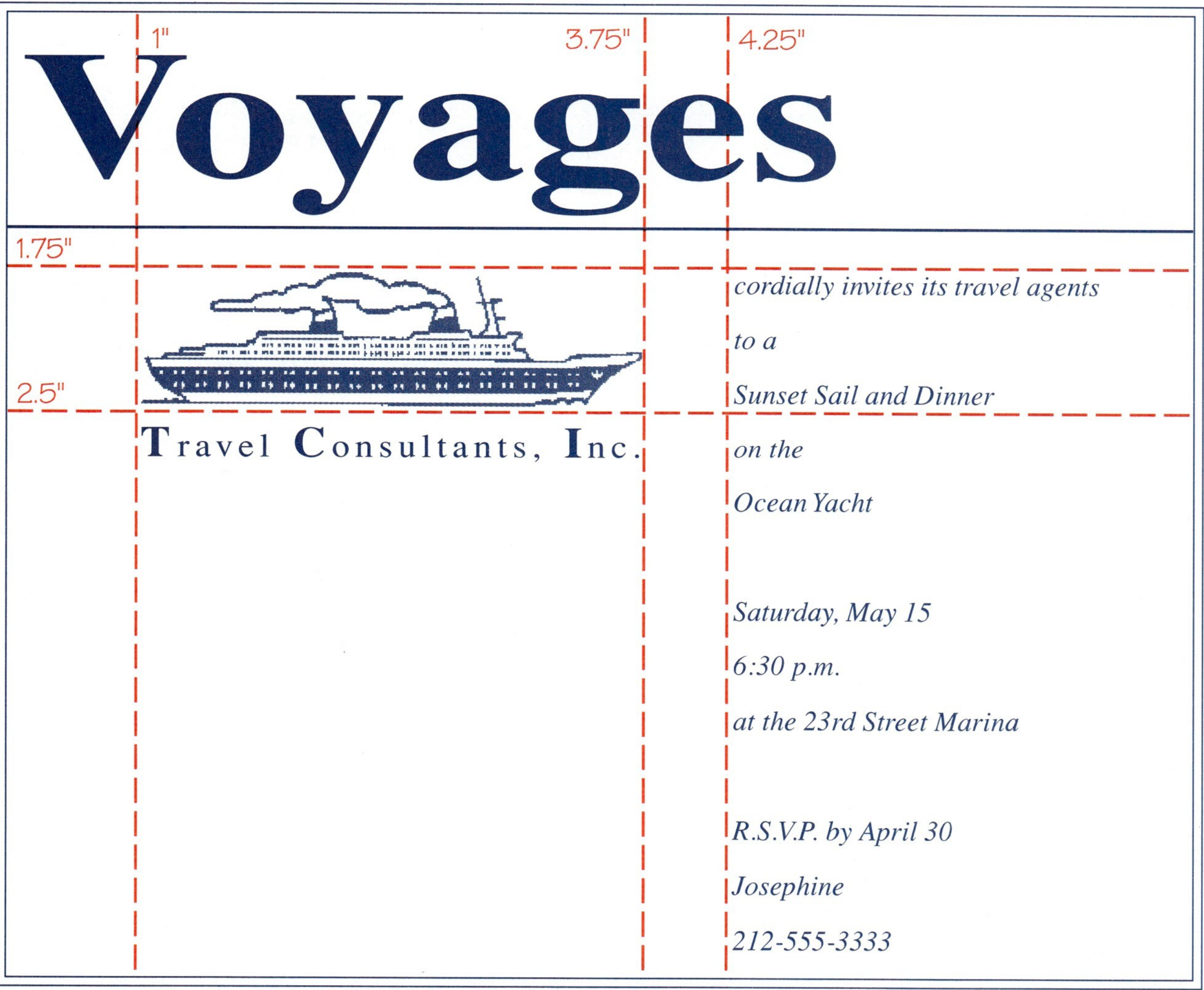

1"
3.75"
4.25"
Voyages
1.75"
2.5"
Travel Consultants, Inc.
cordially invites its travel agents
to a
Sunset Sail and Dinner
on the
Ocean Yacht
Saturday, May 15
6:30 p.m.
at the 23rd Street Marina
R.S.V.P. by April 30
Josephine
212-555-3333

Learning Objectives

Format an announcement

Desktop Techniques Applied

Use a custom page size
Key text in different fonts
Force-justify text
Draw a filled rectangle and square
Copy and paste objects

Concepts

An **announcement** publicizes an event, occasion, or happening. In business, an announcement may be sent to clients, customers, or staff publicizing the opening of a new office, the promotion of a staff member, or a merger with another company. Announcements might be sent to family and friends telling of a professional achievement (like becoming a doctor, lawyer, or partner in a company), the engagement of a child, or the birth of a baby.

An announcement tends to be a formal communication. Use a typeface that conveys this kind of message. Announcements are usually printed on cards that are smaller than the standard 8.5" x 11" paper size.

The text of an announcement, like that of an invitation, is usually centered horizontally and vertically on the page. Other formats may be used, however. As in an invitation, bold, italics, and spacing techniques may be used to emphasize text.

INSTRUCTIONS

1. Start a new publication 5" wide by 7" long with a 2" left margin and all other margins 0".
2. Position vertical ruler guides at .5" and 4.5" and a horizontal ruler guide at 1".
3. Key the company name at the .5" vertical ruler guide and below the 1" horizontal ruler guide, in serif 14/14.5 bold.
4. On the next line, key "Attorneys-at-Law" in serif small caps 10/12.
5. Stretch the text block to the 3.5" mark on the horizontal ruler and force-justify the text.
6. Begin a new text block for the text of the announcement. Key the first three lines in serif 12/14 italic, double-spaced. Quadruple-space after the last of the three lines.
7. Key the address and telephone information in serif 14/16 bold, except for the telephone and facsimile numbers, which should be normal. Quadruple-space after the last number.
8. Key the last line ("Effective September 1, 19--") in serif 12/14 italic.
9. Create a solid-fill rectangle 1/8" high just above the 1" horizontal ruler guide and extending between the vertical ruler guides.
10. Create a small paper-filled square with no line (not larger than the height of the rectangle). Place it on the rectangle. Align the top of the square with the top of the rectangle.
11. Copy the square and paste copies .5" inch apart across the rectangle. You may use a multiple paste option with offset, an align and distribute option, or ruler guides.
12. Copy the rectangle and square together and paste a copy at the left margin, above the address information. Center the rectangle and square vertically between the two blocks of information.
13. In the copied rectangle, delete all the squares but the first. Shorten the rectangle as shown.
14. Adjust the square on the copy so it is aligned in the middle of the rectangle rather than at the top. The square should be centered both horizontally and vertically in the rectangle.
15. Copy the rectangle and square you finalized in Step 14 and place the copy at the left margin, centered vertically between the facsimile number and date as shown.
16. Save the file; name it **TELL.**
17. Using all printer defaults, print one copy.
18. Close the file.

EXERCISE 91

Exercise 91

JOHNSON & HICKS
ATTORNEYS-AT-LAW

is pleased to announce

the relocation of

its office to

1301 South Grand Avenue
Los Angeles, CA 90071-2111

Telephone
(213) 555-7777

Facsimile
(213) 555-7779

Effective September 1, 19--

Announcement

Learning Objectives

Format an announcement

Desktop Techniques Applied

Use a custom page size
Format text in different fonts
Draw boxes with fills
Change the alignment of text
Choose an appropriate symbol

INSTRUCTIONS

1. Create a new publication 5" wide x 7" long with .25" margins.
2. Position vertical ruler guides at 1" and 4" and horizontal ruler guides at .5", 1", and 6".
3. Create a box with no line to frame the margins; shade it 60% gray.
4. Create a box with no line to frame the center of the announcement between the vertical ruler guides at 1" and 4" and the horizontal ruler guides at 1" and 6"; fill it white (paper).
5. Key the company name at the 1" vertical ruler guide in sans serif 14-point bold reverse. Move the text block straight up or down so that it is centered between the horizontal ruler guides at .5" and 1".
6. Key the text of the announcement in serif 12/14 small caps, center-aligned. Double-space between sections. Where the diamond symbols appear in the final copy at the right (Step 11), key any four characters for now. Set names in bold/italic.
7. Set the last three lines of the announcement to serif 10-point italic, normal case (not small caps).
8. Move the announcement text block straight up or down to center it vertically in the paper-filled box.
9. Key the address and phone information in sans serif 10/auto bold reverse, right-aligned at the 4" vertical ruler guide. Move the text block straight up or down so that it is centered in the gray area.
10. Create a white rectangle (no border) above the company name.
11. Choose an appropriate symbol from a symbol typeface to create a separator line between announcement parts as illustrated. (If a symbol typeface is unavailable, create short 2-point lines instead.)
12. Save the file; name it **JOIN.**
13. Using all printer defaults, print one copy.
14. Close the file.

Design Pointers/Hints

- Remember, typefaces have their own personalities. Since the message in this exercise announces lawyers' promotions, the selected typeface should convey a message of dignity and distinction.

EXERCISE 92

Exercise 92

SIMON & ZAHEB

Is Pleased To Announce That

Ray D. Sutherland

Has Become a Partner
in the Firm

and

Carolee Haddad

Has Become an Associate
With the Firm

They will continue to represent clients in matters of Real Estate, Bankruptcy, and Litigation.

**1650 Pennsylvania Ave., N.W.
Washington, DC 20008-4743
(202) 555-0899
FAX (202) 555-6634**

Learning Objectives

Format an announcement

Place graphic elements and adjust spacing attractively

Desktop Techniques Applied

Use a custom page size

Draw a box with rounded corners

Format text in different fonts

Set tracking and character width

Add graphic elements to text

INSTRUCTIONS

1. Start a new publication, 5" wide by 7" long, with a 1" left margin and the other margins .75".
2. Position horizontal ruler guides at .75" and 4.5". Position vertical ruler guides at .5" and 6.5".
3. Draw a 1-point rectangle with rounded corners, using the ruler guides you just set as the borders.
4. Key the word "joy" in sans serif 130-point bold, with very loose tracking and spacing set at 125%, if available, aligned at the right margin.
5. Key the invitation text in a 9/22 italic serif font.
6. Use a graphic or symbol from a symbol typeface for the beginning of each line of serif text. Add color and/or adjust the image control, if appropriate and if the result is attractive. If you are using a graphic, re-size it, if necessary, and set it as an inline graphic followed by an en space, if possible. Otherwise, you can paste copies of the graphic using a multiple paste feature with offset or an align and distribute option, if available. You can also use ruler guides to align the text. In any case, use an attractive amount of space between the graphic or symbol and the following text. The example uses a graphic with lightness and contrast set to 50% and placed as an inline graphic. An en space separates the graphic from the text.
7. Arrange the two text blocks as shown.
8. Save the file; name it **ENGAGE.**
9. Using all printer defaults, print one copy.
10. Close the file.

EXERCISE 93

Exercise 93

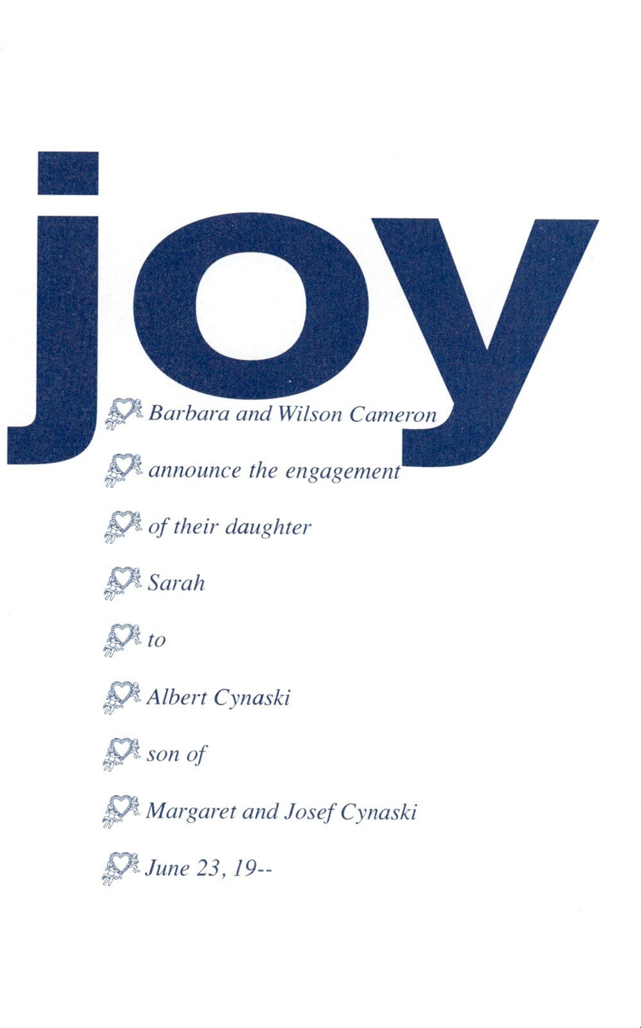

joy
Barbara and Wilson Cameron
announce the engagement
of their daughter
Sarah
to
Albert Cynaski
son of
Margaret and Josef Cynaski
June 23, 19--

EXERCISE 94

Learning Objectives

Format a flyer

Desktop Techniques Applied

Rotate text
Format text in different fonts
Add space after text
Add bullets
Reset tabs
Draw shapes with fills

INSTRUCTIONS

1. Start a new publication with a 2.25" left margin, a 1" right margin, a 2.25" top margin, and a .75" bottom margin.
2. Position horizontal ruler guides at 3/4", 1", 1 1/2", 2", 2 1/4", 2 1/2", and 4 1/2".
3. Position vertical ruler guides at 2 1/8", 2 1/4", 5 3/4", 6", 7", and 7 1/2".
4. Draw a 1-point box to frame the margins.
5. Key the text "MOVING?" in sans serif 72-point bold.
6. Make the text block 8" long and force-justify the text.
7. Rotate the text block and place it so that the "M" is flush with the bottom margin and the text sits on the vertical ruler guide at 2 1/8".
8. Import the template file **MOVE**.
9. Save the file; name it **MOVES.**
10. Select all the text except "MOVING?" and change it to sans serif 14/auto with .125" left and right indents.
11. Set "RE-LO-CATE" to 59/auto.
12. Set "Moving and Storage, inc." to 20/auto with .5" after. Replace the spaces between words with em spaces, and force-justify the line.
13. Insert .25" after the paragraph ending "the Moving Business."
14. Insert desktop publishing software bullets as shown.
15. Reset tabs to 1.5" and 1.75" for the bulleted items.
16. Insert .35" after the last bulleted item.
17. Set the last four lines to 18-point.
18. Adjust the text block so "RE-LO-CATE" sits on the horizontal ruler guide at 4 1/2".

    Note: The snap to guides feature may be helpful for the rest of the steps.
19. To create the top of the truck trailer, draw a rectangle with 60% shade and a 1-point line whose borders are the horizontal ruler guides at 3/4" and 2" and the vertical ruler guides at 2 1/4" and 5 3/4".
20. To create the bottom of the trailer, draw a rectangle with solid fill below the rectangle you just drew whose borders are the horizontal ruler guides at 2" and 2 1/4" and the vertical ruler guides at 2 1/4" and 5 3/4".
21. Drag across the top of the trailer to create a text block. Choose sans serif 59-point bold reverse, center alignment, and key "R."

    Center the text block on the trailer top.
22. Draw a rectangle with solid fill whose borders are the horizontal ruler guides at 1 1/2" and 2 1/4", the right side of the trailer, and the vertical ruler guide at 7 1/2."
23. To create the cab, draw a rectangle with 60% shade and a 1-point line whose borders are the horizontal ruler guides at 1" and 2 1/4" and the vertical ruler guides at 6" and 7".
24. Draw rectangles with a 1-point line and paper fill for the window and door in the cab.
25. To create a wheel, draw a circle .5" in diameter with a 1-point line and 60% shade. Draw a smaller circle with solid fill and place it in the larger circle.
26. Place the wheel at the front of the truck as shown. All wheels should sit on the horizontal ruler guide at 2.5".
27. Copy the wheel (grouping the two circles beforehand would be helpful, if you have that option) and place the copies as shown.
28. Re-save the file.
29. Using all printer defaults, print one copy.
30. Close the file.

EXERCISE 94

Exercise 94

The text, objects, and spacing in this exercise have been reduced because of space constraints.

MOVING?

RE-LO-CATE

Moving and Storage, Inc.

More than 100,000 satisfied customers are familiar with our moving trucks. They're gray with a white "R" on the panel. You see them all over town. And for good reason—the gray truck with the white "R" has come to stand for Excellence in the Moving Business.

- Low, Low Cost
- Last-Minute Moving
- Local and Long-Distance
- Office Relocations
- Large and Small Moves
- Coast-to-Coast Trips
- Senior Citizen Discounts

Call
1-800-555-7777
for a free estimate...and your assurance of a successful move

Learning Objectives

Format a flyer

Place and size graphics attractively

Desktop Techniques Applied

Draw a rectangle

Import text and graphics files

Set text in different fonts

Add space after text

Use the reflect option

INSTRUCTIONS

1. Start a new publication with 2.5" left and right margins, a 1" top margin, and a .75" bottom margin.
2. Set horizontal ruler guides at 2" and 10.25". Set vertical ruler guides at .25" and 8.25".
3. Create a double-line box to frame the margins.
4. Import the template file **GARDEN.**
5. Save the file; name it **GARDENS.**
6. Set all the text to a serif typeface.
7. Set the type size, leading, and spacing as follows:
   - "GREEN THUMB GARDEN CENTER" to 18/17, with .35" after "GARDEN CENTER."
   - "Announces...its annual springtime" to 22/20, with .75" after "springtime."
   - "FLOWER SALE" to 48/40, with .5" after "SALE."
   - The remaining text to 12/14, with .25" left and right indents.
8. Center the text block vertically between the top and bottom margins.
9. Import an appropriate graphic for the top left corner of the flyer (re-size it, if necessary). Place copies of the graphic in the other three corners. Use a mirrored copy for the top and bottom right corners, as in the example, if your software has a reflect option and if the result is attractive.
10. Import another graphic. Re-size it, if necessary, to fit between the vertical ruler guide at .25" and the left border of the flyer (it should not touch the double border). Move and re-size the graphic as necessary until you consider it placed attractively. Then paste a copy of the graphic in the same location on the right side of the page. Again, use a mirrored copy, if your software has a reflect option and if the result is attractive.
11. Re-save the file.
12. Using all printer defaults, print one copy.
13. Close the file.

Design Pointers/Hints

- Flyers should be designed to gain immediate attention. The information in the flyer should be clear and concise.

EXERCISE

95

The text, objects, and spacing in this exercise have been reduced because of space constraints.

Exercise 95

GREEN THUMB GARDEN CENTER

Announces....
its annual
springtime

FLOWER SALE

It's that time of year again to beautify your garden with irises, lilacs, roses, begonias, lilies, geraniums, petunias, or daisies. We have them all.

We also carry a large selection of herbs, shrubs, and small trees.

Arrangements for Every Occasion
Free Garden Layout Consultations
Full Line of Baskets and Vases

All major credit cards accepted.

456 Tenth Avenue
West of 23rd Street
New Haven

203-555-8888

Learning Objectives

Format a flyer

Desktop Techniques Applied

Create a star
Rotate an object and text
Import a graphic file
Place multiple copies of graphics
Adjust the lightness of an image

INSTRUCTIONS

1. Start a new publication with .75" margins.
2. Place vertical ruler guides at 1 3/4" and 7 1/4". Place horizontal ruler guides at 7/8", 3 5/8", 4 1/8", 4 3/8", 7 3/4", 8 1/8", and 8 5/8".
3. Create a polygon with a 2-point line and set it as a star as shown. You may need to stretch the star to get the shape you need. If you do not have a polygon feature with star inset, use an oval.
4. Key the text in the star in sans serif 30/auto bold, center-aligned.
5. Rotate the star and text as shown.
6. Place, re-size (if appropriate), copy, and paste copies of a graphic to the lower right of the star as appropriate. The example uses multiple paste with a horizontal offset of .5".
7. Drag to create a text block framed by the horizontal ruler guides at 3 5/8" and 7 3/4" and the vertical ruler guides at 1 3/4" and 7 1/4". Key the first two paragraphs in sans serif 18/24. Double-space between the paragraphs. Key the address text in sans serif 14/auto bold. Right-align the time and phone number text as shown.
8. Draw a dashed box beginning at 8" on the vertical ruler and extending to the bottom, left, and right margins for the coupons. Draw a dashed line at 4 1/4" on the horizontal ruler to divide the coupon.
9. Draw a box with no line and 60% shade, framed by the vertical ruler guides at 7/8" and 4 1/8" and the horizontal ruler guides at 8 1/8" and 8 5/8". Key "DOORBUSTERS" in sans serif 24/auto, bold, reverse, and center-aligned. Align the text block vertically as well as horizontally in the shaded box.
10. Key the rest of the coupon text as a separate text block in sans serif 14/auto bold, center-aligned. Center the text vertically as well as horizontally.
11. Place as shown the same graphic you used in Step 6, adjusted to 75% lightness and 50% contrast and re-sized if necessary.
12. Copy the completed coupon to the right (the left border of the shaded box should be the vertical ruler guide at 4 3/8"); change "$50" to "$100" and "$100" to "$250." Make sure the two coupons are aligned horizontally.
13. Draw 4-point lines across the top margin and down the left and right margins as far as the coupons.
14. Save the file; name it **FURNISH.**
15. Using all printer defaults, print one copy.
16. Close the file.

EXERCISE
96

Exercise 96

The text, objects, and spacing in this exercise have been reduced because of space constraints.

Spectacular
July 4th Savings!

Don't miss out on our spectacular Fourth of July sale this weekend only at Fabulous Furniture! Living rooms, dinettes, bedrooms—all are on sale, at 40%, 60%, even 70% off our regular low, low prices!

Doors open at 8 a.m. July 3rd, 4th, and 5th for this special sale event! Use the Doorbusters savings coupons below to save even more money!

Fabulous Furniture
14 Cross Street
San Francisco, CA 94102-8836

Open 8 a.m. - 10 p.m.
555-1982

DOORBUSTERS

Save $50
on any purchase over $150

Fabulous Furniture
July 3, 4, 5, 19--

DOORBUSTERS

Save $100
on any purchase over $250

Fabulous Furniture
July 3, 4, 5, 19--

Learning Objectives

Learn advertisement format

Format an advertisement

Desktop Techniques Applied

Set image lightness and contrast

Key text in different fonts

Set a left indent

Draw rules and boxes with fills

Use copy and paste features

Concepts

Advertisements for newsletters, newspapers, magazines, and other publications are often created on the desktop. Advertisements can vary in size from a few inches to an entire page. Advertisements are designed to draw attention to a product or service, to describe and promote it in a few well-chosen words. Advertisements use graphics and text effectively in creating and sustaining a mood.

This design was adapted from an advertisement that appeared in the *Hopkins News-Letter* of Johns Hopkins University, Vol. LXXXIV, No. XXIV, April 18, 1980, p. 13, created by the newspaper's advertising staff.

INSTRUCTIONS

1. Start a new publication with 1.875" left and right margins and 2" top and bottom margins.
2. Place horizontal ruler guides at 2.5" and 7.25".
3. Draw a border as shown to frame the margins.
4. Import a graphic for the upper left corner, as shown. Set it to 75% lightness and 50% contrast.
5. Drag a text block from the top and left margins to the right margin and down to about to the 5" mark on the vertical ruler.
6. Key the first line in serif 12/auto bold, with a .25" left indent. Adjust it so that it sits on the horizontal ruler guide at 2.5". Return three times.
7. Key the next two lines in sans serif 14/auto bold, with no left indent, center-aligned. Return three times.
8. Key "NOTORIOUS" in sans serif 24/auto bold, center-aligned.
9. Key the next line in serif 10/auto bold, center-aligned. Return twice.
10. Key "and" in sans serif 14/auto bold, center-aligned.
11. Draw the staircase using the line tool. Lines should be 1-point; text should be sans serif 24/auto bold. A good method would be to prepare one or two steps, complete with text, and then copy and paste other steps, changing the text after copying.
12. Arrange the completed staircase attractively on the page, as shown. A grouping option would be helpful.
13. Drag a new text block from the left margin and from about 7.25" on the vertical ruler to the right and bottom margins.
14. Key the date, time, location, and admission information in serif 14/ auto bold, center-aligned. Adjust the text block if necessary so that the first line sits on the horizontal ruler guide at 7.25". After the "Admission" line, return twice.
15. Key the last two lines in sans serif 14/auto bold, center-aligned.
16. Draw a box with no line and solid fill to frame the last two lines.
17. Set the last two lines to reverse.
18. Save the file; name it **MOVIES.**
19. Using all printer defaults, print one copy.
20. Close the file.

EXERCISE
97

Exercise 97

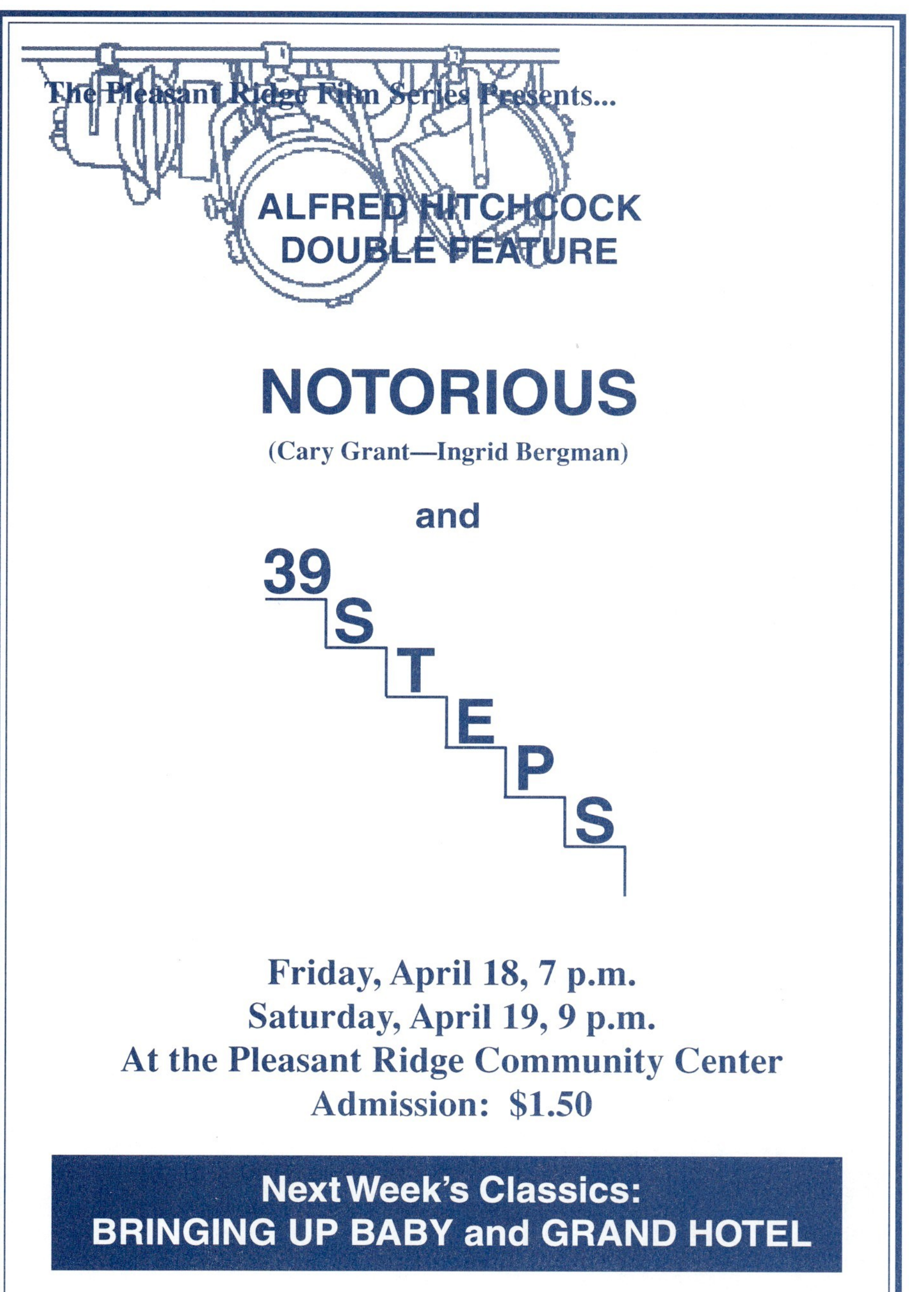

Advertisement

Learning Objectives

Format an advertisement

Desktop Techniques Applied

Drag to create text blocks
Key text in different fonts
Key text with tabs and bullets
Apply color to text and graphics
Set image lightness and contrast

INSTRUCTIONS

1. Start a new publication with 1.625" left and right margins and 3.125" top and bottom margins.
2. Place vertical ruler guides .25" in from the left and right margins.
3. Draw a border with a 4-point line and rounded corners as shown to frame the margins.
4. Import an appropriate graphic for the top of the page, as shown. Re-size it, if necessary. The graphic should extend from the left to the right ruler guide.
5. Key the company name and address text in a sans serif typeface as shown. In the example, the first line is set in 18-point bold/italic with .18" after. The second line is set in 12-point bold. Use en spaces between words and between words and the bullet. (Use a desktop publishing software bullet.) Force-justify both lines.
6. Drag to create a text block stretching from ruler guide to ruler guide. Key the telephone number in sans serif 36-point bold, red, center-aligned.
7. Drag to create another text block stretching from ruler guide to ruler guide. Key the bulleted text in sans serif 11/auto with a left indent of .25", a tab at 2.406", and an em space between each bullet and the text that follows. Choose an appropriate symbol from a symbol typeface for the bullet, or use the desktop publishing software bullet. Set the bullets to red.
8. Import an appropriate graphic to appear behind the bulleted text. Re-size it, if necessary, and set the lightness to 75% and the contrast to 50%.
9. Import an appropriate graphic for the bottom of the page. Re-size it, if necessary.
10. Save the file; name it **LIMO.**
11. Using all printer defaults, print one copy.
12. Close the file.

EXERCISE 98

Exercise 98

Classic Limousine Service
1423 Amity Drive • Orlando, FL 32651-4956
555-0322
Airport service
Birthdays
Weddings
Anniversaries
Nights on the town
Convention services
Gift certificates
Uniformed chauffeurs
Fully licensed and insured
Color TVs
Cellular phones
National reservations
Corporate rates
24-hour service

Learning Objectives

Learn brochure format
Format a brochure

Desktop Techniques Applied

Use landscape orientation
Set text in columns
Kern text
Create a raised cap
Rotate text
Draw rules and boxes with fills

Concepts

A **brochure** is a small pamphlet that provides information about a product or product line, a place, a service, an event, or a schedule. Some brochures are printed on 8 1/2" by 11" paper and folded in thirds or in half. Other brochures use a custom paper size. Brochures can vary from expensively produced booklets using color and high-quality paper, printing, and design, to inexpensive folded pamphlets created with desktop publishing software.

The brochures in this book will be printed on standard 8 1/2" by 11" paper. The first page of this exercise is the inside of the brochure; the second page is the outside page. These two pages will ultimately be printed back to back and folded in thirds.

INSTRUCTIONS

1. Start a new three-page publication with landscape (wide) orientation, .25" left and right margins, and .5" top and bottom margins.
2. On the master page, create three columns with a .5" gutter.
3. On the master page, position a horizontal ruler guide at .75".
4. On page 1 (Panels 2, 3 and 4), draw dashed lines as shown sitting on the top and bottom margin guides for each column. A snap to guides option will be helpful in this step and the steps that follow.
5. Import the template file **CAREER** so that text in each column begins just below the .75" horizontal ruler guide.
6. Save the file; name it **CAREERS.**
7. Cut the beginning information through the dates. Paste it on page 2 in the last panel. This information will be part of the front cover.
8. Go back to page 1 and cut the first three paragraphs. Paste that information in the first panel on page 2 (Panel 5).
9. Go back to page 1 and cut all the registration information at the end of the story, beginning with the title of the conference. Paste that information on page 3.
10. Go back to page 1. Select all the text and set it in serif 11/14.
11. Go through the story on page 1, making the following changes:
    - Set each of the 12 seminar numbers (e.g., CC-01) in sans serif. (If you have a character style feature, create a style and apply it.)
    - Set "CONFERENCE HIGHLIGHTS/Saturday" and "CONFERENCE HIGHLIGHTS/Sunday" to sans serif 13-point.
    - Create a style for conference titles of sans serif 12-point with no hyphenation and apply it.
    - Check for violations of the rules of hyphenation.
12. Align the first lines of each column and the last lines of the first two columns baseline to baseline. Adjust the text as necessary to align it. The third column may be short.

continued on page 194

EXERCISE
99

Exercise 99

CONFERENCE HIGHLIGHTS
Saturday

Careers in Environmental Services
Saturday, 9:00 a.m. **CC-01**
Career opportunities are available in waste management, pollution control, and recycling. Panelists include representatives from major consulting firms as well as industry leaders.

Interviewing Techniques
Saturday, 9:00 a.m. **CC-02**
Resumes may get you the interview, but interviews get you the job. This workshop covers appropriate attire, effective responses to commonly asked questions, and highlighting your strengths.

Actors' Workshop: Getting the Job
Saturday, 10:30 a.m. **CC-03**
This workshop gives you information on how to increase the odds of landing jobs. Topics include: acting jobs—where to find them; casting executives—who they are and what to do; and dramatics classes—what to take to enhance your career.

Advertising: Basic Functions and Practices
Saturday, 11:00 a.m. **CC-04**
This workshop introduces participants to the fundamental practices of advertising and related areas. Topics include marketing and advertising, advertising's role in the economy, creativity in advertising, production, account services, and public relations. Educational background and career paths will also be discussed.

Panel 2

To Be A Teacher: Opportunities and Rewards
Saturday, 1:00 p.m. **CC-05**
Seven teachers with experience in public and private instruction at all levels will discuss the rewards of teaching, educational and licensing requirements, and career paths.

Career Options in Social Work
Saturday, 2:00 p.m. **CC-06**
Topics include kinds of jobs available, career planning, and educational and licensing requirements. This workshop will be taught by a licensed social worker from the Department of Child Services.

Nursing Careers
Saturday, 2:30 p.m. **CC-07**
Courses needed, career paths, and opportunities in this rewarding profession will be discussed. Guest speakers include two registered nurses from St. Luke's Medical Center.

CONFERENCE HIGHLIGHTS
Sunday

Careers in Computer Technology
Sunday, 9:00 a.m. **CC-08**
This seminar explores starting career positions in programming, data communications, and software development. Degree requirements, courses available, career paths, and options will be discussed. Guest speaker will be Mary Larsen, Professor of Information Systems at Whitmore College.

Panel 3

The Fashion Makers: Careers and Opportunities
Sunday, 10:00 a.m. **CC-09**
Meet, learn from, and question contemporary fashion designers. Guests include designers and officers of well-known apparel corporations.

Financial Analysis and Accounting Careers
Sunday, 11:30 a.m. **CC-10**
Topics include the role of the financial planner in today's economy, educational requirements, career paths, and opportunities in this exciting field. Discussion will include careers in auditing and accounting.

Starting a Career in Travel and Tourism
Sunday, 2:00 p.m. **CC-11**
This introduction to the exciting world of travel and tourism includes tour operations, travel agencies, and career paths. Guest speakers include Robin Jones, author of *A Complete Guide to the Travel and Tourism Industry.*

Hotel and Food Management
Sunday, 3:00 p.m. **CC-12**
This seminar will focus on careers in the hospitality fields, including certificate programs in hotel and motel management, food and beverage management, and hospitality accounting. This seminar will be taught by industry professionals with many years of teaching and business experience.

Panel 4

This is page 1 of the brochure.

continued on page 195

Brochure

The text, objects, and spacing in this exercise have been reduced because of space constraints.

INSTRUCTIONS continued from page 192

13. Go to page 2 (Panels 5 and 6 and the front cover).
14. Draw dashed lines as shown sitting on the top and bottom margin guides for Panel 5. Draw a dashed box around the borders of Panel 6 as shown. At the bottom and top, the border should sit on the margins, as in Panel 5.
15. For Panel 5, change the description text to serif 14/24 and the "W" in "Whether" to 36-point bold. If the space between the "W" and the rest of "Whether" looks excessive, kern the letters.
16. For Panel 5, adjust the text to begin just under the horizontal ruler guide at .75". Check for violations of the rules for hyphenation.
17. Go to page 3. Adjust the text block to 7" wide. The text block should not exceed 3" high. You may wish to set horizontal ruler guides at the top of the block and at 3" from the top to help you keep it within 3".
18. Set all the text to serif 10/auto. Set the first three lines to sans serif. Set the first line to 11-point; right-align the dates.
19. Add bullets, en spaces, and a .5-point paragraph or drawn rule to the second line as shown.
20. Add .1" after the lines that begin as follows: "Whitmore College," "Fees," "To register," "Telephone," "Enter the number," "Signature."
21. Add 1-point paragraph or drawn rules as shown. For paragraph rules, you will need to adjust the left indent for each line and set the rules to be flush with the baseline of the text (0" below the baseline).
22. Select the two "Method of payment" lines and reset the tabs. The example uses tabs set at 1.375", 1.625", 2.75", 3", 3.75", and 4".
23. For the same two lines, insert an appropriate character symbol for the check box. If you do not have a symbol, draw a 1-point line for each item to be checked.
24. Rotate the finished form as shown, cut it, and go to page 2. Paste the form in Panel 6. Center it vertically and horizontally.
25. Draw a box to frame the front cover panel, 60% gray with no line.
26. Cut the title and paste it in a different location.
27. Insert returns between text as shown (use two for the larger spaces).
28. Set the text to sans serif 14/auto reverse, with a 1.15" left indent.
29. Adjust the text block to begin just under the ruler guide at .75".
30. Draw 8-point reverse lines as shown. The lines should be vertically centered between the text, should be the same length, and should be as long as the longest line of text.
31. Set the title to serif 38/auto; width, 120%. Either set the line under it as a paragraph rule, or draw the line.
32. Rotate and place the title as shown.
33. Delete the third page.
34. Re-save the file.
35. Using all printer defaults, print one copy.
36. Close the file.

EXERCISE

99

Exercise 99 continued from page 193

Whether you are looking for your first job, changing careers, or deciding what to do next, the Whitmore Career Conference will help you focus your energies.

This two-day conference will include workshops and seminars on career options, career planning, and personal development, as well as programs of study to advance your career choices. Guest speakers from many professions will be available to answer your questions.

For registration information, see the back page of this brochure.

Panel 5

THE ROAD NOT TAKEN **10th Annual Career Conference** **September 8 and 9, 19—**

Whitmore College • 1438 Dice Street • New York, NY • 10007-9786

Fees: Per Seminar: $30. Entire Conference: $250.

To register by telephone, call (212) 555-7657 Monday through Friday, 9:30 a.m. to 7:00 p.m.

Name ____

Address ____

Telephone ____

Enter the number for each seminar (CC-XX): ____

Method of payment: ☐ Check (made payable to *The Road Not Taken*)

☐ Credit card: ☐ Omnex ☐ EarthCard

Card number: ____ Exp. Date: ____

Signature: ____

This form may be mailed to the address above or faxed to (212) 555-7658.

Panel 6

THE ROAD NOT TAKEN

10th Annual Career Conference

Whitmore College Main Building

Saturday and Sunday, September 8 and 9, 19—

Front cover

This is page 2 of the brochure.

Brochure

The text, objects, and spacing in this exercise have been reduced because of space constraints.

Learning Objectives

Format a brochure

Desktop Techniques Applied

Use landscape orientation
Set text in columns
Import text and graphics files
Change the font of text
Adjust the lightness of an image

INSTRUCTIONS

1. Start a new two-page publication with landscape (wide) orientation and 1" margins.
2. Create two columns with a .167" gutter on the first page and four columns with a .5" gutter on the second page.
3. On page 1, place a vertical ruler guide at 6.5".
4. Import the template file **COMPUTER** beginning at the top and left margins of Panel 1. In Panel 2, start text at 1.5" on the vertical ruler. In all other panels, text should begin at the top of each column.
5. Save the file; name it **COMPUTEX**.
6. Set all text to sans serif with auto leading.
7. Set the text that will appear in Panel 1 (see the illustration on page 197) in 10-point. Adjust the bottom windowshade handle so only that text appears in Panel 1.
8. Cut the "4" (in Panel 2) from "4 Service" and paste it outside existing text blocks. Set it to 150-point.
9. Insert a return between "SERVICE" and "COMPUTER," and "COMPUTER" and "INC." so that each word appears on its own line.
10. Set "SERVICE COMPUTER, INC." to 34-point with a 1.5" left indent.
11. Drag the "4" to the left of "SERVICE COMPUTER, INC." Align it as shown. The vertical line in the "4" should be just inside the vertical ruler guide at 6.5".
12. Set "THE COMPLETE COMPUTER FACILITY" to 12-point.
13. Set all remaining text in the story to 9-point.
14. Give the four lines from "TRAINING" through "COMPUTER USE/ RENTAL" a 1.5" left indent.
15. Create a rectangle with no line and solid fill around "TRAINING" as shown. The rectangle should extend from the vertical ruler guide at 6.5" to the right margin.
16. Place copies of the rectangle around the remaining services. The example uses a multiple paste feature with a vertical offset of .3".
17. Set each service title to reverse.
18. Import an appropriate graphic. Re-size it, if necessary, and place it slightly to the left of the vertical ruler guide at 6.5", aligned with the first rectangle.
19. Place copies of the graphic to the left of each rectangle as shown. The example uses a multiple paste feature with a vertical offset of .3".

continued on page 198

Design Pointers/Hints

- The first page of this exercise is the outside of the brochure; the second page is the inside. These two pages will ultimately be printed back to back and folded in half.

Exercise 100

Visit either of our locations:

EAST SIDE

399 EAST MAIN STREET
PROVIDENCE, RI 02903-1419
401-555-7666

WEST SIDE

7112 KELLY BOULEVARD
PROVIDENCE, RI 02904-1456
401-555-9977

THE COMPLETE COMPUTER FACILITY

At 4 SERVICE, we offer you the following services:

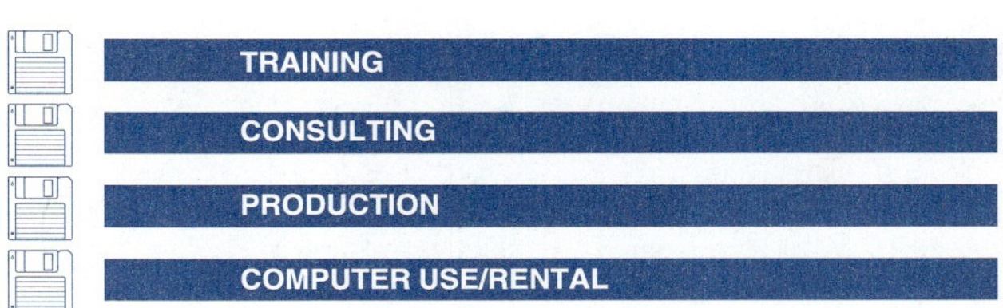

Stop in at either of our two locations. Our friendly, knowledgeable staff is ready to serve your every computer need.

Our services are described in detail inside this brochure.

Panel 1

Panel 2

This is page 1 of the brochure.

continued on page 199

The text, objects, and spacing in this exercise have been reduced because of space constraints.

INSTRUCTIONS

continued from page 196

20. Adjust the bottom windowshade handle in Panel 2 so that the panel includes only the text that appears in the illustration on page 197.

21. Go to page 2, and set the text to full justification.

22. Adjust the windowshade handles so that the appropriate text appears in each column as shown.

23. Draw a rectangle with solid fill and no line across the top of Column 1 in Panel 3 as shown.

24. Copy the rectangle to the other three columns.

25. Make the text of each heading reverse and center-aligned as shown.

26. Adjust the text block in the first column straight down slightly so that the text is centered vertically in the rectangle.

27. Using a ruler guide, align the text blocks in the other three columns so that the headings are even baseline to baseline.

28. Paste a copy of the same graphic used on page 1 next to "TRAINING" on page 2 as shown. Re-size the graphic, if necessary.

29. Paste additional copies of the graphic next to the other three headings. Use a ruler guide to align the graphics.

30. Import another appropriate graphic (the example uses a computer). Re-size it, if necessary, and place it as shown.

31. For the new graphic, set the lightness to 75% and the contrast to 50%.

32. Re-save the file.

33. Using all printer defaults, print one copy.

34. Close the file.

EXERCISE 100

Exercise 100 continued from page 197

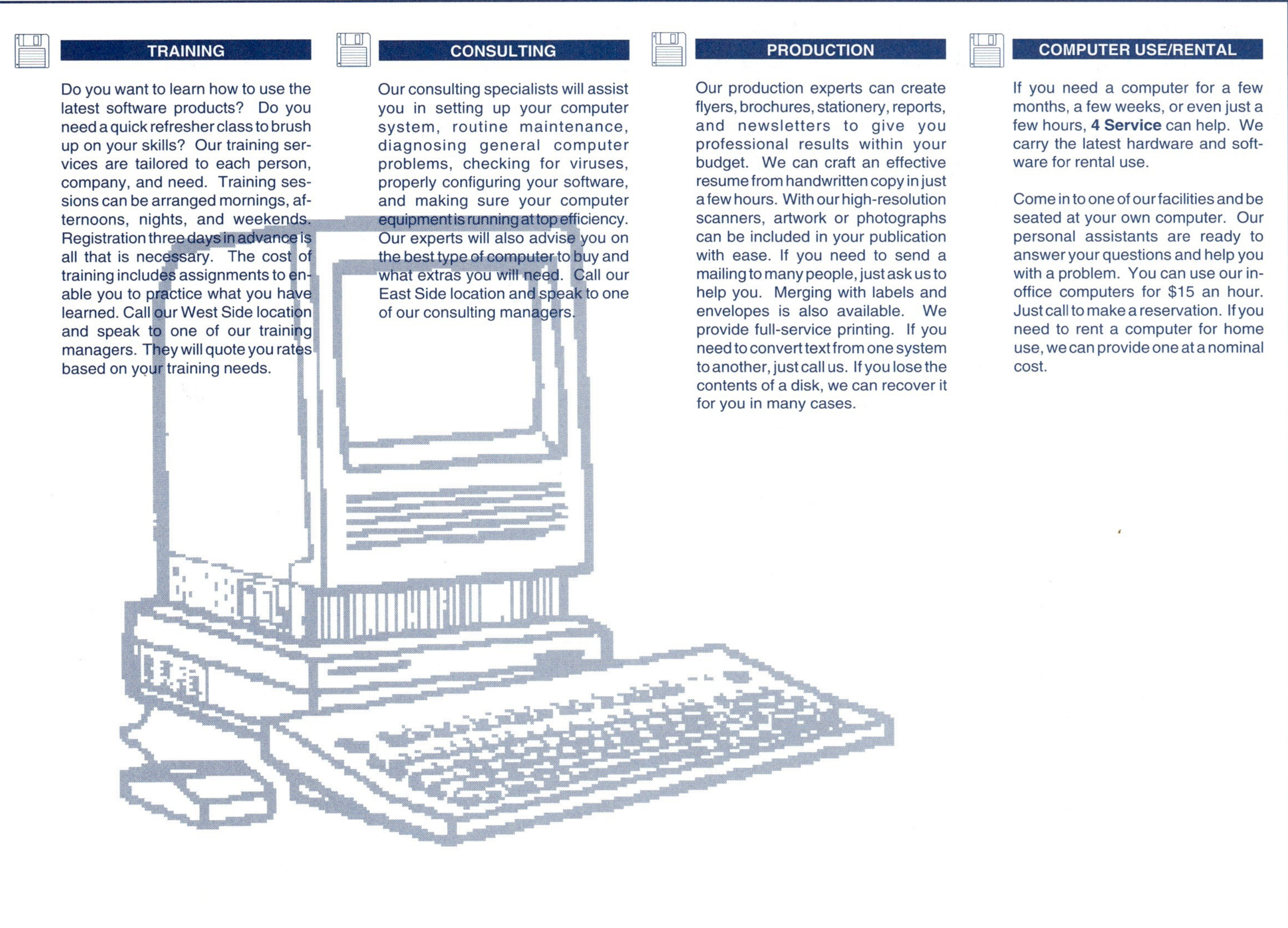

TRAINING

Do you want to learn how to use the latest software products? Do you need a quick refresher class to brush up on your skills? Our training services are tailored to each person, company, and need. Training sessions can be arranged mornings, afternoons, nights, and weekends. Registration three days in advance is all that is necessary. The cost of training includes assignments to enable you to practice what you have learned. Call our West Side location and speak to one of our training managers. They will quote you rates based on your training needs.

CONSULTING

Our consulting specialists will assist you in setting up your computer system, routine maintenance, diagnosing general computer problems, checking for viruses, properly configuring your software, and making sure your computer equipment is running at top efficiency. Our experts will also advise you on the best type of computer to buy and what extras you will need. Call our East Side location and speak to one of our consulting managers.

PRODUCTION

Our production experts can create flyers, brochures, stationery, reports, and newsletters to give you professional results within your budget. We can craft an effective resume from handwritten copy in just a few hours. With our high-resolution scanners, artwork or photographs can be included in your publication with ease. If you need to send a mailing to many people, just ask us to help you. Merging with labels and envelopes is also available. We provide full-service printing. If you need to convert text from one system to another, just call us. If you lose the contents of a disk, we can recover it for you in many cases.

COMPUTER USE/RENTAL

If you need a computer for a few months, a few weeks, or even just a few hours, **4 Service** can help. We carry the latest hardware and software for rental use.

Come in to one of our facilities and be seated at your own computer. Our personal assistants are ready to answer your questions and help you with a problem. You can use our in-office computers for $15 an hour. Just call to make a reservation. If you need to rent a computer for home use, we can provide one at a nominal cost.

Panel 3

Panel 4

This is page 2 of the brochure.

The text, objects, and spacing in this exercise have been reduced because of space constraints.

Learning Objectives

Learn about menu formatting
Format a menu

Desktop Techniques Applied

Use landscape orientation
Draw shapes with fills and rules
Import a text file
Set a right-aligned tab with leaders
Adjust the spacing of text

Concepts

Menus list food items and their prices. A restaurant's menu not only lists food items sold and their costs, but also creates an appeal and an image. Many companies create menus for corporate breakfasts and luncheons.

INSTRUCTIONS

1. Start a new two-page publication with landscape orientation and .5" margins.
2. On page 1, position vertical ruler guides at 7" and 9" and horizontal ruler guides at 1", 1 1/8", 1 1/4", 1 3/4", 1 7/8", 2", 2 5/8", 3 1/4", 3 3/8", 3 1/2", 4", 4 1/8", 4 1/4", 4 3/4", 4 7/8", 5", 5 5/8", 6 1/4", 6 3/8", 6 1/2", 7", 7 1/8", and 7 1/4".
3. If you have a snap to guides option, select it. It will be very helpful in the steps that follow.
4. Draw a box with solid fill to frame the left, top, and bottom margins, extending to the vertical ruler guide at 7".
5. To create the top black piano key, draw a rectangle with solid fill, the borders of which are the vertical ruler guides at 7" and 9" and the horizontal ruler guides at 1" and 1.25".
6. To create the other black piano keys, paste copies of the rectangle between the appropriate horizontal ruler guides as shown in the exercise.
7. To create the white piano keys, draw (or draw and copy) 1-point horizontal lines from the vertical ruler guide at 9" to the right margin and on the horizontal ruler guides at the following positions: 1 1/8", 1 7/8", 3 3/8", 4 1/8", 4 7/8", 6 3/8", and 7 1/8". Then draw two additional 1-point lines from the vertical ruler guide at 7" to the right margin and along the horizontal ruler guides at 2 5/8" and 5 5/8".
8. Save the file; name it **SYMPHONY.**
9. Drag a text block from about 3" to about 5.5" on the vertical ruler and extending between the vertical ruler guides at 7" and 9" (end the text block slightly short of the vertical ruler guide at 9"). Choose serif 12/auto bold reverse, right-aligned, and key, with a return between each word, THE SYMPHONY GRILL.
10. Select all the text you just keyed and add .55" after. Adjust the text block so that the text appears on the three black keys as shown.

continued on page 202

EXERCISE 101

Exercise 101

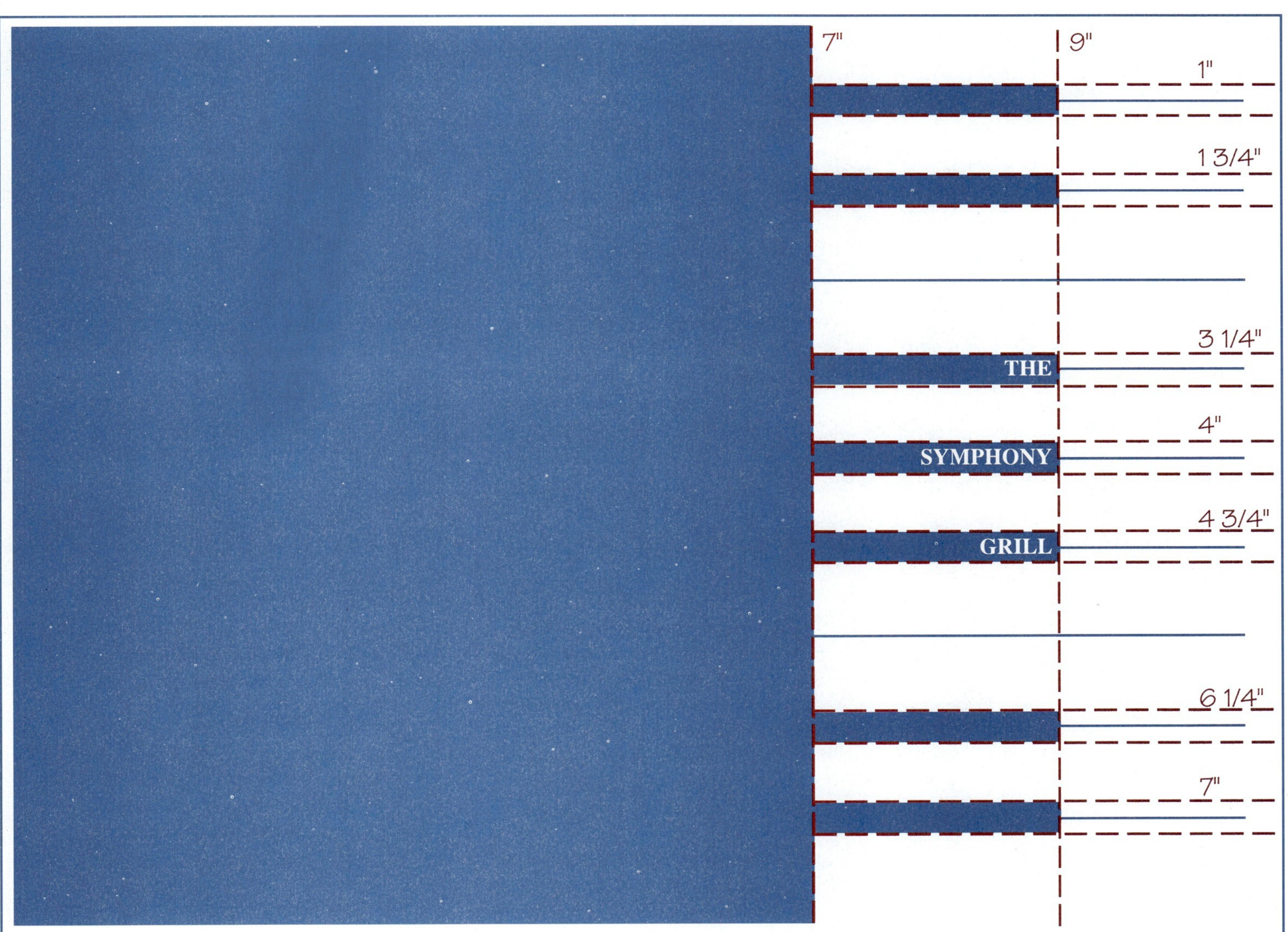

continued on page 203

This is page 1 of the menu.

Menu

The text, objects, and spacing in this exercise have been reduced because of space constraints.

EXERCISE 101

INSTRUCTIONS continued from page 200

11. Go to page 2 and create two columns with a .167" gutter.

12. Import the template file **SYMPH.**

13. Select all the text and set it to serif 10/15. Set a right-aligned tab with leaders for the prices. The example uses a tab at 4.906".

14. Insert additional space as necessary between the first two courses so that two courses appear in the left column and three in the right, with the first and last lines aligned baseline to baseline across the columns and the columns ending evenly, as shown. The example uses added space after "ROASTED WILD MUSHROOM PIZZA" of 1.47".

15. To create a scale, draw a hairline rule below the first course title, extending from one side of the column to the other. If you have a multiple paste feature with offset, copy the rule, and paste four copies with .05" vertical offset. If you do not have a multiple paste feature, change the measurement system on your vertical ruler to picas and, using ruler guides, paste 4 copies of the rule 3 points apart.

16. To create the musical note, if you have an option for grouping objects and re-sizing them as a group, open the data file **SHAPES1,** group the objects that comprise the musical note, and copy the group to **SYMPHONY.** Then re-size the group and place copies of the note on the scale.

    If you do not have a grouping option, create a musical note using the circle and line tools, copy it, and paste several copies on the scale.

17. Copy the completed scale and place it after each course title as shown. The scales at the top of the page should align across columns.

18. Re-save the file.

19. Using all printer defaults, print one copy.

20. Close the file.

EXERCISE 101

Exercise 101 continued from page 201

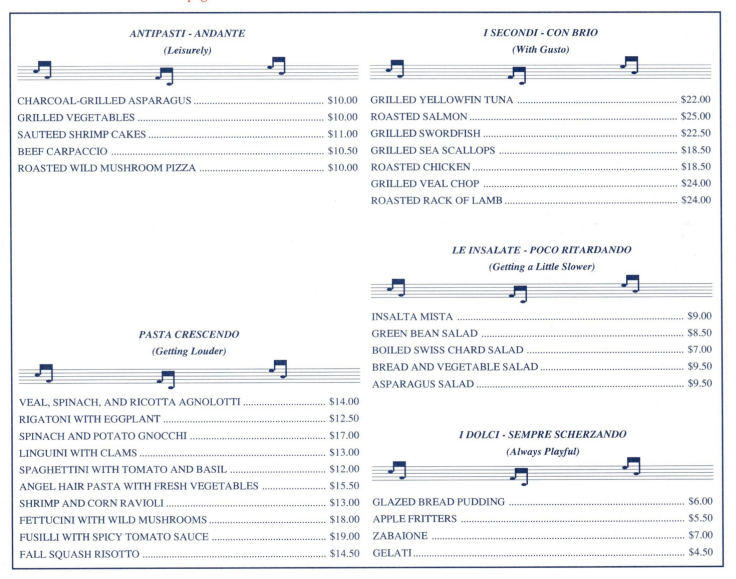

ANTIPASTI - ANDANTE

(Leisurely)

CHARCOAL-GRILLED ASPARAGUS	$10.00
GRILLED VEGETABLES	$10.00
SAUTEED SHRIMP CAKES	$11.00
BEEF CARPACCIO	$10.50
ROASTED WILD MUSHROOM PIZZA	$10.00

PASTA CRESCENDO

(Getting Louder)

VEAL, SPINACH, AND RICOTTA AGNOLOTTI	$14.00
RIGATONI WITH EGGPLANT	$12.50
SPINACH AND POTATO GNOCCHI	$17.00
LINGUINI WITH CLAMS	$13.00
SPAGHETTINI WITH TOMATO AND BASIL	$12.00
ANGEL HAIR PASTA WITH FRESH VEGETABLES	$15.50
SHRIMP AND CORN RAVIOLI	$13.00
FETTUCINI WITH WILD MUSHROOMS	$18.00
FUSILLI WITH SPICY TOMATO SAUCE	$19.00
FALL SQUASH RISOTTO	$14.50

I SECONDI - CON BRIO

(With Gusto)

GRILLED YELLOWFIN TUNA	$22.00
ROASTED SALMON	$25.00
GRILLED SWORDFISH	$22.50
GRILLED SEA SCALLOPS	$18.50
ROASTED CHICKEN	$18.50
GRILLED VEAL CHOP	$24.00
ROASTED RACK OF LAMB	$24.00

LE INSALATE - POCO RITARDANDO

(Getting a Little Slower)

INSALTA MISTA	$9.00
GREEN BEAN SALAD	$8.50
BOILED SWISS CHARD SALAD	$7.00
BREAD AND VEGETABLE SALAD	$9.50
ASPARAGUS SALAD	$9.50

I DOLCI - SEMPRE SCHERZANDO

(Always Playful)

GLAZED BREAD PUDDING	$6.00
APPLE FRITTERS	$5.50
ZABAIONE	$7.00
GELATI	$4.50

This is page 2 of the menu.

The text, objects, and spacing in this exercise have been reduced because of space constraints.

EXERCISE 102

Learning Objectives

Format a menu

Desktop Techniques Applied

Import text and graphics files
Use em spaces and en spaces
Force-justify text
Create a style based on text
Draw a filled box

INSTRUCTIONS

1. Start a new publication with .5" margins.
2. Position horizontal ruler guides at 2" and 2.25".
3. Import the template file **PALM.**
4. Save the file; name it **PALM1.**
5. Set the restaurant name to sans serif 14-point, replace the spaces between the words with em spaces, and force-justify the text.
6. Set the rest of the text to serif 9/18 italic.
7. Position vertical ruler guides to the left and right of the longest food item ("Vanilla Ice Cream with Hot Chocolate Mousse - $4.00").
8. Set "APPETIZERS" to sans serif 10-point with loose tracking (if available). If you have a paragraph rule feature, give the heading a .5-point rule below, with left and right indents so that the rule extends only as far as the vertical ruler guides you drew in Step 7. The example uses left and right indents of 2.4". If you do not have a paragraph rule feature, draw, copy, and paste copies of the rule after completing Step 11.
9. Create a style based on the "APPETIZERS" text and apply it to the other three course headings.
10. For each course heading, insert a small measured amount of space, such as a thin space, between each pair of letters. In the line listing the beverages, replace the spaces between "$2.50" and "Tea" and "$2.50" and "Soft Drinks" with an em space plus an en space.
11. Drag the text block down so the restaurant name is centered between the two horizontal ruler guides as shown.
12. Create a rectangle with solid fill to fit over the restaurant name, extending between the two horizontal ruler guides and from the left to the right margins.
13. Set the restaurant name to reverse.
14. Import a graphic that complements the restaurant title and place it above the word "PALM." Re-size it, if necessary.
15. Re-save the file.
16. Using all printer defaults, print one copy.
17. Close the file.

Design Pointers/Hints

- If a restaurant's menu changes daily, a master page might be created on which alterations could easily be made or new menu items added.
- The design of the menu sets the tone for the type of restaurant. If the restaurant is a contemporary one, you might use a sans serif typeface, which tends to have a more modern appeal. A serif typeface has a more formal look.

EXERCISE 102

Exercise 102

APPETIZERS

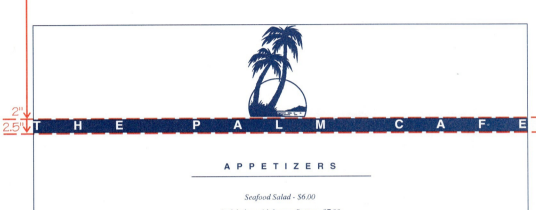

Seafood Salad - $6.00

Artichokes with Lemon Butter - $7.00

Melon wtih Prosciutto - $6.50

Carpaccio with Caper-Parsley Sauce - $7.50

Cold Sorrel Soup - $5.00

ENTREES

Red Snapper Baked in Parchment - $12.00

Filet of Sole Wrapped in Spinach - $11.00

Mussels with Pesto - $9.50

Crusty Mustard Chicken - $12.50

Pork Chops with Fennel - $13.00

Pan-Fried Filet of Beef - $17.00

DESSERTS

Cranberry Kuchen - $5.00

Express Sorbet - $3.00

Vanilla Ice Cream with Hot Chocolate Mousse - $4.00

Sour Cherry Clafouti - $5.00

BEVERAGES

Coffee - $2.50 *Tea - $2.50* *Soft Drinks - $2.50*

Ask to see our wine list.

The text, objects, and spacing in this exercise have been reduced because of space constraints.

Learning Objectives

Format a menu

Desktop Techniques Applied

Drag-place a text file
Reset a tab
Draw rules and shapes with fills
Use copy and paste features
Import and re-size graphics

INSTRUCTIONS

1. Start a new publication with .5" margins.
2. Position vertical ruler guides at 2", 2.25", and 4.5" and horizontal ruler guides at 1" and 2.5".
3. Drag-place the template file **SUNSET** beginning at the 2.25" vertical ruler guide and the 2.5" horizontal ruler guide. Drag down to the right and bottom margins.
4. Save the file; name it **SUNSETS.**
5. Set all the text to sans serif 9/auto with a tab at 2.5" (clear all other tabs).
6. Set the title to 14-point.
7. If necessary, adjust the text block so the title is just under the 2.5" horizontal ruler guide.

TO CREATE THE DESIGN AT THE TOP OF THE MENU:

8. Draw a rectangle with no line and solid fill, the borders of which are the top, left, and right margins and the horizontal ruler guide at 1".
9. Draw a 4-point line from the left to the right margin 1/8" below the black rectangle.
10. Either copy the line and paste two copies with a vertical offset of .125", or draw two lines 1/8" below the previous one, 1/8" apart. The first line should be 2-point; the second, 1-point.
11. Either copy the bottom line and paste two copies with a vertical offset of .25", or draw two lines 1/4" below the previous one, 1/4" apart. The first line should be 1-point; the second, .5-point.
12. Either copy the bottom line and paste two copies with a vertical offset of .5", or draw two lines 1/2" below the previous one, 1/2" apart. Both should be hairlines. The last line should be below the title.
13. Import a graphic relating to a desert or southwest theme. Place and re-size the graphic five times to appear as shown in the exercise. You may find ruler guides and a magnified view helpful.
14. Create a white circle with no border (to represent the setting sun) on the black "horizon" as shown in the exercise.
15. Draw vertical dotted lines on the 2" and 4.5" vertical ruler guides, extending from the top of the menu items to the bottom margin.
16. Re-save the file.
17. Using all printer defaults, print one copy.
18. Close the file.

EXERCISE

103

Exercise 103

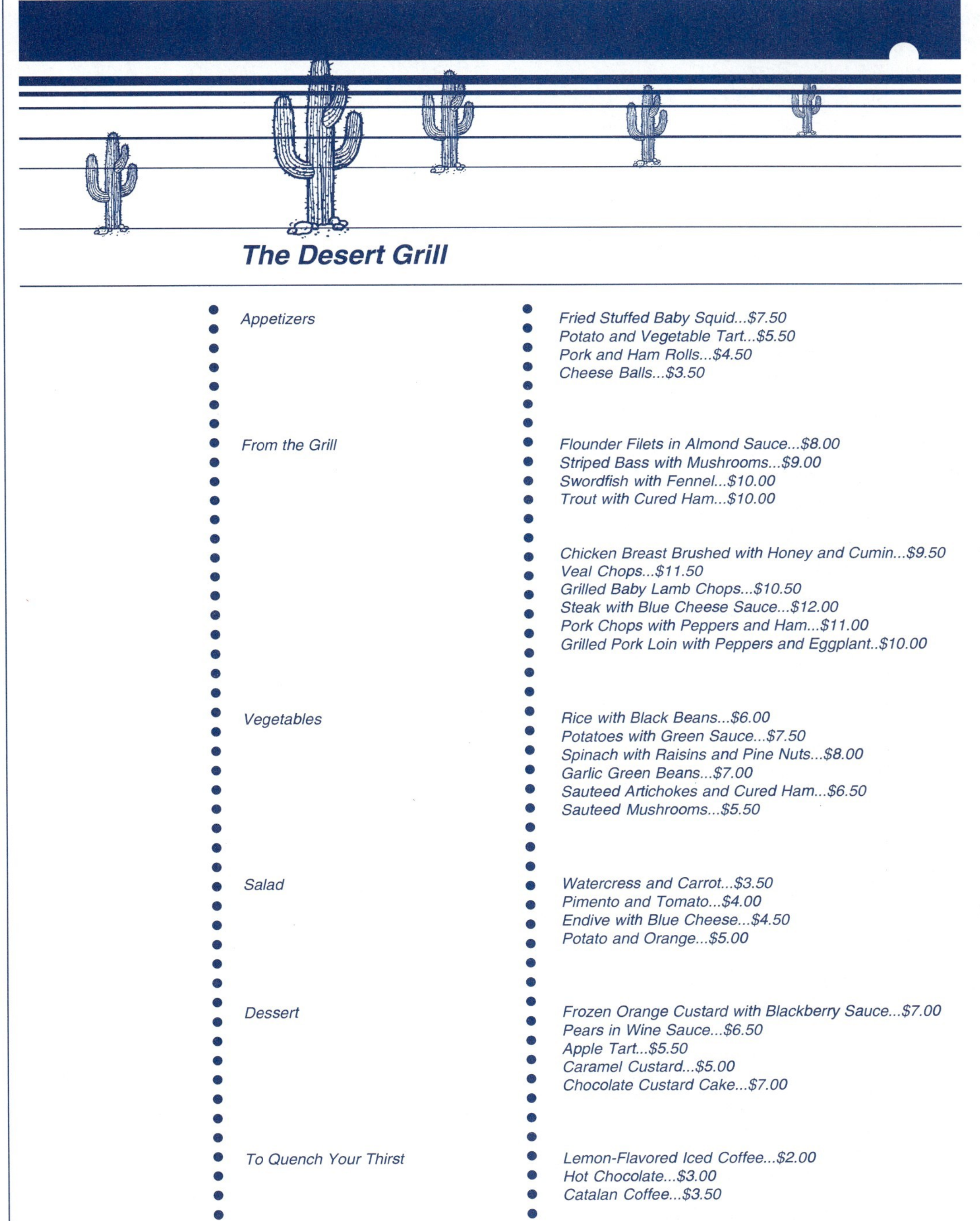

The Desert Grill

Appetizers

Fried Stuffed Baby Squid...$7.50
Potato and Vegetable Tart...$5.50
Pork and Ham Rolls...$4.50
Cheese Balls...$3.50

From the Grill

Flounder Filets in Almond Sauce...$8.00
Striped Bass with Mushrooms...$9.00
Swordfish with Fennel...$10.00
Trout with Cured Ham...$10.00

Chicken Breast Brushed with Honey and Cumin...$9.50
Veal Chops...$11.50
Grilled Baby Lamb Chops...$10.50
Steak with Blue Cheese Sauce...$12.00
Pork Chops with Peppers and Ham...$11.00
Grilled Pork Loin with Peppers and Eggplant..$10.00

Vegetables

Rice with Black Beans...$6.00
Potatoes with Green Sauce...$7.50
Spinach with Raisins and Pine Nuts...$8.00
Garlic Green Beans...$7.00
Sauteed Artichokes and Cured Ham...$6.50
Sauteed Mushrooms...$5.50

Salad

Watercress and Carrot...$3.50
Pimento and Tomato...$4.00
Endive with Blue Cheese...$4.50
Potato and Orange...$5.00

Dessert

Frozen Orange Custard with Blackberry Sauce...$7.00
Pears in Wine Sauce...$6.50
Apple Tart...$5.50
Caramel Custard...$5.00
Chocolate Custard Cake...$7.00

To Quench Your Thirst

Lemon-Flavored Iced Coffee...$2.00
Hot Chocolate...$3.00
Catalan Coffee...$3.50

The text, objects, and spacing in this exercise have been reduced because of space constraints.

Learning Objectives

Learn newsletter format
Format a newsletter

Desktop Techniques Applied

Set up columns
Draw rules and boxes with fills
Import text and graphics files
Change the font of text
Adjust the spacing of text

Concepts

A **newsletter** is a communication that allows people who share a common interest to exchange ideas, developments, and information on a regular basis. In some organizations, newsletters are prepared weekly, while other organizations distribute them monthly, bimonthly, quarterly, or semiannually. Some newsletters are distributed within an organization or to customers. Some people subscribe to organizations and pay to receive their newsletter.

Newsletters are used by business organizations and educational institutions to make announcements and to deliver messages about new products, promotions, and achievements.

Formatting of newsletters vary. Most, however, have the following features:

- **Masthead** or **nameplate**—may include the newsletter's title, the intended audience, the division or organization publishing the document, the volume and/or issue number, and the date of the issue.
- **Contents**—lists the articles or topics featured in the issue.
- **Headlines**—indicate the contents of the articles.
- **Body copy**—comprises the text of the articles.

INSTRUCTIONS

1. Start a new publication with .75" left and right margins, a 2.5" top margin, and a 1" bottom margin.
2. Position vertical ruler guides at the left and right margins (.75" and 7.75") and horizontal ruler guides at 1", 2", and 2.25".
3. Create two columns with a .167" gutter.
4. Draw a .5-point vertical line in the middle of the gutter (4.25" on the horizontal ruler) that extends from the top to the bottom margin.
5. Draw 1-point horizontal lines at the 1" and 2.25" horizontal ruler guides, extending from one vertical ruler guide to the other.
6. Import the template file **CONEWS** beginning in the left column just below the top margin.
7. Save the file; name it **CONEWS1.**
8. Cut the masthead (date, title, and subtitle) and drag-place it above the top margin, extending from one vertical ruler guide to the other.
9. Set all text except the masthead to sans serif 12/13.
10. Set headings to 14/14 (you may wish to create and apply a style).
11. Import a sports graphic and place it below the "EMPLOYEE ACTIVITIES" heading as shown. Re-size the graphic, if necessary. Use text wrap or insert space around the graphic as appropriate.
12. Align the first and last lines of each column baseline to baseline. Adjust spacing, if necessary, so the columns end even with each other as shown.
13. In the masthead, set the date to sans serif 15/auto with very loose tracking.
14. Set "JOB TALK" to sans serif 55/auto with very loose tracking.
15. Set the next line to 18/auto; make the first five words small caps.
16. Adjust the text block, if necessary, so that the date is slightly above the horizontal ruler guide at 1".
17. Insert space before the line beginning "A Weekly Publication" so that it falls between the horizontal ruler guides at 2" and 2.25". The example uses .08".
18. Create a box around the date with no border; shade it 40% gray.
19. Set the date to reverse.
20. Import (and re-size, if necessary,) a clock or another appropriate office graphic to replace the "O" in "JOB." You can delete the "O" and place the file as an inline graphic or put a paper-filled box with no line over the "O" and place the graphic in the standard way.
21. Re-save the file.
22. Using all printer defaults, print one copy.
23. Close the file.

Exercise 104

Newsletter

August 16, 19—

JOB TALK

A WEEKLY PUBLICATION OF THE ABC INVESTMENT GROUP

MARKET OUTLOOK

Dollar Declines Against the Mark

In the past week, the dollar has fallen 2.9 percent against the Deutsche mark. The dollar's decline against other currencies has been less dramatic by comparison. The primary reason for this decline against German currency is the difference between United States and foreign interest rates. We expect that the dollar will continue to weaken and that the Deutsche mark and other continental currencies will strengthen further.

Economic Recovery Strengthening

While the economy is not yet showing signs of a recovery, we believe that recovery is just around the corner. Economic data on employment, retail sales, housing, production, and orders for equipment and goods are all showing positive growth. We feel that recovery will be slow, as in the past. In the first six months of 1970, the economic growth rate was 5.4 percent.

NEWSBRIEFS

Organizational Changes

Jonathan Stuart, Associate, Private Banking, has been transferred to Corporate Finance, Healthcare. He is now located on the 26th floor, Extension 4-7869.

David Washington has been appointed Vice President, Capital Markets. Mr. Washington comes to us from Davis, Cercer, & Howell. He is located on the 34th floor, Extension 4-9458.

Milestones

Pamela Blass, Vice President, Mergers and Acquisitions, celebrates 25 years with ABC Investment Group. Please join her at a breakfast celebration in the 9th floor conference room on Friday, September 6, at 8 a.m.

EMPLOYEE ACTIVITIES

Intramural Softball

Private Banking beat the Conquerors by forfeit. The Slammers beat the Knockouts 6-4. Current standings:

Conquerors (6-1)
Slammers (5-3)
Private Banking (4-4)
Knockouts (3-5)
Misfits (1-7)

Volunteer Day

Our annual Volunteer Day will be Wednesday, October 2. Join us at the Good Neighbors Community Center for a day of painting, cleanup, and other volunteer services. Contact Hector Benavides in Human Relations at Extension 4-1990.

The text, objects, and spacing in this exercise have been reduced because of space constraints.

Learning Objectives

Format a newsletter

Desktop Techniques Applied

Draw rules and boxes with fills
Import text and graphics files
Drag-paste text
Set tracking and character width
Adjust the spacing of text

Concepts

Newsletters can be one page or multiple pages. They range in size from the traditional 8 1/2" by 11" page size to tabloid 11" x 17" size.

INSTRUCTIONS

1. Start a new two-page publication with .75" margins.
2. Go to the master page, and set up two columns with a .167" gutter.
3. On the master page, position a horizontal ruler guide at 2".
4. On page 1, position a horizontal ruler guide at 1.5".
5. On page 1, draw a 6-point line along the top margin that extends from the left to the right margin.
6. Import the template file **ALUMNI** beginning on page 1 in the left column at the 4 3/8" mark on the vertical ruler. Place the remainder of the text in each column below the horizontal ruler guide at 2".
7. Save the file; name it **ALUMNI1.**
8. Set all the text to serif 12/auto.
9. Cut the masthead (title, subtitle, and date) and drag-place it in the area between the top margin and the horizontal ruler guide at 2", across both columns from the left margin to the right margin.
10. Set "WESTLAKE CLUB" to 45-point and the next line to 18-point.
11. For "Alumni Association Newsletter," set the tracking to very loose and the width to 130%, if available.
12. In the same line, right-align the date as shown.
13. Adjust the text block so that "WESTLAKE CLUB" sits on the horizontal ruler guide at 1.5" and the next line is slightly above the horizontal ruler guide at 2".
14. Set "Calendar of Upcoming Events" and each date to 14-point.
15. For the calendar, create a hanging indent of 1.5".
16. Set the text to be boxed in 11/auto with a .125" left and right indent and .083" after each paragraph.
17. Adjust the bottom windowshade handle in the left column so that that column contains only the calendar and the text to be boxed.
18. Adjust the text block in the right column so that it begins at 2.5" on the vertical ruler. Place a ruler guide under the last line of text in the column so that the text is sitting on the line.
19. Insert space before the material to be boxed so that, when the box is drawn, the bottom of the box will sit on the ruler guide you just drew. The example uses .2".
20. Draw the box; use a 1-point rule and 10% shade.
21. At the horizontal ruler guide at 2" and at the right side of Column 1 as shown, create a box 2" tall by 2" wide with a 6-point border. Draw a 6-point line from the left margin to the top border of the box.

continued on page 212

Exercise 105

WESTLAKE CLUB

Alumni Association Newsletter Fall 1997

THE PRESIDENT'S MESSAGE:

We are asking our fellow alums to help save our newsletter. Unless some loyal and generous friends of Westlake High School come forth to rescue us from fiscal crisis, we cannot publish again, as we simply do not have the resources. Each mailing costs more than $1,000 to distribute. Our dues and occasional contributions no longer cover costs.

We are appealing to our alumni to help us collect dues and volunteer their time to the production of our newsletter. We also need suggestions, recommendations, good wishes, and news of Westlakers, near and far; but most of all, we need $$$. To volunteer your time, call Janie Weston at 203-555-7574. We look forward to hearing from you.

Thomas Shaunessy

Calendar of Upcoming Events

NOVEMBER 15 ***Class of 1957 Reunion***

JANUARY 18 ***Retirement Party for Dr. Patterson***

APRIL 4 ***Westlake Concert Production***

JUNE 18 ***Class of 1973 Reunion***

The Westlake Club Alumni Association Newsletter
Volume 20, Number 3
Fall 1997
A publication for alumni of Westlake High School published four times a year.
Editor: Janie Weston
Contributing Writers: Gloria Barba, Alex Best-Hamilton, Betty Quinsey, Scott Rigby
Send your suggestions to the ***Westlake Club Alumni Association Newsletter,*** Westlake High School, 6 Forster Street, Bethel, CT 06829-1416.
E-mail address: weston@xwestlak.com

FORTHCOMING REUNIONS

Class of 1957

Members of Westlake Class of 1957 held a meeting at Janet Wilson's home to review plans for their 40-year reunion, to be held at MARNIE'S RESTAURANT in Bethel on November 15. The festivities will begin at 8 p.m. There will be a hot and cold buffet. The price is $40 per person. Entertainment will be provided by The Ed Mobley Big Band. If you have not yet reserved your place for this special event, contact one of the committee members listed below.

Dorothy Watson (203) 555-7575
Shirley Arnold (203) 555-3838

The text, objects, and spacing in this exercise have been reduced because of space constraints.

continued on page 213

EXERCISE 105

INSTRUCTIONS continued from page 210

22. Import an appropriate graphic; re-size it, if necessary; and place it in the box you just drew as shown.
23. Copy the graphic, with the box and line.
24. Go to page 2. Position horizontal ruler guides at 5/8" and 3 1/2" and a vertical ruler guide at the left margin (.75").
25. Key "page 2" in serif 10/auto on the horizontal ruler guide at 5/8" and at the vertical ruler guide.
26. Drag the text block in the second column down to begin below the 3.5" horizontal ruler guide.
27. Paste the graphic with the box and line so that the box is at the top of the right column but slightly to the left of the column guide as shown. The left border of the box should be in the gutter.
28. Extend the rule to the left margin as shown.
29. Adjust the text as necessary so that the two columns are even and aligned baseline to baseline at the bottom. You may adjust the right column to begin slightly above the ruler guide at 3.5" if necessary.
30. Re-save the file.
31. Using all printer defaults, print one copy.
32. Close the file.

Design Pointers/Hints

- You can save time in producing a newsletter by creating a template. Place repeating elements on master pages. Create a style sheet. Use dummy text files and graphics placeholders. For each new issue, simply replace the text and graphics with the new material.

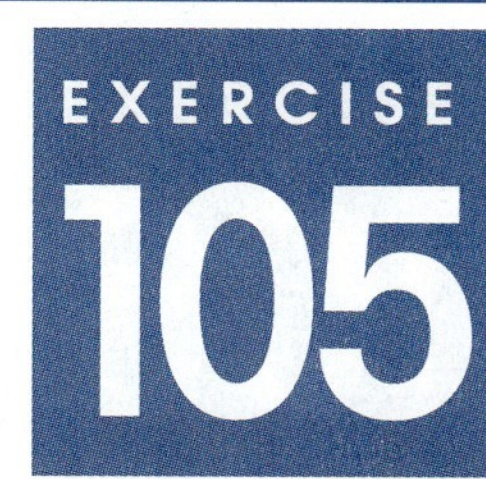

Exercise 105 continued from page 211

page 2

Class of 1973

Westlake Class of 1973 will hold their 25-year reunion at Westlake Lodge in Bethel on June 18 at 7:30 p.m. The Reunion Committee is preparing to notify classmates. Anyone needing information should contact:

Michael Armenia	(203) 555-2434
John Simon	(203) 555-6767

RETIREMENT OF DR. PATTERSON

Dr. Richard Patterson will be retiring after 40 years of service as an educator. Dr. Patterson began his career as an English teacher in New York City. In 1965, he moved to Connecticut and started teaching English at Westlake High. Dr. Patterson became an assistant principal in 1970 and then became principal in 1975. While he was principal, Dr. Patterson continued to teach one English class. He always maintained that his love of the subject and his students required him to be in the classroom at least one period a day. Join us for dinner at the Swan Club in Bethel on January 18 to honor Dr. Patterson for his commitment and dedication to his profession. For additional information, call Beth Soranik at Westlake High School at (203) 555-3666.

CONCERT PRODUCTION

The Westlake Orchestra will perform an all-Mozart program on April 4 at 7:30 p.m. in the Westlake High School auditorium. Proceeds will go to the Alumni Association. Please support our organization by attending.

WHAT'S UP CORNER

1960 - Paul Bergman, Esq.
Paul is a senior partner with West and Shih in New York City. He and his wife, Gina, live in New York City and have a son and a daughter.

1968 - Donna Newman, M.D.
Donna is an internist in private practice in Manalapan, New Jersey. She and her husband, Victor Perez, live in Manalapan and have two daughters.

1975 - David Wikstrom, Ph.D.
An astrophysicist, David lives in Huntsville, Alabama, where he is coordinator for the Starr Project.

1978 - Bea Albanee
Bea is now volunteer coordinator for the Good Neighbors Community Center. She lives with her husband, Robert, and their three sons in Worthington, Ohio. Bea wants to know when her 20th reunion will be. Is anybody planning one?

Now that you have enjoyed reading about some of your old friends and former classmates, tell us what's happening in your life! Send an update to WHAT'S UP CORNER, Ms. Betty Quinsey, 25 Hallow Street, Bethel, CT 06850-3426.

The text, objects, and spacing in this exercise have been reduced because of space constraints.

Learning Objectives

Format a newsletter

Desktop Techniques Applied

Set up columns
Import text and graphics files
Drag-paste text
Set tracking and character width
Adjust the spacing of text

Concepts

Some newsletters are prepared so that the back page contains space for the address and return address. A newsletter containing a **mailing area** becomes a self-mailer, eliminating the need to insert the document into a separate envelope. The document you will produce in this exercise is a self-mailer.

The first page of this exercise is the inside page of the newsletter; the second page is the outside page. The two pages will ultimately be printed back to back, folded, and stapled. A label containing the addressee's name will then be affixed to the mailer, which will be ready for postal delivery.

INSTRUCTIONS

1. Start a new two-page publication with 1" left and top margins, a .75" right margin, ana a 1.25" bottom margin.
2. On the master page, and set up three columns with a .167" gutter.
3. On the master page, position a horizontal ruler guide at 2".
4. On page 1, position horizontal ruler guides at 3", 7", and 8.5".
5. On page 2, position horizontal ruler guides at 2.25" and 5.5".
6. Import the template file **VITAMIN.** On page 1, place it in each column below the horizontal ruler guide at 3". On page 2, place it in each column below the horizontal ruler guide at 2.25".
7. Save the file; name it **VITAMINS.**
8. Cut the masthead (title, subtitle, and date) and drag-paste it between the top margin and the horizontal ruler guide at 2" and across the second and third columns.
9. Set "HEALTH" to sans serif 55-point, with 70% width and very loose track.
10. Set "WATCH" to sans serif 38-point, with 120% width and tight track.
11. Adjust the text block so that "HEALTHWATCH" sits on the horizontal ruler guide at 2".
12. Set the next line to sans serif 12-point, with 80% width and very loose track. Right-align the date.
13. Draw a 12-point horizontal line below "HEALTHWATCH" extending the width of the second and third columns.
14. Set all the "In This Issue" text to sans serif 12/12, with 90% width.
15. Draw (or set as paragraph rules) a 1-point horizontal line above and below the "In This Issue" text.
16. Set the text of the first two articles to serif 10/11.
17. Adjust the text block in the first column to end at the horizontal ruler guide at 8.5". Adjust the text block in the second and third columns to end at the horizontal ruler guide at 7".
18. Align the first and last lines in Columns 2 and 3 baseline to baseline, and make sure the two columns end evenly as shown. You may need to adjust the spacing to achieve these goals.
19. Import an appropriate graphic. Place it (re-sizing it, if necessary) in the first column between the top margin and the horizontal ruler guide at 3" .
20. Import another appropriate graphic; place it in the first column (re-sizing it, if necessary) below the 8.5" horizontal ruler guide.

continued on page 216

EXERCISE **106**

Exercise 106

HEALTH**WATCH**

A Newsletter from the Eastview Fitness Center Fall 19—

In This Issue

Vitamin C Shown To Reduce Heart Disease

Putting It All Together—What To Eat

Eating for Energy

VITAMIN C SHOWN TO REDUCE HEART DISEASE

Recent studies have shown that high blood levels of vitamin C are associated with higher levels of "good" cholesterol in the blood and lower the risk of coronary heart disease. Research shows that vitamin C appears to prevent cholesterol from being oxidized in the blood; this may decrease the chance that the cholesterol circulating in the blood will end up in the arteries, increasing one's risk of acquiring heart disease.

Good sources of vitamin C include papayas, oranges, cantaloupe, strawberries, broccoli, orange or grapefruit juice, brussels sprouts, and cauliflower. Be sure to get your vitamin C—your life depends on it!

PUTTING IT ALL TOGETHER—WHAT TO EAT

To obtain essential nutrients, it is important to consume fruits and vegetables as part of your regular diet. In fact, four servings of fruits and vegetables are recommended daily. A serving might be 1/2 cup of chopped vegetables or fruit, half a grapefruit, a medium potato, or a bowl of salad. At least one serving should be rich in vitamin C; at least one other should be a dark green or deep yellow vegetable. Fresh or steamed fruit and vegetables provide more nutrients to the body than canned ones.

From the bread, grain, and cereal group, you should eat four servings daily, including at least one whole-grain serving. A serving might be an ounce of dry cereal (low in sugar and salt, please!), 3/4 cup of pasta or rice, or a slice of bread.

To maintain a healthy diet, one should eat only two servings of protein a day. A serving might be 2 to 3 ounces of chicken, fish, beef, or cheese; a cup of dry beans served with rice; or half a cup of cottage cheese.

Finally, from the dairy group, men, pregnant or nursing women, and teens need four servings daily; women and older children, three; and small children, two to three. A serving might be a cup of milk, yogurt, or calcium-fortified orange juice; 2 cups of cottage cheese; or 1 1/4 ounces of hard cheese.

Avoiding excessive salt and fat will help prevent many health problems. And don't forget exercise—it is the foundation of a healthy body. A brisk walk three times a week for 20 minutes will keep you in good health.

Tips for Your Overall Diet

- ❖ Always eat breakfast, even if you only have a piece of fruit and a glass of milk. Your blood sugar level is very low in the morning.
- ❖ Eat five or six small meals during the day. This will help to keep your energy levels high.
- ❖ Avoid overeating. Large amounts of food require a lot of time to digest, draining the body of energy. Eat until you are satisfied, and then stop.
- ❖ Drink plenty of water throughout the day, especially after exercising.
- ❖ Do not consume high-fat, high-protein, or high-sugar meals before any major activity. These foods can take up to eight hours to digest and, therefore, divert blood away from your muscles.
- ❖ Above all, listen to your body. Though you may eat well, the body also needs adequate rest to compensate for an active lifestyle!

The text, objects, and spacing in this exercise have been reduced because of space constraints.

continued on page 217

EXERCISE 106

INSTRUCTIONS continued from page 214

21. Go to page 2 and cut the text for "Tips for Your Overall Diet."
22. On page 1, drag-place the "Tips" text in the second column between the 7" horizontal ruler guide and the bottom margin and stretching across Columns 2 and 3.
23. Set the heading to sans serif 12/13; center it.
24. Set the "Tips" body text to sans serif 9/11.
25. Choose an appropriate symbol (or drawn object) for the bullet. Set it in 9/11 like the body text.
26. Set a hanging indent so that the bullet is at .125" and the text to the right of the bullet is at .375". Give the text a .125" right indent and add .05" after paragraphs.
27. Draw a dotted box around the "Tips" text as shown.
28. Go to page 2 and cut "EATING FOR ENERGY." Drag-paste it across the second and third columns above the 2" horizontal ruler guide.
29. Set "EATING FOR ENERGY" to sans serif 24/32, with very loose track and 110% width.
30. Draw a 2-point line across the 2" ruler guide extending from the left to the right margin.
31. Adjust the "EATING FOR ENERGY" text block, if necessary, so the text is just above the horizontal ruler guide at 2".
32. Set "Carbohydrates," "Fats," and "Protein" to sans serif 14/14, centered. You may wish to create a style and then apply it.
33. Set the body text in each column to 12/12, justified. You may wish to create a style and then apply it.
34. Adjust the text so each food group is in its own column. Align the headings baseline to baseline. Text columns should be just under the 2.25" horizontal ruler guide.
35. Import an appropriate graphic. Place it in the first column (re-sizing it, if necessary) below the top margin and above the horizontal line.
36. Draw a dashed line at the 5.5" horizontal ruler guide that extends from the left to the right margin.
37. Cut "HEALTHWATCH" and the address text through the ZIP Code. Drag-paste it below the 5.5" horizontal ruler guide from the left to the right margin.
38. Set "HEALTH" to sans serif 40-point, with 70% width and loose track.
39. Set "WATCH" to sans serif 35-point, with 120% width and tight track.
40. Draw a 6-point line below the title.
41. Set the return address information in sans serif 10/12, with 90% width and very loose track.
42. Cut the postmark information. Drag-paste it in Column 3, below the horizontal ruler guide at 5.5".
43. Set the postmark information to sans serif 9/12, with 90% width and very tight track, center-aligned.
44. Place the postmark information as shown. Draw a hairline box around it.
45. Re-save the file.
46. Using all printer defaults, print one copy.
47. Close the file.

Exercise 106 continued from page 215

EATING FOR ENERGY

Carbohydrates

Carbohydrates are your body's primary fuel. In the body, carbohydrates are broken down into simple sugar glucose. The glucose is carried by the blood and stored as glycogen in your liver and muscles. Complex carbohydrates, found in unrefined whole grains, beans, and vegetables, are high in fiber, while simple carbohydrates are sugars for the most part and generally have almost no nutritional value.

Fat

Fat reserves in the body help energize aerobic activities. Your muscles and liver have limited capacities for storing glycogen. Once their stores are depleted, the fat that is stored in your body is put to use. Fatty acids, which make up fats, are removed from storage and sent to the body's muscles, where they are broken down and used for energy.

Protein

Though it is required for muscle growth and repair, protein is not a major source of energy. During exercise, protein will not contribute greatly to the energy that you use, but it will be vital to you as your muscles recover and rebuild themselves after you are through. The best sources of protein are eggs, fish, meat, beans, and dairy products.

HEALTH**WATCH**

Eastview Fitness Center
455 Highbridge Road
San Francisco, CA 94120-7807

BULK RATE
U.S. POSTAGE PAID
PERMIT NO. 3456
SAN FRANCISCO, CA

Learning Objectives

Learn formatting guidelines for electronic publishing

Convert a document to electronic format

Concepts

As the number of people making use of the Internet increases, electronic publishing and distribution of documents has become more popular and practical. In the next two exercises, you will use features of your desktop publishing software to prepare two documents for electronic distribution.

Documents can be converted from prepared versions intended for print distribution, or they can be designed from the ground up with electronic publication in mind. Unless you think your document will be printed by the recipient rather than read on-screen, designing for the screen is best. Designing for the screen is also best when your intended audience may have a different World Wide Web browser application than yours.

Differences in screen resolution, colors, and fonts across different computers and platforms are other considerations in designing or converting a document for electronic distribution. Some file conversion applications can embed in the electronic file the fonts used in the original publication. If it is not necessary to preserve the exact font, such applications can usually create a working version.

These two exercises are written for users of PageMaker 6.0 Windows with Adobe Acrobat. Where appropriate, substitute the equivalent steps and applications for the equipment you are using.

With Adobe Acrobat, you can convert a document from a Macintosh or Windows application to Portable Document Format (PDF). The PDF file will retain the page layout, typography, graphics, and color of the original. The PDF file can be viewed on-screen or printed using either of two Acrobat viewers: Reader or Exchange.

INSTRUCTIONS

1. Open the data file **VITAMINS.**
2. Choose the option for creating a PDF file or the equivalent.
3. Select Distill Now or the equivalent to prepare a converted version of your file.
4. If available, select the View PDF Using option and the name of your viewer from the pop-up menu (or the equivalent) to view your PDF file immediately after creation.
5. Click on Create or the equivalent.
6. If necessary, specify a filename and location, and click on Save or the equivalent.

   If your file is not immediately displayed in your viewer, open the viewer application separately and open your new PDF file.
7. Examine the file in your viewer. It should look quite similar to the original file.
8. In your viewer application, using all printer defaults, print one copy.
9. Close the file.

EXERCISE 107

Exercise 107

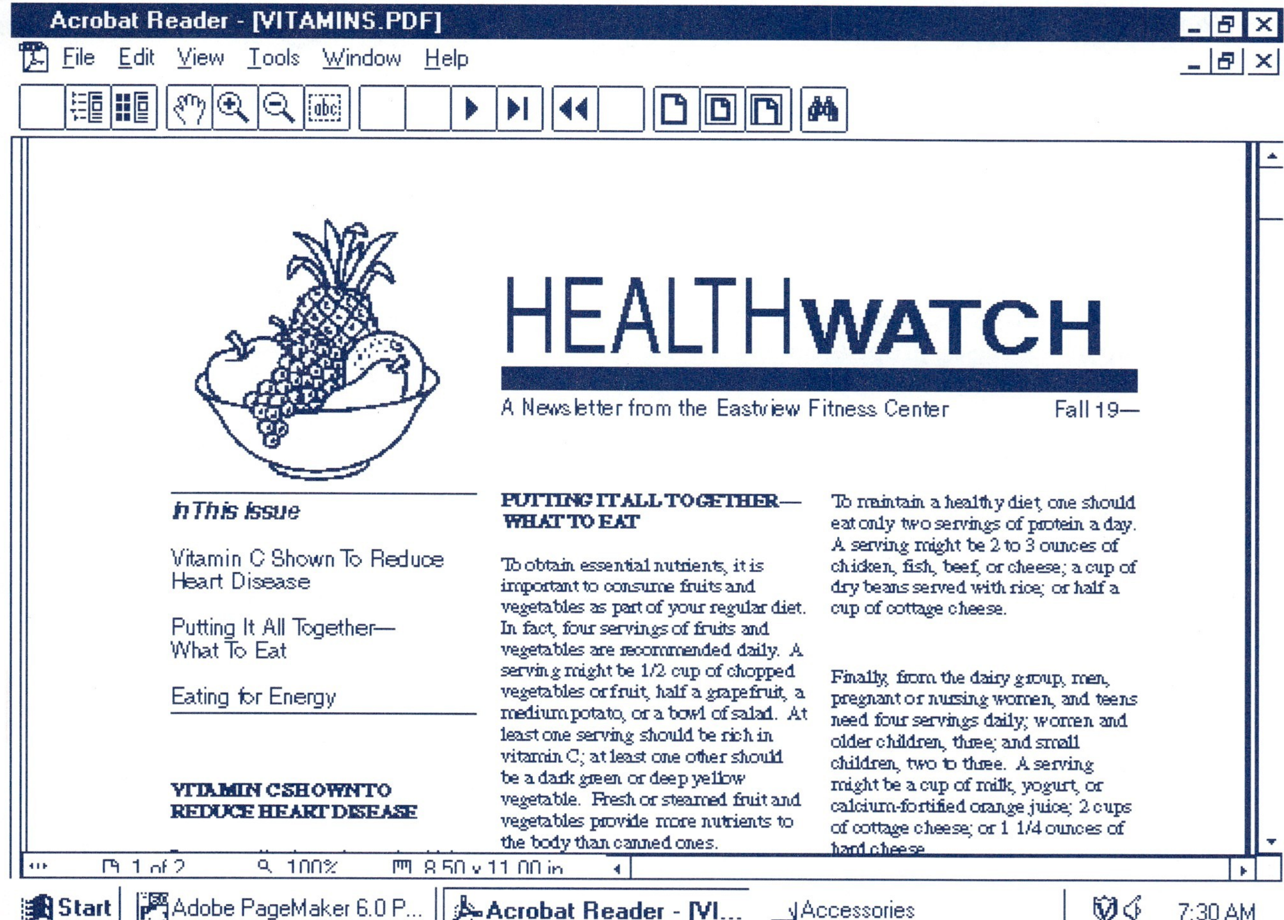

Acrobat Reader - [VITAMINS.PDF]

File Edit View Tools Window Help

HEALTHWATCH

A Newsletter from the Eastview Fitness Center Fall 19—

In This Issue

Vitamin C Shown To Reduce Heart Disease

Putting It All Together—What To Eat

Eating for Energy

VITAMIN C SHOWN TO REDUCE HEART DISEASE

PUTTING IT ALL TOGETHER—WHAT TO EAT

To obtain essential nutrients, it is important to consume fruits and vegetables as part of your regular diet. In fact, four servings of fruits and vegetables are recommended daily. A serving might be 1/2 cup of chopped vegetables or fruit, half a grapefruit, a medium potato, or a bowl of salad. At least one serving should be rich in vitamin C; at least one other should be a dark green or deep yellow vegetable. Fresh or steamed fruit and vegetables provide more nutrients to the body than canned ones.

To maintain a healthy diet, one should eat only two servings of protein a day. A serving might be 2 to 3 ounces of chicken, fish, beef, or cheese; a cup of dry beans served with rice; or half a cup of cottage cheese.

Finally, from the dairy group, men, pregnant or nursing women, and teens need four servings daily; women and older children, three; and small children, two to three. A serving might be a cup of milk, yogurt, or calcium-fortified orange juice; 2 cups of cottage cheese; or 1 1/4 ounces of hard cheese.

1 of 2 100% 8.50 x 11.00 in

Start Adobe PageMaker 6.0 P... Acrobat Reader - [VI... Accessories 7:30 AM

Electronic Document

Learning Objectives

Learn formatting guidelines for the World Wide Web

Create and format a document for Web distribution

Desktop Techniques Applied

Format text with styles

Concepts

On the World Wide Web, information is displayed in pages constructed using **hypertext markup language (HTML).** Hypertext markup language employs standard styles for formatting text, similar to the formatting styles used in many desktop publishing programs. For example, there is an **H1** style for main headings and a **Body Text** style for body text.

In some desktop publishing software, documents intended for publication on the Web can be converted to HTML documents, or you can design a document from the ground up in HTML format. In this exercise, you will do the latter. The exercise is written for the PageMaker 6.0 HTML Author plug-in. Where appropriate, substitute the appropriate steps for the software you are using.

This exercise takes you through the steps to prepare a document for distribution on the Web. But you will need to have Web server hardware and software, or an account with someone who runs a server, in order to publish your file on the Internet.

Desktop publishing software that supports HTML formatting also lets you set up **hypertext links**—text pointers that take the user to other specified parts of the document, to other documents, or to other computers, for additional information. In a Web browser, the hypertext link appears highlighted. In this exercise, you will create a hypertext link to text within your document.

Your desktop publishing software may also permit you to format text as an **anchor.** In HTML, an **anchor** is a hypertext link destination within a document. The user of a Web browser can click a hypertext link to an anchor, and the browser will jump to that location in the document. In this exercise, you will create two anchors to text within your document.

When you are designing a page for the World Wide Web, consider that the size of the monitors or windows in which different users will view the file will vary. In addition, most formatting ordinarily applied in your desktop publishing software will not be preserved in a browser, including font; type size; leading; tracking; font width; most type styles; color except for hypertext links; indents; tabs; and paragraph alignment. For Web distribution, simple is best.

INSTRUCTIONS

1. Start a new document. Use the default settings.
2. Place the template file **PF.**
3. Save the file; name it **PF11.**
4. Add in the same font as the rest of the text the title and two headings at the right, with line returns as shown.
5. From the Utilities menu, choose PageMaker Plug-ins/ HTML Author.
6. Click on OK.
7. Select all the text, and apply the HTML Body Text style.
8. Apply the HTML H1 style to the title.
9. Apply the HTML H2 style to the two headings.
10. Select the first heading, and choose HTML Author.
11. In the Create Links dialog box, choose Anchor from the Create pop-up menu.
12. For the anchor label, key "Planning." Click on Create and then on OK.
13. Repeat Steps 10-12 for the second heading, with "Templates" for the anchor label.
14. Select the second heading again. Choose HTML Author.
15. Select Hyperlink from the Create pop-up menu.
16. Choose Link to Anchor from the Link Type pop-up menu.
17. In the Choose Anchor Label box, select Templates, click on Create, and click on OK. The heading should appear underscored and in a different color.
18. Using all printer defaults, print one copy.
19. Save and close the file.

EXERCISE 108

Exercise 108

USING PRACTICE TEXT

This is practice or "dummy" text that you can use for importing, placing, and playing purposes. Desktop publishers often use dummy text. When you are first designing a publication, you can flow a dummy text file in to see how your design will look with type. Desktop publishers also use dummy text for publications that will be produced periodically, such as a monthly newsletter. The dummy text serves as a placeholder for the different articles that will appear in each issue. You will learn more about using dummy text in this way in later exercises.

Some desktop publishing programs give you practice or "dummy" text that looks like Latin (but it's not). It is called a *lorem ipsum* file. Really, any file can serve as dummy text. The more it looks like the kind of text you will be using in your final publication, the better. You can manipulate and move sections of practice text as you desire. You can experiment with different elements such as typefaces, type styles, type sizes, and leading.

Planning a Publication

Later in this book, you will be given the opportunity to create your own projects. Before you tackle them, you will learn to plan your publication ahead by drawing a "thumbnail" sketch on a piece of blank paper. Drawing a thumbnail will give you direction in creating your page layout on the computer. The sketch should define the approximate positions of all the text and graphic elements that will appear on each page. Of course, the design may be changed as you are working on your project in the desktop publishing program.

There are countless ways to design a document. Professional designing requires education and skill, but you do not have to be a professional designer to create simple, attractive publications in your desktop publishing software. The exercises in this book will give you the general guidelines you need for document design, as well as ideas to consider and examples to follow. Looking at different publications will give you other ideas to try.

Using Templates

Desktop publishing software often comes with sample documents, or *templates*, already designed and formatted for you. Your software may provide templates for letters, memos, newsletters, reports, and other common documents. Templates can be used as is or modified as needed. You will learn more about templates later in this text.

When you begin to design a publication, try different typefaces, type styles, type sizes, and leading options. Change the margins, and vary the space between columns. Stretch your text boxes to varying lengths. Don't be afraid to experiment! If you are not happy with your work, delete the story, or close your desktop publishing file without saving it and place the file again. You can place files as many times as you like without altering them.

Remember, this is practice text. You can read the copy if you like, but all the information contained here will be given to you formally in later exercises.

The text and spacing in this exercise have been reduced because of space constraints.

Learning Objectives

Learn presentation graphics format
Format presentation graphics

Desktop Techniques Applied

Use landscape orientation
Set elements on a master page
Key text in different fonts
Use graphic symbols
Replace text with new text

Concepts

Oral presentations can be enhanced by the use of **presentation graphics.** Prepared as slides or transparencies, presentation graphics can underscore important points and, like other graphics, can effectively present data, particularly statistical data.

All graphics in a presentation should have a consistent format. Borders, boxes, lines, arrows, color, and blank space are effective tools for creating a theme. Do not overdo these elements, however. A simple, consistent layout is best.

Each graphic in a presentation should focus on one idea or topic. Often, the first graphic is an agenda or overview of the presentation, which may be shown again at the conclusion.

Presentation graphics may include clip art, charts, and other graphic elements. Like graphics for a publication, presentation graphics should be integrally related to the points you are trying to make. Charts should not be too complex and should be in a format the audience will readily understand.

When writing text for presentation graphics, avoid unfamiliar terms. Use simple, direct statements. Bulleted lists should contain no more than seven items. Use parallel structure, and be concise.

INSTRUCTIONS

1. Start a new two-page publication with landscape orientation and 1" margins.
2. On the master page, draw a border as shown to frame the margins.
3. On the master page, set a vertical ruler guide at .25" and a horizontal ruler guide at 1.75".
4. On the master page, key the logo at the vertical ruler guide and sitting on the horizontal ruler guide in sans serif bold 24/auto. In the logo, use an appropriate graphic or symbol from a symbol typeface or a star created with the polygon tool.
5. On page 1, position a horizontal ruler guide at 3".
6. On the ruler guide you just drew, key "Sales Meeting Agenda" in sans serif 36/auto bold, center-aligned, with .25" after.
7. In the same text block, key the enumerated items in sans serif 24/auto bold, left-aligned, with a 2" left indent, .25" after, and a tab at 3".
8. Copy the text block to page 2. Place a horizontal ruler guide at 3.5", and place the text block so the title is sitting on the ruler guide.
9. Key over the page 1 copy with the page 2 copy as show at the right. You will need to delete one of the enumerated items.
10. Replace the numbers and periods with an appropriate bullet item. Use a graphic, a symbol from a symbol typeface, or a drawn object.
11. Save the file; name it **STARR.**
12. Using all printer defaults, print one copy.
13. Close the file.

Exercise 109

Sales Meeting Agenda

1. 1997 Goals
2. Auto Insurance
3. Life Insurance
4. New Disability Insurance
5. Summary

Auto Insurance Selling Points

- ☛ Low Rates
- ☛ Important State Coverages
- ☛ Customer Satisfaction
- ☛ Good Driver Dividends

The text, objects, and spacing in this exercise have been reduced because of space constraints.

Presentation Graphics

Learning Objectives

Format a presentation graphic

Desktop Techniques Applied

Replace text with new text
Add a page to a document
Create a pie or bar chart

INSTRUCTIONS

1. Open the data file **STARR.**
2. Go to page 2, and copy the contents of the page.
3. Insert a new page after page 2.
4. On the new page, position a horizontal ruler guide at 2.75".
5. Paste the copy on the page so that the title sits on the horizontal ruler guide at 2.75".
6. Key "Subscriber Savings Account" to replace "Auto Insurance Selling Points."
7. Change the space after for "Subscriber Savings Account" from .25" to .12".
8. Delete the rest of the text block.
9. Key the subtitle, "1997 Investments," in sans serif 30-point auto, with no left indent, center-aligned.
10. Create a pie chart or bar chart using the information in the chart at the right. If you need help, refer to pages 136-139 of your text.
11. Arrange the chart attractively on the page.
12. Using all printer defaults, print one copy.
13. Save and close the file.

Design Pointers/Hints

- Text in presentation graphics should be keyed in uppercase and lowercase letters, rather than in all capital letters. For overhead transparencies, the type should be 36- to 48-point for headings and 18- to 24-point for bulleted items. A rule of thumb for checking type size is to place the copy on the floor. If you can read the text fairly easily, it should be large enough when projected.

Exercise 110

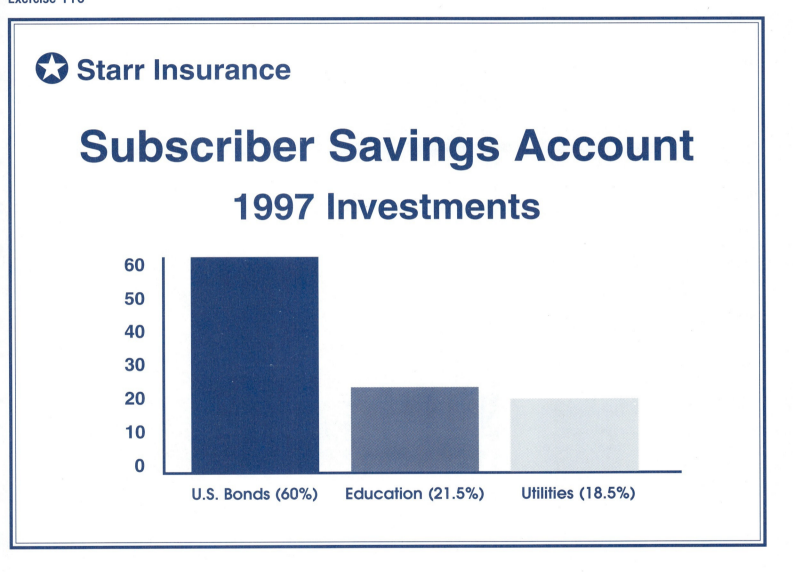

Starr Insurance

Subscriber Savings Account

1997 Investments

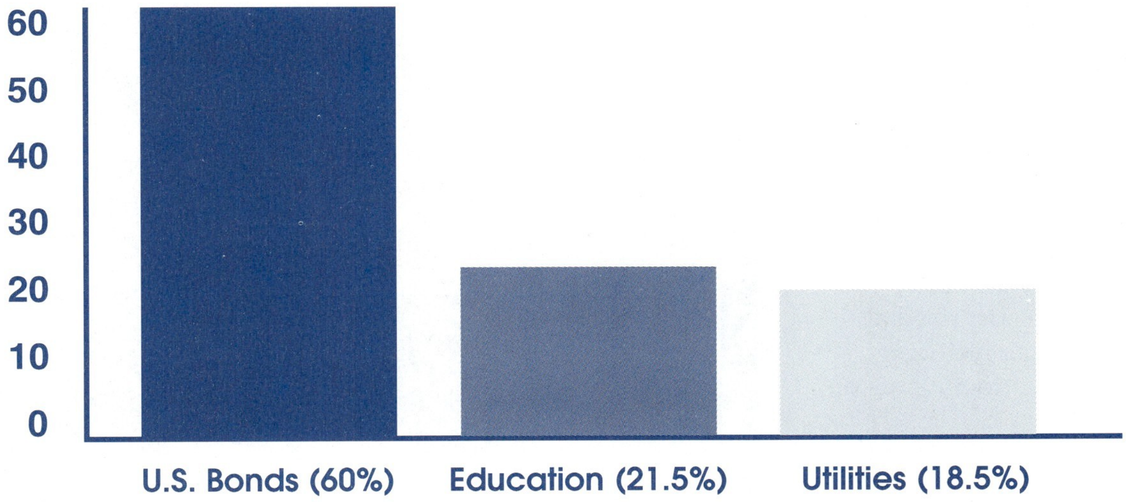

60
50
40
30
20
10
0

U.S. Bonds (60%) Education (21.5%) Utilities (18.5%)

The text, objects, and spacing in this exercise have been reduced because of space constraints.

Concepts

In the exercises that follow, you will complete desktop publishing projects with very little direction. Create these documents using the desktop publishing features and guidelines for design you have learned. Use clip art, drawn art, and text art as you consider appropriate.

The exercises and applications you have completed should give you options and ideas. You can also study the work of professional designers. Looking at examples of the kind of publication you are designing will help as well.

Before creating a document on your desktop publishing software, you may wish to draw a thumbnail sketch of the document on paper. The sketch should define the approximate positions of all graphic elements that will appear on each page. Of course, you may modify a plan as you work.

Creating your own designs may be difficult, at first. The more you work at it, however, the better you will be. You will be surprised at how quickly you are producing professional-looking documents on your own.

INSTRUCTIONS

1. Create a resume for yourself in chronological or functional format.
2. Save the file; name it **RESUME.**
3. Using all printer defaults, print one copy.
4. Close the file.

INSTRUCTIONS

1. Create your own letterhead. Include your name, address, city, state, ZIP Code, phone number (with area code), and Internet address, if appropriate.
2. Save the file; name it **LETTERHD.**
3. Using all printer defaults, print one copy.
4. Close the file.

INSTRUCTIONS

1. Create an advertisement for a bookstore to be placed in a national publication. The advertisement must measure 4.5" by 2" and should include the following information:

   Appletree Books
   Books, music, and software
   Rare books a specialty
   14 Gilchrist Street
   San Francisco, CA 94102-4483
   Telephone: 800-555-2468
   FAX: 415-555-0010
   http://wwx.grand.net/applbks
2. Save the file; name it **APPLTREE.**
3. Using all printer defaults, print one copy.
4. Close the file.

INSTRUCTIONS

1. Create an engagement announcement that measures 5" by 7" using the following wording:

   Marivel and Raymond Malagos
   announce the engagement
   of their daughter
   Josephine
   to
   Michael Ramos
   son of
   Maria and Roberto Ramos
   December 21, 19--

2. Save the file; name it **ENGAGE.**

3. Using all printer defaults, print one copy.

4. Close the file.

INSTRUCTIONS

1. Create a flyer announcing a jazz festival. Use the following information:

   The New York City Jazz Festival

   What better way to spend spring...visiting New York City...and listening to jazz bands from all over the country. For seven nights, you can listen to performances of:

   The Rider International Drums Competition
   The Quincy Adams Big Band
   The Lincoln Center Orchestra (tunes from the jazz-band era)

   May 1-8, 19--

   For complete ticket information, call 212-555-3333.

   The New York City Jazz Festival is sponsored by the Eye-On-New York Association.

2. Save the file; name it **JAZZ.**

3. Using all printer defaults, print one copy.

4. Close the file.

INSTRUCTIONS

1. Using the template file **BROCHURE,** create a two-page brochure for the Country Lane Dinner Theater announcing its summer schedule. This brochure will be printed back-to-back and folded into three panels (six panels total, three for each page).

   Some hints on the creation of the brochure: Put the "SENSATIONAL" information on one panel. Another should contain the return address of the theater; on this panel, address labels eventually will be affixed for mailing to potential customers. Make another panel the title panel, listing the names of the shows in the summer schedule. Use another panel for the menu, another for the details of the summer schedule, and another for pricing and policies.

2. Save the file; name it **DINNER.**
3. Using all printer defaults, print one copy.
4. Close the file.

INSTRUCTIONS

1. Create an invitation for a benefit homes tour. The invitation must measure 5" by 7" and should include the following information (not necessarily line for line):

   The Blue Skies Society invites you
   on a tour of ten historic houses of Walnut Hills
   Saturday, December 17
   12 p.m. - 7 p.m.

   Reception to follow at Spicer House

   Proceeds to benefit Kids First

   Tickets: $50.00

   R.S.V.P. by Saturday, December 10
   Ms. June Alford
   555-1432

2. Save the file; name it **INVITE.**
3. Using all printer defaults, print one copy.
4. Close the file.

EXERCISE 118

INSTRUCTIONS

1. Create a logo for Party Bonanza, a party supplies discount store. The store is at 15 McGee Avenue, Berkeley, CA 94703-2280. The telephone number is (415) 555-8200.

2. Save the file; name it **LOGO.**

3. Using all printer defaults, print one copy.

4. Close the file.

EXERCISE 119

INSTRUCTIONS

1. Create page 14 of a catalog for EarthNow, a retailer of environmentally sensitive products. Include at least three items on the catalog page. Write brief descriptions of each item, and use clip art or drawn objects to illustrate them. Give each item a product number and a price.

2. Save the file; name it **CATALOG.**

3. Using all printer defaults, print one copy.

4. Close the file.

EXERCISE 120

INSTRUCTIONS

1. Using the template file **LEGAL,** create an agenda for a legal seminar on ethics, sexual harassment, and substance abuse in the workplace.

2. Save the file; name it **SEMINAR.**

3. Using all printer defaults, print one copy.

4. Close the file.

EXERCISE 121

INSTRUCTIONS

1. Create a presentation graphic for a regional teachers' conference on adult education. Use this information:

EDUCATIONAL ATTAINMENT
Persons Age 25 and Over

Graduate Degree	35,000
Bachelor's Degree	80,000
Associate Degree	39,000
Some College	108,000
High School Graduate	140,000
Grade 9-12, No Diploma	63,000
Less Than 9th Grade	29,000

2. Save the file; name it **PREGRAPH.**
3. Using all printer defaults, print one copy.
4. Close the file.

EXERCISE 122

INSTRUCTIONS

1. Using the template file **HISTORIC,** create a grant proposal for a nonprofit organization called Carapace to renovate historic houses.
2. Develop a title for the proposal. The title should be brief, easy to remember, and to the point.
3. Create a title page.
4. Save the file; name it **GRANT.**
5. Using all printer defaults, print one copy.
6. Close the file.

EXERCISE 123

INSTRUCTIONS

1. Using the template file **ENVIRON,** create a two-page newsletter for the Kona Club, an organization involved with environmental issues.
2. Save the file; name it **KONA.**
3. Using all printer defaults, print one copy.
4. Close the file.

EXERCISE 124

INSTRUCTIONS

1. Using the template file **LATCHKEY,** create a registration form for the Pattison School Latchkey Program.
2. Save the file; name it **LATCHKEY.**
3. Using all printer defaults, print one copy.
4. Close the file.

EXERCISE 125

INSTRUCTIONS

1. Using the template file **FINANCE,** create a page of financial data from the semi-annual report of the Baedeker Fund to shareholders. Your challenge is to present these data in a visually attractive and readable format.
2. Save the file; name it **BAEDEKER.**
3. Using all printer defaults, print one copy.
4. Close the file.

The Glover, Massachusetts, Visitors Bureau

Glover, Massachusetts, is an old maritime community of 36,108, located in Essex County, on Massachusetts Bay. The town dates from pre-Revolutionary War days and figured colorfully in that conflict. Under the mandate of General George Washington, Nathaniel Westcott, a Glover privateer, assailed 17 British merchant ships and captured their crews and cargoes. The town underwent bombardment twice, as the cannonball marks on the sea wall attest.

The town was once an important port and center of the China trade. Its principle sources of income were fishing, farming, and several factories until well into the 1900s, when the factories began closing down or moving out, and farms were sold to home builders or made into larger, corporate-run entities. Now the primary business is the fishery, with some light industry scattered about town and a few high-tech companies out on the freeway.

Glover has well-kept houses and churches, some dating back to the 1600s. Several are National Historic Sites and are open to the public. A few residents have set up their historic homes as bed and breakfasts. Glover has a pleasant downtown area with many small businesses and restaurants. The town offers parks--two on the beach--with beautiful native flowers, cobblestone walkways, playgrounds, cookout grills, and picnic benches. One park has a band shell where local bands play every weekend evening in the summer. The well-tended local beaches are suitable for swimming, beachcombing, and sunbathing. At two local marinas, sailboats and row-boats can be rented.

The Glover Visitors Bureau, Town Council, and Chamber of Commerce are agreed that more needs to be done to promote Glover as a pleasant year-round tourist attraction. They recently hired Norma McRae, a lifelong resident of Glover, as Director of Communications, and she has hired you as her Publications Assistant. For Ms. McRae, you will be using your desktop publishing skills to produce a variety of documents to attract tourists to the town. Your tasks will also include some research, editing, and writing.

Ms. McRae is relying on your ability to complete your work independently, without much direction. She knows that you have a basic knowledge of document formats and the desktop publishing skills to make your work attractive. Use what you have been taught in this class to complete the following eight assignments. Refer to your textbook as needed.

The Glover Visitors Bureau
14 Cabot Street
Glover, MA 01915-4459
(508) 555-2000

Norma McRae
Director of Communications

JOB 1

We've decided to put out a four-page semimonthly shoppers' newsletter. We'll call it The Downtown Glover Shopping Gazette. I want it to have a volume and issue number. The masthead should have our address and phone number, as well as your and my name and title. We're going to print it on 8.5- by 11-inch paper. It will be handed out in the downtown stores and bed-and-breakfasts and mailed to residents. Half of one page should be a mailing panel; for mailing, the newsletter will be folded in half, stapled, and labeled. We're sending it bulk rate. Our permit number is 7580.

A lot of the newsletter will be advertising. We're selling one- and two-column ads in different lengths: 1.75", 2", 3", 3.5", and 4". We're also going to have write-ups of local businesses and events. We don't need bylines, since either you or I will be doing the writing. We have a few regular features that should appear in the same place in every issue: "Band Shell Banter," three paragraphs or so about the band shell concerts; "Bed-and-Breakfast News," about the same length; "The Itinerant Gourmet," a restaurant review, five or six paragraphs; and a movie review, five or six paragraphs, again.

Please create a template for the newsletter with formats for text and graphics, a masthead, and space set aside for regular features.

JOB 2

Great job on the newsletter template! Everyone was very pleased with your work.

Your next assignment is to produce the June 1-15 issue of the newsletter. I've typed up six articles on the word processor. They're called **TOURS, MAGIC, B&B** (that's the bed-and-breakfast feature), **GOURMET** (the restaurant review), **MOVIE** (the movie review), and **GORDONS.** I'm not a very good speller, so please check my work. If you need to cut my writing because of space constraints, go ahead.

I didn't have time to write up the "Bandshell Banter" piece. Could you please develop it from my notes? It's called **BANTER** on the disk.

We have quite a few advertisers for our first issue. The **ADCOPY** file lists advertisers, ad size, ad copy, and any special offers. Please design the ads from the information given. Feel free to use clip art in the ads and anywhere else you think it looks attractive.

JOB 3

In last night's meeting, the Town Council finally finished up the schedule of activities for Heritage Days. I'd like you to develop a flyer listing these activities. The flyer will be on display and available for people to take at all the downtown stores and supermarkets. We're also going to include it with the Door Delivery advertisements for Glover, Beverly, and Salem the week before Heritage Days. As you probably know, Door Delivery packets go to every house in town. Please make the flyer the standard size, 8.5 by 11 inches.

I took notes on the activities on my laptop at the meeting. They're in a word processing file called **HERITAGE.** There's a lot of copy, and it's quite jumbled up—people kept changing things!—please organize it for me, will you? And check it for typos. Put in some appropriate clip art, and add that the Visitors Bureau is conducting bus and foot tours at 10, 2, and 4 each day, starting from Glover Common.

Thanks,
Norma

JOB 4

The Glover Visitors Bureau
14 Cabot Street
Glover, MA 01915-4459
(508) 555-2000

Norma McRae
Director of Communications

I agree that we need to update our Guide to Services brochure. Your ideas for the brochure are first-rate.

As you suggested, let's make the brochure so that it can be folded into three panels. We'll print it on 8.5- by 11-inch paper, back to back, with three panels on each side.

I've found the text for the old brochure; it's in a word processing file called **VISIT.** We'll have the printer put in a photograph on the front panel. On that panel, please add "Welcome to Glover" and "The Glover Visitors Bureau Guide to Services."

The tour information should be placed so that it begins where people open the brochure. I don't have a very big budget on this project, so please add some clip art to illustrate the text.

The back panel should have just the "Other Services" material and the Visitors Bureau name, address, and telephone number. Please make sure the latter information, particularly the phone number, is in large type.

Thanks,
Norma

JOB
5

We're going to put together a visitors guide booklet for tourists. The booklet will be available free here, at all the historic sites, and at any restaurant, shop, or accommodation that wants to carry it. We'll also mail it out in response to inquiries. I want you to design the booklet and produce the first edition.

Page size should be 5.25" by 8.5". We'll use photographs we have on file. Except for the one color photograph, which I want in a large size on the cover, I want you to decide which photos to use, what size each photo should be, and where each photo should appear. The commercial printer will make stats of the photos and strip them in. I've typed up a list of photos you can use in a word processor file called **PHOTO.** There are about two dozen of them. Use as many as you like.

For each photo you choose, you'll need to draw a box on the document page, which will show the printer where and at what size the photo will appear. Include a statement in the box saying something like, "Put Photo A here." Then you"ll need to provide a key of the photos. The printer will mask out the words and the boxes you've drawn before stripping in the stats.

In the photo key document that you prepare, remind the printer of the final page size and to remove the boxes and statements. Make your instructions as clear as possible.

The title of the booklet will be "Visitors Guide to Glover." The cover should also say, "Compliments of the Glover Visitors Bureau" and "A Guide to historic attractions, dining, shopping, and accommodations."

For the rest of the booklet, we'll be using black plus another color—I think you call it spot color? I'd like you to choose and apply an appropriate color.

Since we just hired a part-time photographer a few months ago, we don't have many photos of events from past years for the calendar section. Feel free to add clip art to enliven it.

The bulk of the information to go into the booklet is in a file called **GUIDE.** On the second page, please prepare a table of contents. Please add where appropriate write-ups of Marcel's Pharmacy, the Magic Carpet, Gordon's, Findlay's Fruit and Vegetable Market, the Ryder Bike Shop, the Depot Coffee Shop, and Hancock House. You should be able to get what you need from the June 1-15 newsletter.

The calendar, which should be the last item in the booklet, is in a separate file called **EVENTS.** Please add to the calendar information about the two band shell concerts you wrote about in the newsletter, and put something about Heritage Days from the flyer you prepared.

Don't worry about whether your text ends on an even or uneven number of pages. I may decide to add a few more things, and I haven't figured out what to put on the back cover. Any suggestions?

JOB

6

The Glover Visitors Bureau
14 Cabot Street
Glover, MA 01915-4459
(508) 555-2000

Norma McRae
Director of Communications

I'd like to get some feedback from tourists on what they liked about their visit to Glover and what they think could be improved. We have a database of persons who have taken our tours or who have stopped in to the Bureau for information. Let's survey those people.

I remember from your interview that you have some expertise in developing surveys, so I'm going to give you this assignment. The survey should not exceed one 8.5- by 11-inch page, but we can print on the back of the page as well as the front. We'll include a self-addressed, postage-paid envelope.

Here are some of the things I'd like to know:

If they took a tour, which one—Morning Walkers, Afternoon Walkers, Weekend Walkers, Senior Citizens Bus, Garden Bus, or Family Bus. Did they like their tour? If not, what particularly didn't they like? Do they have suggestions for additions/deletions/other tours?

What they thought of particular attractions: the Foxx House, Abbott Gardens, Bancroft House, the First Baptist Church, Nathaniel Westcott's House, the sea wall, Pickett Park, City Gardens, Moriah Arboretum, Broughton Gardens, The Olde Meeting House, Glover Common, Lighthouse Beach, and the Glover Museum.

What else they did while they were in town that they particularly enjoyed or disliked, and why.

If they stayed overnight, where, and any comments on their accommodations.

Did they do any shopping, and did they enjoy their shopping experience?

If they ate in town, how were the restaurants?

Would they consider coming back? Why or why not?

Was the Visitors Bureau helpful?

Please add anything else you think is appropriate.

JOB

7

The Glover Visitors Bureau
14 Cabot Street
Glover, MA 01915-4459
(508) 555-2000

Norma McRae
Director of Communications

As you know, one of my concerns as a resident of Glover and as an employee of the Visitors Bureau is beachwater pollution. We've had several beach closings in the past few years, and there was a problem with underground septic systems, which quite a few of our homes near the shore still have, leaching wastewater into the bay last summer.

I'm giving a talk next week at Glover Community College on this important topic. But the data I've used in past speeches are from several years ago. I need some fresh facts and figures. I know that you work a lot on the Internet. Would you please see if you can find a few articles on beachwater pollution? If you don't have access to the Net, please use library resources to complete this assignment. Then create two or three presentation graphics based on some of the data in the articles. Please include a complete source citation on each graphic.

There was a piece on environmental Internet sites in the *Glover Times* a few weeks ago. I've copied down addresses for six sites that sound promising:

National Resources Defense Council - Ocean Web Site
http://nrdc.org/dire/tocean.html

Governmental World Wide Web Resources Relating to the Environment
Australian, Canadian, and United States environmental Web sites
http://envirolink.org/envirogov.html

National Oceanic and Atmospheric Administration
Information on sustainable fisheries, protected species, and healthy coasts
http://www.noaa.gov/

National Marine Fisheries Service
Oceans and their living resources
http://kingfish.ssp.nmfs.gov

Environmental News Network
Latest environmental news, updated daily
http://www.enn.com

Whale Times
Whales, sharks, seals, and penguins
http://www.whaletimes.org/whagray.htm

JOB 8

The Glover Visitors Bureau
14 Cabot Street
Glover, MA 01915-4459
(508) 555-2000

Norma McRae
Director of Communications

I've finally decided what to do with the back cover of the visitors guide booklet you prepared. I'd like you to put together several indexes—alphabetical lists of names of places with page numbers in the booklet on which they are discussed. Let's have one index each for Attractions, Restaurants, Shopping, Accommodations, and the Summer Calendar of Events (for the Calendar, don't list each individual event, just the page numbers on which the Calendar appears).

I can't remember whether the visitors guide ends with an even or an odd number of pages, but it doesn't matter—if it ends with an even number of pages, we'll just add a blank page for the inside back cover.

Please include on the back page a coupon entitling the bearer to $1 off any Visitors Bureau tour. Give it an expiration date of September 8.

Thanks,
Norma

Learning Objectives

Perform basic mouse actions

Terms

- Mouse
- Point
- Click
- Double-click
- Drag

Concepts

Most desktop publishing programs require you to use a mouse. A **mouse** is a hand-held device that controls the pointer and lets you select options from the screen. With a mouse, you can edit text and graphics, access desktop features, and create shapes and designs more quickly and easily than with a keyboard.

A mouse has one, two, or three buttons. Most functions require the use of the left button. Unless otherwise instructed, use the left button for the exercises in this text.

As you move the mouse, the pointer moves correspondingly. If the mouse is lifted and placed back on the tabletop or mouse pad, the pointer will not move. Only the rolling of the ball underneath the mouse (moving the mouse on the work surface) causes the pointer to move.

In desktop publishing software, the pointer usually appears initially as an arrow. It assumes other shapes depending on the task you are performing or the tool you select. For example, when you choose the PageMaker ellipse tool, the pointer looks like this: +

You can perform any task with the mouse if you learn these four mouse actions:

- **Point**. Move the mouse (roll it on the work surface) so that the pointer points to an item, usually the item you are going to work with next.
- **Click.** Tap the mouse button once quickly. Clicking has different functions in different programs. Generally, you click on an object to single it out for your next action. For example, clicking on a graphic may select it for editing. Clicking in text may insert the text cursor so you can key and edit. Clicking on an icon may execute an action (for example, clicking on a printer icon starts a document printing).
- **Double-click.** Rapidly tap the mouse button twice. Double-clicking generally executes an action. For example, double-clicking on a Windows application icon loads the application. Double-clicking on a word usually highlights it for editing.
- **Drag.** While holding down the left mouse button, move the mouse to another location. Dragging is generally used to make menu selections; select text; and move, resize, and crop graphics.

INSTRUCTIONS

1. Start any program that uses a mouse and allows you to work with text. If you need help, ask your instructor.
2. Open a document that contains text. Again, if you need assistance, ask your instructor.
3. Identify the pointer. If you are using a word processor, or working with text in a desktop publishing program, the pointer may resemble a capital **I**.
4. Hold the mouse so that your index finger rests on the left mouse button.
5. Roll the mouse on the work surface up, down, left, and right. Note that the pointer moves as the mouse does.
6. Practice clicking, double-clicking, and dragging on text. When text is highlighted, click elsewhere to remove the highlighting.
7. Close the document without saving it.

Learning Objectives

Select menu items
Select dialog box items

Terms

- Menu
- Menu bar
- Dialog box (pop-up box)

Concepts

To perform most tasks in a desktop publishing program, you will work with menus. A **menu** is a list of related commands or options. The File menu, for example, usually contains commands for creating, retrieving, and printing publications, as well as for exiting from the software. The names of all the menus appear in the **menu bar** at the top of screen.

To open a menu:

- Click on the menu name (for some programs, point to the menu name and hold down the mouse button).
- Press Alt + the bold, underscored, or different-colored letter in the menu name (for many programs that run under Windows).

To choose a menu command:

- Open the menu and click on the command (for some programs, drag down from the name of the menu to the command).
- Use the keyboard shortcut that appears to the right of the command as listed on the menu. Keyboard shortcuts execute the command immediately, bypassing opening the menu.
- Open the menu and key the bold, underscored, or different-colored letter of the command (for many programs that run under Windows).
- Highlight the command using the arrow keys and press Enter (for many programs that run under Windows).

A Layout Menu

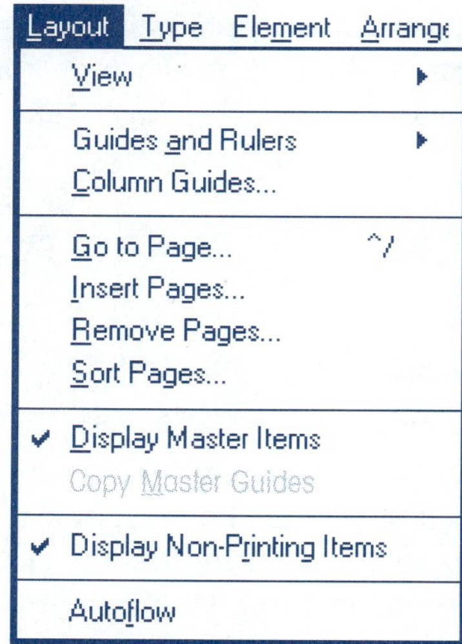

To close a menu without executing a command, click anywhere off the menu (for some programs, release the mouse button).

How menu options appear tells you something about their use. Black options are currently available for use; gray options are not. A check mark next to a menu item indicates that the option is currently selected. Menu commands with arrows take you to submenus. On some software, an

Concepts (continued)

ellipsis (...) indicates that a dialog box will be forthcoming (see the dialog box below). In a **pop-up** or **dialog box,** you select options and provide additional information in order to complete a task.

Dialog boxes contain different types of buttons and boxes from which you make choices. Options with an arrow open to reveal a submenu of options. Options with an ellipsis (...) take you to another dialog box. For some options, you have to key information. To exit from a dialog box without executing the options you have selected, click on Cancel or press Escape.

To make choices in dialog boxes, use these methods (not all methods work for all software):

- Click on a command button, check box, radio or option button, icon, or choice in a list box.
- Press Tab until you reach the item (Shift + Tab moves you backwards); then press Enter or Return.
- Key information in a text box.
- For many programs that run under Windows, key the number or the underscored, highlighted, or different-colored letter of the option (you may need to press Alt + the letter).

A Document Setup Dialog Box

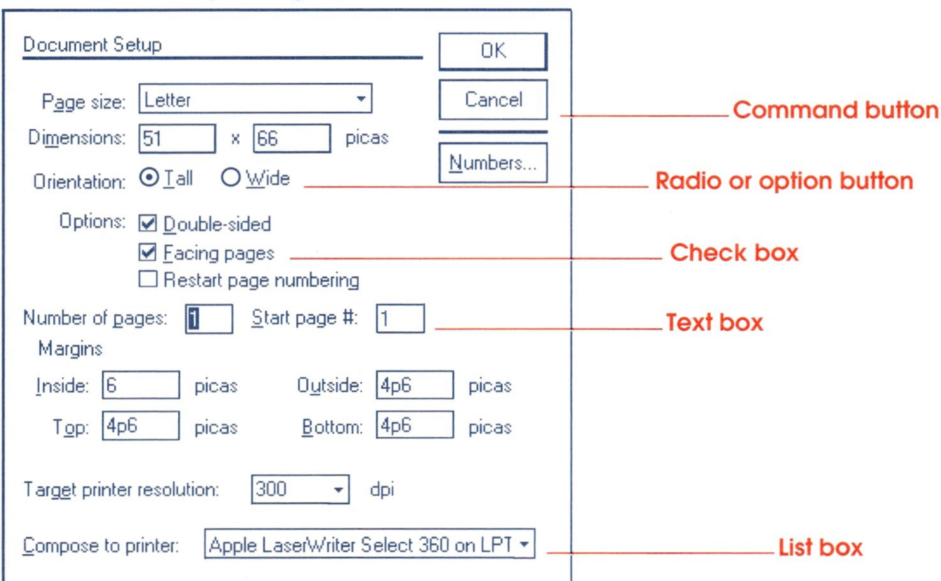

INSTRUCTIONS

1. Open the File menu, using a method from the Concepts appropriate for your software. Examine the commands on the menu.
2. Click somewhere away from the menu, or release the mouse button, to close the File menu.
3. Open each of the other menus, noting the selections available. Look for menu commands with check marks, ellipses, and arrows, as well as gray options.
4. If you have a menu command with an arrow, select it, using a method from the Concepts appropriate for your software. Examine the resulting submenu.
5. Click somewhere away from the menu, or release the mouse button, to close the menu and submenu.
6. If you have a menu command with an ellipsis, select it.
7. Try some of the methods described at the left for making dialog box selections.
8. Click on Cancel or press Escape to close the box without executing the selections you have made.

Learning Objectives

Work with windows

Terms

- Window
- Title bar
- Close box
- Maximize (zoom) box
- Minimize box
- Size box
- Scroll bars
- Scroll bar arrow
- Scroll box
- Icons
- Folders
- Program groups

EXERCISE 3A

Concepts

In most computer software, you will work with **windows.** Open applications appear in windows; within an application, a number of different documents may be open, each in its own window. Windows generally contain a **title bar, a close box,** and a **maximize** or **zoom box.** For Microsoft Windows and software that runs under it, windows also contain a **minimize** box. Macintosh windows contain a **size box.** Depending on the application, windows may have additional features.

Windows may contain one or two **scroll bars** (horizontal and vertical). To view any additional information in the window, you can click on the scroll bar. Clicking on a **scroll bar arrow** changes your view of the screen in small increments. Clicking on a large rectangle moves you through a file in larger increments. You can drag the small square in a scroll bar (the **scroll box**) to move a precise distance.

Icons are small pictures that represent folders or program groups, programs, documents, tools, and features. (**Folders** and **program groups** are disk versions of a file cabinet drawer, a place where individual files are stored, used for organizational purposes.) Double-clicking on a program icon loads the program; within programs, clicking on icons lets you perform many tasks without having to navigate through menus or use keyboard commands. Icons appear on the desktop; within program groups or folders; and, within applications, in button bars, toolboxes, ribbons, etc.

You can run windows full-screen or re-size them. For Windows and software that runs under it, windows can be re-sized manually by dragging the sides or corners with the mouse or by using the Control menu Size command and the cursor keys. You can also have the software arrange the windows for you using the Cascade or Tile command. For Macintosh software, the size box can be dragged to re-size the window.

To work in different windows, click on the title bar of the window in which you want to work (Windows) or on the icon at the right of the MultiFinder menu bar (Mac). For Windows versions before Windows 95 and software that runs under them, you can also use the switch command (Ctrl + Esc) to switch between applications; to switch between files within an application, the command generally appears in the application's Window menu. In Windows 95, you can switch between applications by clicking on buttons in the Taskbar. On the Mac, you can also choose the application from the Apple menu.

To move windows, drag them by the title bar. For Windows and software that runs under it, you can also use the Control menu Move command and the cursor keys.

INSTRUCTIONS

1. Open any window. If you need help, ask your instructor.
2. Practice using the scroll bars to move around in the window.
3. If you have a minimize button, use it to shrink the window to an icon or button.
4. Double-click on the icon, or click on the button, to restore the window.
5. Click on the maximize or zoom box to enlarge the window.
6. Click on the button again (it may have a slightly different appearance) to restore the window to its size before maximizing.
7. Practice re-sizing the window, using the size box or dragging the sides or corners.
8. Open a new application (if you need help, ask your instructor). Practice switching between the two windows, using the method described in the Concepts that is appropriate for your software.
9. If you are working with Microsoft Windows, practice cascading and tiling your windows.
10. Practice moving your windows by dragging them by the title bar.
11. Close your windows by clicking on the close box.

GLOSSARY

alignment The placement of text relative to the margins.

analysis A type of writing that states a problem, question, or issue; examines it; and proposes a solution.

automatic text flow A text flow option in which text placement proceeds automatically.

block format A popular letter format in which all letter parts begin at the left margin.

bullets Special characters used for emphasis, in lists when the order of the items does not matter, and to add graphic interest.

character view A control palette view in which you can change attributes such as typeface, type style, type size, and leading.

click To tap the mouse button once quickly.

clicking an insertion point Clicking the I-beam in text in order to work with the text.

clip art Collections of ready-made illustrations that may be purchased on disk.

clipboard A temporary storage area for text and graphics.

close box A box on which you can click or double-click to close a document, dialog box, or application.

color matching system A standard set of colors that can be matched precisely by a commercial printer.

color separations Printouts of a page containing only all elements of the same color.

colors palette A window used for applying color.

column break A text flow option in which text flows above a graphic and then jumps to the next column.

control palette A window that lets you change several attributes for selected text or graphics at once.

copy To copy text or a graphic to the clipboard.

crop To trim a graphic image.

crossbar The shape the pointer becomes once the tools for shapes and drawing lines are selected.

cut To remove text or a graphic to the clipboard.

default A preset condition of the software, which the software uses if no other option is selected.

dialog box (pop-up box) A box in which you select options and provide additional information in order to complete a task.

distributing objects An option for putting an even amount of space between objects.

double-click To tap the mouse button twice quickly.

double-sided An option for printing documents on both sides of the page.

drag To move the mouse while holding down the mouse button.

drag-place Dragging to create a precise placement area for text or a graphic.

drawing tools Tools in the toolbox with which you can create simple objects or designs.

drop cap Text art: a letter (usually the first letter of a paragraph) much larger than and embedded into the surrounding text.

dummy text (*lorem ipsum*/copyfit file) Practice text used for placement and formatting purposes.

ellipsis marks Three dots separated by spaces, usually representing omitted material.

em space A space produced with a special keyboard combination equal to the point size of your type.

en space A space produced with a special keyboard combination equal to half an em space.

enclosure/attachment notation A notation a double space below the body of a letter that indicates a separate item is included with the letter.

facing pages An option for working with pages that will face each other in the printed publication side by side.

feasibility report A type of report that explains actions that must be taken and barriers that must be surmounted to make a change.

feathering Adding small amounts of space after paragraphs or increasing the leading slightly to align text.

flush left Text alignment in which text is even at the left and ragged at the right.

flush right Text alignment in which text is even at the right and ragged at the left.

folders Places on the computer where individual files are stored.

font A set of characters in one style and one size of one typeface. Example: Times Roman 12-point bold.

footer Text that appears at the bottom of a page.

force-justified Text alignment in which text is stretched to extend to both side margins of the text block.

grabber hand An icon resembling a hand used to move around in the publication window.

grid A setup of nonprinting lines; e.g., margin, column, and ruler guides.

group An option that allows you to group selected objects permanently.

gutter The space between columns.

handles Boxes surrounding an object indicating that it has been selected.

hanging indent An indent in which the first line of a paragraph begins farther to the left than the remaining lines.

hyphenation zone The area at the end of a line of type in which an automatic hyphenation feature will divide words.

I-beam Icon used for highlighting text or to click an insertion point.

icon A symbol or miniature picture that represents a program, document, tool, or feature.

inline graphic An imported or drawn graphic set in text and functioning as a text character.

insertion point The cursor location indicating where the next character will be keyed.

jump over A text flow option in which text flows above a graphic, jumps over it, and continues flowing below the graphic.

justified Text alignment in which the text is even at both the left and the right margins.

keep with option An option that keeps lines of text together so text will not be broken inappropriately.

kerning The process of "fine-tuning" spacing by adjusting the space between characters.

keyline A method of determining where to set columns in tables.

landscape orientation A paper orientation that is wider than it is tall.

layering shapes Stacking one shape on top of another.

leading The vertical distance between lines of type.

letterhead Stationery used by an individual or a company that contains name and address information.

library feature A feature that allows you to store frequently used text and graphic objects.

logo A symbol, picture, or saying that creates an image of a company.

manual text flow A text flow option in which you place text manually page by page or column by column.

marquee A box drawn around objects with the pointer tool to select them all at once.

mask To hide part of an object so that only a portion of it appears.

master pages Pages on which you can set guides, text, and graphics that you want to appear on every page of the publication.

maximize (zoom) box A box that toggles the size of the window between an enlarged size and the size the window was before enlarging.

menu A list of related commands or options.

menu bar The screen location where the names of all the menus appear.

minimize box A box that reduces a window to an icon.

mixed punctuation A letter punctuation style in which a colon follows the salutation and a comma follows the complimentary close.

modified block letter A letter format similar to the block letter except that the date and closing lines start near the horizontal center of the paper. Body text paragraphs may be indented.

monospace A typeface in which the same amount of space is allotted to each letter.

mouse A hand-held device that controls the pointer and lets you select options from the screen.

negative leading Leading that is less than the point size of the type.

no wrap A text wrap option in which text flows through a graphic.

offset In a power paste feature, the distance between objects; in a custom text wrap option, the space between the edge of the graphic and the beginning of the text.

open punctuation A letter punctuation style in which no punctuation follows the salutation or complimentary close.

orphan The last line of a paragraph appearing by itself at the top of a column or page.

pan To move a cropped image around in its frame.

paste To insert cut or copied text or graphics.

paragraph Any unit of text that ends in a hard return.

paragraph view A control palette view in which you can change formatting features such as alignment and indents for one or more paragraphs.

personal-business letter A letter format used for correspondence between an individual and a business.

pica A unit of measurement used with type. Six picas equal an inch.

placeholder Text or an object that holds a place for the final text or graphic that will come later.

point A unit of measurement used with type. Also, to move the mouse so that the pointer points to an item, usually the item to be worked on next.

portrait orientation A paper orientation that is taller than it is wide.

power paste A feature that lets you paste multiple copies of an object, often at equal distances.

process color Color derived from cyan, magenta, yellow, and black, seen as an unlimited range of colors.

program groups Places on the computer where individual files or programs are stored.

proportional A typeface in which the space allotted to each character is proportional to the width of the character.

pull quote Text art, generally in a box and in a larger size than the surrounding type, consisting of important, interesting, or provocative text from the body copy.

raised cap Text art: a letter (usually the first letter of a paragraph) that sits on the same baseline of the surrounding text but is much larger.

reference initials The initials of a person other than the author who keys a letter, at the left margin a double space below the writer's name, title or department, whichever comes last.

reflect An option that lets you make an object into a mirror image of itself.

registration Proper alignment of two or more elements.

registration marks Marks placed in the same location on every color separation of a publication page, used to position the separations precisely so colors print in the proper location.

resolution Sharpness or depth of detail of an image, usually expressed in dots per inch.

resume A document that lists your experience, skills, and abilities, used in ob-seeking.

rotate An option for turning a graphic, text, or group to different positions.

ruler guides Nonprinting horizontal and vertical lines used for aligning text and graphics on the document screen.

rulers The horizontal and vertical measurement scale that appears on the op and left of a screen on some desktop publishing programs.

ans serif (typeface) A typeface that s straight-edged.

scanning Making a digitized copy of printed text or graphics, which can be placed in a desktop-published document as a graphic.

screen captures Shots of the computer screen made with standard or eparately purchased software.

scroll bar arrow An arrow on which you can click to change your view of he screen in small increments.

croll bars Bars on which you can lick or drag to view different parts of window or a list box.

croll box A box that you can drag to nove a precise distance to see a lifferent area of a document.

elect To choose a command, object, r text to work with next.

emiautomatic text flow A text flow ption in which the text flow icon ppears automatically.

ervice bureau A company that rovides services such as high-quality rinting and file conversion.

set width A feature that enables you to expand or condense type.

script (typeface) A typeface that resembles handwriting.

serif (typeface) A typeface with lines or curves extending from the ends of the letters.

size box A box that can be dragged to re-size a window.

skew An option that lets you distort objects such as text blocks, drawn or imported graphics, or groups for a special effect.

spot color The assignment of color to selected page elements.

story A single unit of text.

story editor A mini-word processor available in some desktop publishing programs.

style A set of formatting characteristics that can be applied to a paragraph or selected text.

style sheet The set of styles used in a particular document.

styles palette A window used to apply styles.

table editor A feature of some desktop publishing software that enables you to create tables with ease.

target printer The printer on which you will print the final version of a document.

template A designed and formatted document on which new documents are based.

text art Graphic elements created from text (e.g., raised or drop caps, text boxes, or rotated text).

text block A unit of text bounded by windowshades containing all or part of a story.

text cursor A blinking vertical line or other icon showing the location of the insertion point.

text flow An option for controlling how text flows around a graphic or other object.

text wrap An option for controlling whether and how text wraps around a graphic or other object.

textual citation A popular method of formatting references: parenthetically, following the relevant text.

title bar A bar containing the name of an application or document.

toolbox A display of symbols or miniature pictures that represent selections for performing certain tasks.

top of caps leading A leading option in which leading is measured from the highest point on any character of the largest font in the line.

tracking A feature that enables you to adjust the relative space between characters for selected text.

typeface A collection of all the characters of a single type design (e.g., Helvetica or Times Roman).

type size Measurement of characters in points by vertical height.

type style Modification of typefaces to add emphasis or contrast (e.g., bold or italic).

unbound reports Short reports fastened in the upper left corner by a staple or paper clip.

white space The nonprinted space of margins and gutters.

widow The first line of a paragraph appearing by itself at the bottom of a column or page.

window A rectangular box on the screen that contains icons, an active application, or an open file.

windowshade handles Handles used to adjust the size of a text block, to indicate when a story continues to another text block, or to show when more of a story remains to be placed.

windowshades Lines with handles appearing at the top and bottom of a text block when it is selected.

wrap all sides A text flow option in which text flows around all sides of a graphic.

zero marker A pair of dotted intersecting lines at the upper left corner of the document window where the rulers intersect, used to reset where zero appears on a ruler.

INDEX